PASSAGE TO WALDEN

PASSAGE TO WALDEN

by

REGINALD L. COOK

Second Edition

Containing a Key to References and Citations

NEW YORK / RUSSELL & RUSSELL

1966

SECOND EDITION, CONTAINING A KEY
TO THE REFERENCES AND WORKS CITED

AND PUBLISHED BY RUSSELL & RUSSELL
A DIVISION OF ATHENEUM HOUSE, INC.
BY ARRANGEMENT WITH HOUGHTON MIFFLIN COMPANY, BOSTON
L. C. CATALOG CARD NO: 66—24680

PRINTED IN THE UNITED STATES OF AMERICA

FOR

NITA

IN LOVE AND GRATITUDE

ACKNOWLEDGMENTS

FOR QUOTATIONS from copyrighted material I have been granted permission by the following: Little, Brown and Company for Bronson Alcott's *Journals,* edited by Odell Shepard, and *Pedlar's Progess: The Life of Bronson Alcott* by Odell Shepard; Dodd, Mead and Company for J. Henri Fabre's *The Life of the Spider*; Harvard University Press for William Brewster's *October Farm*; E. P. Dutton & Co., Inc., for W. H. Hudson's *Far Away and Long Ago,* and *The Naturalist in La Plata*; the Atlantic Monthly for Walt Whitman's *An American Primer.*

It is obvious that it would have been impossible to publish this book without quoting copiously from the Walden edition of Henry David Thoreau's *Collected Works,* which include the extremely valuable *Journal,* edited by Bradford Torrey in 1906. The copyright of this edition is held by Houghton Mifflin Company.

I have quoted frequently also from the following Houghton Mifflin publications: Ralph Waldo Emerson's *Complete Works,* Centenary Edition (1903–1904), and *Journals* (1909–1914); John Burroughs's *Works* (1893); John Muir's *Works,* Sierra Edition (1916); *John of the Mountains,* edited by Linnie M. Wolfe (1938); and Donald Culross Peattie's *Road of a Naturalist* (1941). For the use of all these invaluable materials and for editorial assistance, I am very grateful to Houghton Mifflin Company.

A portion of the prefatory note and a few other passages appeared previously in the University of Kansas City *Review.* I wish to acknowledge, finally, the kindness of the Henry E. Huntington Library and Art Gallery for permitting me to study the Thoreau manuscripts in their collection.

I am especially grateful to Doctor Viola C. White, Curator

of the Abernethy Library at Middlebury College, for invaluable technical assistance and friendly encouragement, to Francis H. Allen for many helpful suggestions and emendations in the manuscript, to Frederick B. Wilcox for reading and criticizing the manuscript, and to Wyman W. Parker and W. Storrs Lee whose interest and help certainly contributed to the writing of this book, but most of all to my wife for her unstinting help.

PASSAGE TO WALDEN

"So we saunter toward the Holy Land, till one day the sun shall shine more brightly than ever he has done, shall perchance shine into our minds and hearts, and light up our whole lives with a great awakening light, as warm and serene and golden as on a bankside in autumn."

CONTENTS

PREFATORY

SUCH A STARTLING array of contradictory interpretations of Henry Thoreau has appeared that we inquire, even as Edwin Arlington Robinson inquired of the man Flammonde, "What was he, and what was he not?" He has been represented as a recluse – cold, humorless, inhuman; as a skulker; as a stoic; as a sentimentalist; as an Emersonian odd-jobber. To some he has appeared a frail, freakish, thin-blooded intellectual, gnarled as an oak, characteristically a New England Yankee in that he was a bundle of inhibitions. It is asserted that his life was a denial of life itself; that his soul-searching was merely a manifestation of latter-day Puritanism; that his skepticism and conscientiousness were negative rather than positive.

The representation of Thoreau as the devotee of a consecrated life has been the most persistent interpretation, and it cannot easily be ignored. Because he kept journals so assiduously over a period of twenty-five years, he has become for some the symbol of the New England sense of duty. True, he was sedulous in what he was doing, but the symbol does not reach deep enough. Why did he perform this duty? – not, what does he resemble? – is the real question to answer. Others have ascribed to Puritanism his sense of duty and his exaltation of principle. That he was partly a stoic, partly a mystic, who can deny? but the emphasis must be placed on partly. That he was a cold, humorless, inhuman hermit his relationship to his fellow men readily disproves. That his paradoxes are often irritating, and that his theorizing and assertions are sometimes impracticable is only too true. Many persons who otherwise might be predisposed to enjoy him are either annoyed or left simply cold by these qualities.

Thoreau's way of life and a careful reading of *Walden* attest that he did not skulk from the obligations of this world. His short life has a proportion which some critics either myopically miss or indifferently ignore. The classical humanist contends that Thoreau's actions represent a denial of life. But wasn't he an in-worldly man, not a worldly one? He turned to nature, which is not to abandon the world but only to prefer one aspect of experience to another – the natural for the factitious. That he turned inward and that he was self-absorbed are both apparent. He was introvertive. Unless introversion becomes anti-social, it is not to be deprecated. Extraversion, a counter-characteristic of the human personality, is also to be deprecated when it is socially aggressive.

His ascetic inclinations – his rice and water – represent to many a narrowing rather than an expanding standard of living. Beside Walt Whitman's exaggerated expansiveness – life "immense in passion, pulse, and power" – Thoreau's contracted diet appears thin-blooded, notional, faddish. Yet the effect his tonic and sanguine gospel has upon us is hardly contracting.

One may also feel about Thoreau, as Henry James did, that his genius was "a slim and crooked one," and that he was "imperfect, unfinished, inartistic," and "parochial." Or, one may regard him, as Hawthorne did, as a man in whose presence one felt ashamed of having any money or two coats to wear or a house to live in, since his own mode of life was "so unsparing a criticism on all other modes, such as the world approves." Some critics see only the twist in the fibre, the knot in the grain; others feel only the implied criticism of their private way of life. We acknowledge the crooked bent of his genius, but as for its slimness, who shall say?

Perhaps in the sense that idealists rarely realize their ideals, and consequently fail to consummate perfection, he is "imperfect." But by what token is he "inartistic"? As for parochialism, he was aware of the problem. In a letter to Emerson, Thoreau wrote, "Concord's little arch does not span all our fate, nor is what transpires under it law for the universe." If Thoreau's experience appears circumscribed in horizon, nevertheless it is deep and strong. He did not range far and wide, but near and close. If he did not carry kingdoms in the shelter of his eye, he had at least pierced the surface to elemental essences, had glimpsed the world in a grain of Cochituate sand, heaven in a spiked orchis, held infinity in the cupped palm of his muscular hands, and experienced eternity in an hour by his Walden doorstoop.

If, like the hunting hawk, he worked close to field and hedge, still he nested within hum of human voices. His "Indian life," as Hawthorne described it, was not lived in tepee, and its physical necessity – food – secured with bow and arrow. As a stream-follower and field-tramper, he was nature's eye-witness, and by his apprehension of the dramatic life within natural phenomena he excites our interest and shows us how the fields and woods and streams are also necessary sources of culture, which supplement schools, libraries, museums, churches, laboratories, concert halls, newspapers, and the political institutions of democracy.

Passage to Walden attempts neither to tell the story of Henry Thoreau's life, nor to evaluate his relationship to "the golden day" and the era of atomic energy. Its chief aim is to penetrate the essential quality and evoke the richness of his correspondence with nature. The source of his vitality was nature; the ultimate end of this vitality was the cultivation of the human spirit. This book will fall short of its goal if either the exploration of the source or the ultimate end expressed in his writings fails of clarification and intensity.

Thoreau is as near the Emersonian concept of Man Thinking as any writer of his or our time. The whole man stands back of the effort. What he sought was wholly sought. What he realized was wholly realized. When he says injunctively, "We must *live* all our *life*," he is reporting the singleness of purpose in his own effort. Because his writings embody acts of life, one must first see and feel what he lived in order to share his experience.

PASSAGE TO WALDEN

I

The Saunterer

I wish so to live ever as to derive my satisfactions and inspirations from the commonest events, every-day phenomena, so that what my senses hourly perceive, my daily walk, the conversation of my neighbors, may inspire me, and I may dream of no heaven but that which lies about me.

JOURNAL, March 11, 1856

PLANTED CASUALLY in the lean soil of Concord, Thoreau struck root in its pleasant rural landscape, matured, bore fruit, was early stricken and died, unvanquished in spirit, mingling his earth with the earth of Concord. The spirit of his temperament was as native to the region as the mists that hover over the Musketaquid. He loved Concord's low hills, slow-pulsed winding river, wildwood openings, and fields like thresholds, and he carried, as he said, figuratively, Concord ground in his boots and in his hat. "A man dwells in his native valley," he thought, "like a corolla in its calyx, like an acorn in its cup. *Here,* of course, is all that you love, all that you expect, all that you are."

Yet Concord was in no way exceptional as a natural environment; it represented, on the contrary, a relatively tame landscape for a naturalist. In *Far Away and Long Ago,* W. H. Hudson described the teeming life of the pampas, amid which he grew up—a region that was not only abundant in natural phenomena but various and wide. Thoreau was almost as restricted in natural phenomena as Jean-Henri Fabre at Sérignan, but we know with what skill the Provençal master of insects studied spiders and gnats and bees and caterpillars and beetles in his harmas, a narrow tract of stony wilderness at the foot of Mont Ventoux.

Like Fabre, who studied the habits and psychology of spiders in near-by rosemary hedges and holm-oak copses, Thoreau made the most of what lay not far from his door-stoop. "To live within limits," wrote Goethe, "to want one thing, or a very few things, very much and love them dearly, cling to them, survey them from every angle, become one with them—that is what makes the poet, the artist, the human being." Most assuredly Thoreau was such a poet, such an artist, such a human being, who, within the limits of the original Concord township, moved and had his being. He had very few things, most of which he cherished dearly and clung to, and literally surveyed from every angle, becoming one with them. What Concord may have lacked he made up for in imagination. Enlightenment too frequently implies reason only; to a poet it also implies imagination. Imagination was one of Thoreau's inherent resources. "Olympus," he declared, "is but the outside of the earth everywhere." Not only was Concord home, for there was his coat and tent, his books and friends; it was, for him, as truly a microcosm. It contained his tundra, sea bottom, mountain range, jungle floor, bush, steppe, heath, and mead.

What the Frome Vale of Dorsetshire was to Hardy, what Ayrshire hill and dale were to Burns, what the hamlet of

Coate, Wiltshire, with its fir plantations, tumuli, stone circles, and down were to solitary Richard Jefferies, what the glacial alpine meadows of the spiny Sierra were to John Muir, the hills and streams, woods and swamps, lakes and pastures of Concord were to Thoreau. The Musketaquid, "with the moccasined tread of an Indian warrior," wound leisurely through the sandy soil, watering the wide, grassy meadows. The Great Meadows extended to the northeast of the town, and the wild, rich tract called the Easterbrooks country, where Thoreau cropped huckleberries and gathered a winter's supply of tangy wild apples, lay to the north. His vantage-ground was a hilltop south of Nut Meadow from which he surveyed the Indian-named hills – Annursnack, Ponkawtasset, Nashoba, and Nawshawtuct – that rose amid the meadows "like eggs that belong to one nest though scattered." Walden Wood was his forest walk; Fair Haven Cliff was his lookout. Conantum, which lay across Fair Haven Bay, was his retiring spot, "where one may have many thoughts and not decide anything." It included an old deserted farmhouse, a desolate pasture rising to a bleak cliff, open wood, a river-reach, a green meadow, and a moss-grown wild-apple orchard.

Poet-like, Thoreau named the spots that attracted him: Cardinal Shore, where the cardinal flowers grew in abundance on the shore of the Musketaquid under Fair Haven Hill; and similarly he named Alder Spring at Clamshell Hill; Mount Misery; Utricularia Bay; Cohosh Swamp; Blue Heron Rock; Pleasant Meadow; Scrub Oak Plain; Curlypate Hill. Who better than he knew the Concord ambit? The best show of water-lilies was to be found in Cyrus Hosmer's meadow; of lady's-slippers in Ministerial Swamp; swamp pinks on the banks of Heather Meadow Brook, and wild roses northeast of Trillium Wood. Arrowheads dotted the light, dry soil of the Great Fields and Clamshell Hill. The oven-bird's nest lay in Laurel Glen "near the edge of an open pine wood, under a fallen pine twig and a heap of dry oak leaves." "The universe," he once said, "expects every man to do his duty in his parallel of latitude." Thoreau did his duty; literally, he helped to put Concord on the map.

Concord was a satisfying environment for an imaginative and self-contained human being. Though tardily Thoreau discovered the Boxboro Woods, eight miles to the west, he made up for his tardiness by ardent praise. Jefferies had the old forest of Savernake; he had the Boxboro Woods. He discovered that Concord had a greater luxuriance of the same species of plants in its lean soil than had upland New England. No vista that he glimpsed in the Connecticut Valley at Brattleboro, Vermont, or at Walpole, New Hampshire, could equal either in variety or richness the interesting horizon of the Musketaquid from Nawshawtuct, or the view from Fair Haven Cliff. On fresh spring days he sat on the cliff and watched the awakening woods and the river. Pine-covered islands lay to the south in Fair Haven Bay. The hickories put out fresh young yellowish leaves, and the oaks light-grayish ones. The oven-bird thrummed its "sawyer-like strain," chewinks rustled through the dry leaves, and the wood thrush called clearly and thrillingly. At such times Concord appeared to him transcendently beautiful, as if it were not actual but painted "far off, as in [a] picture." Although it neither teemed with abundant flora and fauna nor proliferated new and strange fruits, nevertheless it nourished him.

2

Henry Thoreau was slightly undersized and sparely built, but tough and wiry – a man of lean, concentrated energy. His hair was brown, his mouth pursed, his nose aquiline – "Emersonian" some called it – and his bluish-gray eyes were deeply set under the formidable brows of his weather-beaten face. His forehead was both high and broad; his arms long, and while talking, his hands were often vigorously clenched, indicative of intensity. His feet were big and gripped the earth, and his strong legs, as Emerson remarked, were no insignificant part of his armor. A short man, a slight man, surely, but not a puny one.

It was difficult to distinguish him from the woodlots and pastures he threaded when he wore his loose-textured suit of dark and light browns and green. In clothes that resembled a pasture covered with patches of withered sweetfern and lechea, he passed unperceived half a mile in front of a farmer's window. Wild animals, undaunted by his natural clothing, fearlessly approached him. Once a mink came within twenty feet, and he thought that it would have come even closer had he worn corduroys.

He sauntered through fields and woods, as Emerson enumerated, "with music-book under his arm, to press flowers in; with telescope in his pocket, to see the birds, and microscope to count stamens; with a diary, jack-knife, and twine; in stout shoes, and strong gray trousers, ready to brave the shrub-oaks and smilax, and to climb the tree for a hawk's nest." His hat served as his botany box. The lining gathered in midway, made a shelf, and the darkness and the vapors arising from his head preserved the flowers through a long walk. Orchises carried all day in this improvised herbarium retained their freshness for a day or two after withdrawal. In the freezing March rains, when the north wind kept him under the shelter of the hills and woods — "along their south sides" — he wore an india-rubber coat and boots for protection. And there was his ubiquitous umbrella which prompted at least one countryman to mistake his business.

Since his shoes were a very important part of his gear, it was a matter of grave deliberation when he ventured into the bootmaker's and bought a pair of tawny cowhide boots intended for his winter walks when the mizzling rains made sloshy walking. They had to be stout. He noted that frequently the negligent bootmakers did not completely peg the heels of the boot, and, dissatisfied with boots that were only wooden-pegged at the toes, he required the seller to add an extra row of iron heel-pegs. With iron-pegged heels he crossed very wet and miry places dry-shod by moving rapidly on his heels. Perplexed by the untying of leather thongs, he finally hit upon a hard knot! Instead of a granny's knot (two simple knots one over the other), he tried a square knot (two running slip-nooses, called by sailors a reef-knot) to withstand the wringing and twisting he gave the leather thongs in his walks. Equipped with good stout shoes tied in a square knot, he felt like an armed man.

Essentially a lover of field and woods, life in gardens and in parlors was unpalatable to him. A great part of our troubles he considered to be domestic and originated from living indoors. A house bred insanity; was, in a sense, a hospital; but in the world of nature he recovered his sanity at once. Certainly he was not, in Nietzsche's epithet, a "house-animal."

Feeling the necessity to re-ally himself with nature each day, to make root and send out some little fibre, even on a winter day, he struck out from his doorstoop, easily walking ten, fifteen, or twenty miles, without going by any house, by following the river, then the brook, then the meadow and the woodside. A journey two hours long brought him to a strange land where an old farmhouse was a proper orientation from the vapidity and triviality of village life. Four hours in the open restored his well-being. Sun and wind thickened the cuticle over a few of his finer qualities, but he thought he gained more from "the tan and callus of experience" than he lost.

Poet-fashion, he spent his days anticipating the sunrise, trying to hear what was in the wind, watching from cliff or tree, waiting at evening on the hilltop for the sky to fall so that he might catch something. He was a self-appointed inspector of snowstorms and rainstorms, a surveyor of forest paths and all across-lot routes. Like a faithful herdsman he looked after the wild stock of the town and he kept an eye on the unfrequented nooks and corners of a farm. He watered the red huckleberry, sand cherry, nettle-tree, red pine, black ash, white grape, and yellow violet, "which might have withered else in dry seasons." It was wise to be outdoors early and late, sauntering far and earnestly, in order to re-create the whole body and to perceive the phenomena of the day. There was no way of knowing when something might turn up. When he thought his walk was profitless or a failure, it was then usually on the point of becoming a success; "for then," as he surmised, "you are in that subdued and knocking mood to which Nature never fails to open." When the day sometimes seemed a vain one, and the world appeared trivial, then, with the dropping of sun and wind, he caught its reflex. The dews purified the atmosphere and made it transparent, and the lakes and rivers acquired "a glassy stillness, reflecting the skies." He felt renewed, and he took what Keats called "the journey homeward to his habitual self." He exulted in the fact that he was at the top of his condition for perceiving beauty.

It was a shrewd Thoreauvian remark in *Walden* that if he had remembered how the same sun which ripened his beans illumined a whole system of earths, it might have prevented some mistakes. This had not been the light in which he hoed them, but he was reminded that there was a light—the light of relativity and universality—in which things might be regarded. There was, for instance, a light in which walking might be regarded. He was not, strictly speaking, a walker or a tramper or a hiker or a journeyman; he was a saunterer—"a Sainte-terrer, a Saunterer, a Holy-Lander"—who extended his sauntering to Monadnock, Wachusett, Uncannunuc, Greylock, the Catskills, Mount Washington, the Maine Woods, and Cape Cod. Sauntering was the light in which he regarded walking. "For every walk is a sort of crusade, preached by some Peter the Hermit in us, to go forth and reconquer this Holy Land from the hands of the Infidels."

He sauntered to pine groves that were like "fleets at sea, full-rigged, with wavy boughs"; to the cedar wood beyond Flint's Pond, "where the trees, covered with hoary blue berries, spiring higher and higher, are fit to stand before Valhalla" and where creeping juniper covered the ground; to swamps where the usnea lichen hung in festoons from the black spruce trees, where toadstools—"round tables of the swamp gods"—covered the ground, where swamp pinks, dogwood, wild holly, and red alderberry, glowing "like eyes of imps," grew. He visited particular trees in pasture, woodland, swamp, and hilltop: the black birch, yellow birch, beech, bass, hornbeam, *Celtis occidentalis,* pine, or hemlock. "These were the shrines I visited both summer and winter," he declared. Frequently he tramped eight or ten miles through deep snow "to keep an appointment with a beech-tree or a yellow birch, or an old acquaintance among the pines . . ."

3

Surely Thoreau had a genius for sauntering, the art of which consisted not solely in exercising either legs or body, nor solely in recruiting the spirits, "but positively to exercise both body and spirit." He set out upon his walks "in the spirit of undying adventure"; they were a sort of crusade carried on through every season year after year without diminution in discovery or enthusiasm. Moreover, he responded to a subtle magnetism in nature which drew him irresistibly toward the southwest. What Thoreau felt privately ("I must walk toward Oregon, and not toward Europe"), Donald Culross Peattie sees as a national inclination. "Always Americans have turned west, body and soul," says Peattie in *The Road of a Naturalist.* "They love the national tradition of unbreathed air, and they welcome a solitude that is not lonely but free." In the force of the subtle magnetism in nature, Thoreau thought he perceived the general truth of our going eastward for history, art, literature – "retracing the steps of the race" – and our going westward – "as into the future, with a spirit of enterprise and adventure." Since the old, meandering, dry, uninhabited Marlborough road led southwest, his inward needle generally settled in that direction.

The West was synonymous with the wild. Wilderness represented the preservation of the world. "From the forest and wilderness come the tonics and barks which brace mankind," he asserted. Where forest covered virgin soil the strength and marrow of nature lay. There man was refreshed. When the vegetable soil became exhausted, human cultures weakened. So with a characteristically exaggerated gesture, Thoreau exalted the untamed but nourishing wilderness where the Northern Indians ate raw the marrow of the Arctic reindeer, and he exulted in the wilderness where the Hottentots lived on the marrow of kudus. Once he felt a powerful impulse to seize and down a woodchuck raw, which he resisted. He would have approved of the wilderness areas now open to a highly urbanized people, areas like the Porcupine hardwood forest on the Michigan peninsula, or Hell's Canyon on the Oregon-Idaho boundary between the Devil's Range and the Wallowa Mountain, or Okefenokee Swamp in Georgia, or the High Sierra out of Carson City, Nevada, or the Grand Tetons out of Jackson, Wyoming, or the Bitterroot wilderness area out of Butte, Montana.

Thoreau sought acquaintance with nature "to know," as he said, "her moods and manners." The primitive, wild, and non-human were as essential aspects of her moods and manners as the more gentle, delicate, and elusive aspects. To study nature without the wild aspect was like attempting to study a tribe of Indians that had lost all its warriors. Others might prefer nature's tamer and more domesticated mood and manner, but in himself he found "a peculiarly wild nature," one that acknowledged a stronger kinship with the lichen on the rocks than with books. He liked best wild lands where no settler had squatted, the drearest prospect of ocean, desert, or wilderness, the darkest wood, the most dismal swamp. When he saw a redbird on his friend's string, he thought that deeper woods might reveal redder birds. He threaded woods and waded swamps, but discovered no wilder bird kindred to them. On a trip to Ktaadn in 1846, he praised the "primeval, untamed, and forever untamable Nature" in the Maine forests. It was pure nature, not the mother earth with which he was acquainted in Concord, a vast and terrific matter, and he felt there "the presence of a force not bound to be kind to man." "Talk of mysteries!" he exclaimed. "Think of our life in nature, — daily to be shown matter, to come in contact with it, — rocks, trees, wind on the cheeks! The *solid* earth! The *actual* world! The *common sense! Contact! Contact! Who* are we? *Where* are we?"

Concord excited an unsatisfied expectation of redder birds than the redbirds. He also missed "the nobler animals" — the cougar, lynx, wolverene, wolf, bear, moose, deer, beaver, panther — in Concord. Nature without these wild denizens appeared maimed and imperfect. Bear and moose, which had once been killed on Fair Haven Hill, and wolves, which were once caught along the Assabet River, had disappeared. Only a few of the "nobler animals" survived. Otter tracks had been seen in his day near the mouth of Pole Brook (he called it Bidens Brook), and when John Adams of Carlisle caught a Canadian lynx near the north line of the town, George Melvin fetched Thoreau to see it.

So strenuous was his devotion to the doctrine of the wild, only a swamp "impervious and quaking," like Becky Stow's or Gowing's, where the dense beds of andromeda covered the quaking sphagnum, could satisfy an appetency for the marrowy soil in which the strength of nature lay. When he made an expedition to Becky Stow's swamp on a midsummer's day in 1856, he rolled up his trousers to his knees and waded about, intently examining the sphagnum, filling his pockets with cranberries, and, much to his surprise, found an anthill in the sphagnum, full of ants with their young. "It consisted of particles of sphagnum like sawdust, was a foot and a half in diameter, and my feet sunk to water all around it!" Yet it was the discovery of small black hairy huckleberries in which he particularly rejoiced, for here, not far from the centre of Concord, was a swamp where grew wild berries – insipid, inedible, tough, and hairy. Here was a manifestation of a primitive and vigorous nature, still untamed, and it seemed to him that he had truly reached a *new world.* Of course there was no greater wilderness – not even in the wilds of Labrador – than he imported into Concord.

All good things were wild and free. It was the wildness in literature that chiefly appealed to him. So he praised wild fancies of serpents, griffins, flying dragons; wild strains of music; wild friends and neighbors; domestic animals that reasserted their wildness or native vigor; the "vast, savage, howling mother of ours, Nature"; and the wild and dusky knowledge which redeems a man from cultivated precocity. "A truly good book," he thought, was "something as wildly natural and primitive, mysterious and marvellous, ambrosial and fertile, as a fungus or a lichen." Chaucer, Spenser, Milton, and Shakespeare were, comparatively speaking, tame. The untamed thinking in *Hamlet* and the *Iliad* appealed to him, but he could not recall any poetry which adequately expressed his yearning for the wild. Even Robin Hood was tame. Mythology and the Oriental Scriptures more nearly represented what he liked. One book, however, which satisfied his craving for wildness was Samuel Purchas's *Purchas his Pilgrimes*. "It affected me," he said, "like looking into an impassable swamp, ten feet deep with sphagnum, where the monarchs of the forest, covered with mosses and stretched along the ground, were making haste to become peat."

4

On the move from the built-up sections, Thoreau represented an expeditionary force of one man. He acquired considerable skill while crossing a country in avoiding houses and too-cultivated parts. He learned how "to shut every window with an apple tree," and there was no better fence to put between the saunterer and the village than a storm into which the villagers did not venture. When he was safely off the roads and in the open fields, the sky had a new appearance for him, and with the rising of his spirits he stepped along buoyantly. The fields he loved best were bare, extended, rolling, sandy beneath the thin sod, bordered by copses, with brooks and meadows in sight. He crossed lots like a hunting dog, with tireless energy, striking directly through the brush and up the side-hills. He burst forth from a thick shrub-oak lot and immediately dove into another. Or he followed where the foxes made their paths. Sometimes his walks were semi-riparial. In the winter, when walking in the fields was difficult, he struck out toward three great highways raying from one center near his door — down the main river or up its two branches. In the summer he stopped to bathe at Hubbard's Bend in the same tub the muskrat used.

Neither storms nor wetness deterred him. On stormy days he simply preferred the sandy road to the rain-soaked grasses and bushes. The dampness seemed to favor his voice, and so he sang "Tom Bowling," pulling out all the stops. When it rained he put up his umbrella, and while the rain dripped from it he felt comfortable, all compact and his thoughts collected, and listened meanwhile to the ground soaking up the rain and to the robins, sparrows, bluebirds, and the unfailing scream of the jays. He found it pleasant sauntering in the softly subdued light before a storm was over. He gloated in "a long, soaking rain, the drops trickling down the stubble," while he lay "drenched on a last year's bed of wild oats, by the side of some bare hill, ruminating." He counselled: "Take long walks in stormy weather or through deep snows in the fields and woods, if you would keep your spirits up. Deal with brute nature. Be cold and hungry and weary."

He was no "summer soldier" or "sunshine patriot" when it came to experiencing nature. A genuine instinct prompted him to appreciate the variety of nature's aspects, whether dun or fair, melancholy or iridescent, sombre or alluring, drear or bright. In the sunshine one kind of life crawled into its lair, and another kind of life prowled about or flew secretly in the night. It was during the fierce seasonal rainstorms that the geese sailed the waters and the herons advanced to their feeding-grounds. "When it rains and blows, keeping men indoors, then the lover of Nature must forth. Then returns Nature to her wild estate."

There was yet another value in the storm. Its moaning routed the triviality of his fair-weather life. It was a challenge as thrilling as the sound of an enemy's bugle, mustering his energy "to resist the invaders of our life's territory." The cold and wet of a prolonged April rainstorm gave a tone to his system and he revived like a lichen. Thrilled to the core at the advance of the enemy, he hustled out to experience the full force of the spring rainstorms. In the woods were cladonia lichens lustily swollen with moisture into which his feet sank, and he believed that, like the lichens, he was fullest of life when he was wettest. Then he discovered "evidences of immortality not known to divines," and he ceased to die; it was *then* he detected some buds and sprouts of life burgeoning.

He was as sensitively aware of the night as of the day. "What an immeasurable interval there is," he exclaimed, "between the first tinge of moonlight which we detect lighting with mysterious silvery light the western slopes like a paler grass, and the last wave of daylight on the eastern ones! It is wonderful how our senses ever span it, how from being aware of the one we become aware of the other." He was up all hours of the night, to watch the yellow moonshine spreading over the vale below Fair Haven Cliff, to glimpse the phosphorescent arc of a moonlit hillside, to feel the warmer currents of air rising from the valley to the hilltop, to find that the sky was blue and not black, "for we see through the shadow of the earth into the distant atmosphere of day." He showed how necessary it was to see by moonlight as well as by daylight. "I saw by the shadows cast by the irregularities of the clayey mud-bank that it was necessary to see such surfaces by moonlight as well as by sunlight to get a complete notion of them. This bank looked much more flat by day when the light was strongest, but now its lit prominences were revealed and made remarkable by the dark shadows which they cast, and the whole scene was more variegated and picturesque than by day.'

Such was the reanimation of this all-weather, all-season man who believed in atmospheric exposure; who saw nature, not only in its natural habitat, but, as it were, on the wing, that is, in action — the heron trailing its long legs in homeward flight, the painted tortoise laying its eggs, or the wood tortoise rustling through the sedge to the water, the woodchuck browsing in the pasture, the muskrat swimming in the Musketaquid, the bream protecting its fry, and the gray squirrel leaping from tree to tree; who also saw three aspects of nature: the non-human wilderness of nature as in howling swamps; the delicate beauty of nature as in frost tracery, gossamer web, houstonia and Indian grass; and, as well, the domesticated aspect of nature, to be observed in rye-fields or rustic dwelling.

So passionate was Thoreau's love of Concord that he seldom travelled far from it, for there he could watch narrowly the poetic moods of his mind and report the phenomena of his own daily life. He could not be induced to go on expeditions the essence of which might better be realized at home. He rejected Isaac Hecker's invitation to join him in 1844 on a journey across the Atlantic (they would work their passage across), after which they would walk, work, or beg, if need be, through England, France, Germany, and Italy. "Let us see what the genius or stupidity of our honored forefathers have heaped up," wrote Hecker. "We wish to kneel at their shrines and embrace their spirits and kiss the ground which they have hallowed with their presence. We shall prove the dollar is not almighty, and the impossible, moonshine." Thoreau replied that he constantly returned from "every external enterprise with disgust, to fresh faith in a kind of Brahminical, Artesian, Inner Temple life." He was a poet in whom the homing instinct was unerring. His daily journey was, in Keats's words, a constant "reperception and ratification of what is fine" in nature. Some of the truth about nature would be as readily apparent in the earth of Concord as in the Canadian bush or in the wide, barren, fog-hemmed tundra of the North, or on the undulant prairies of the West, or in the High Sierra moraines, or in the heathland of southwest England. By observing warily and recording accurately the seasonal cycles in New England, he showed how it was possible to become naturalized in the American environment.

II

Nature's Eye-Witnesses

How much is written about Nature as somebody has portrayed her, how little about Nature as she is, and chiefly concerns us, i.e., how much prose, how little poetry!

Journal, October 6, 1857

In the history of nature writing, a distinction should be made between those whose contribution to our knowledge is of a scientific order and those whose contribution is mainly literary. Izaak Walton, Gilbert White, Henry Thoreau, Richard Jefferies, John Muir, John Burroughs, Jean-Henri Fabre, and W. H. Hudson belong with the latter group, not with Marcello Malpighi, seventeenth-century microscopist, who disclosed the secrets of the silkworm; not with the Dutch scientist Jan Swammerdam, whose *The Bible of Nature* contains the secrets of the hive which he had discovered; not with the expert Delft lens-grinder, Leeuwenhoek, whose *Secrets of Nature* represents the nascent scientific viewpoint; not with Réaumur, the skilled formicologist, whose *The Natural History of Ants* exposes the caste system among the emmets and the nature of winged ants.

In what relationship, then, does Thoreau stand to the literary nature writers? What distinguishes the nature writing in *Walden* and the *Journal* from *The Compleat Angler, The Natural History and Antiquities of Selborne, Wild Life in a Southern County, My First Summer in the Sierra, Wake-Robin, Souvenirs entomologiques,* and *A Naturalist in La Plata*? Each naturalist and nature classic casts light by which to understand Thoreau. Some point up his skill and viewpoint; others lay bare his limitations and deficiencies.

The Compleat Angler, which appeared in 1653, is a beguiling book. Replete with fable and enthusiasm, it has a meadowy freshness and runs on smoothly like a swift-gliding trout stream between grassy banks. Its value is more a human than a scientific one. True, there is the mouth-watering savor of frying chub in its pages, but the essential quality is the friendly one of the good companion, who invites you to sit in the cool shade under the broad beech tree, and while the birds seem to have a friendly contention with an echo and while the lambs sport in the cheerful sun, to angle pleasurably in the shadowy pools under the shelving bank of the New or the Lea. More significant than the piscatorial art is the natural beauty of the scene, and more interesting than the natural scene is the chatty, gossipy Piscator, who entertains you — little more — with the news that otters smell fish forty furlongs off (five miles by my reckoning), or with specious declamations about how eels are bred of a particular (he doesn't further identify it) dew falling in the month of May and June on the banks of some particular ponds and rivers, or with the implausible information that a certain river turns sheep's wool vermilion if they *drink* of its water.

We may prize *The Compleat Angler* the way Walton says

the French value the greyling. It is so valuable to them they say that it feeds on gold. So valuable is Walton to us we wouldn't have him scientifically accurate, not when his pleasant charm fills us with good feeling toward humanity. We listen raptly while Piscator rings the bell which drew carp to the surface; we inhale with great satisfaction the scent of those sheets of lavender between which he preferred to lie. How one-eyed John Goodwin would have enjoyed old Oliver Hardy who anointed the worms he used for bait with oil of ivy berries so irresistibly attractive was it to the fish! *The Compleat Angler* is as companionable and fond as Edwin Arlington Robinson's Uncle Ananias; we love him, but we do not believe him.

2

Only slightly less engaging than *The Compleat Angler* and far more informative scientifically is *The Natural History and Antiquities of Selborne* (1789). The letters of the bachelor curate to his friends Thomas Pennant and Daines Barrington are full of Fauna Selborniensis. From the inner world of *The Wakes* in Selborne, Hampshire, Gilbert White opened intercourse with the outer world concerning the activity in his district of swallows, field mice, fern owls, stone curlews, tadpoles, house martins, turnip flies, tortoises, aerial spiders, and field crickets. "It is, I find," he says, "in zoology as it is in botany: all nature is so full that that district produces the greatest variety which is the most examined."

Only a nervous and perhaps dull reader would find his

book without charm. The charm of *The Compleat Angler* consists partly in the enticing friendliness of Izaak Walton, and partly, too, in seductive stylistic expression. In *Selborne* the charm consists partly in the personality of Gilbert White, but partly also in his perceptions. We look along his ray of light with some interest and only afterward recall how a thoroughly interesting man has engaged our attention. Threading the discourses on dew ponds, wagtails, redstarts, echoes, and other natural phenomena are slight but informative details. We learn that the punctual goatsucker strikes up its vesper song just at the report of the Portsmouth evening gun, or that two field mice weigh one copper ha'penny, or that swallows drink on the wing while they skim over the surface of pools, or that the grasshopper lark utters a "sibilous note." But *Selborne* interests us chiefly in consequence of the man behind the eyes. The man is honest. He admits his perplexities openly; such, for example, as the "dark and mysterious" fact of the generation of eels. He is also candid, for he describes exactly what he sees: the copulation of swifts on the wing. He is observant, marking the flight of birds, the migration of aphides. He is modest, deferring to Ray and Linnaeus when a point of issue arises. He is gently humorous, referring to the bee-daft boy as "a very *merops apiaster*, or bee-bird." And he is enthusiastic, as he describes the "wonderful procreant cradle" of the field mice.

Selborne is the kind of book *Walden* might have been had Thoreau been less the poet and more the scientific naturalist. This indicates its virtue and marks its limitation. "Through all his pottering and gossiping you will perceive that he is out for nothing less than the biota of a sample area in the temperate zone," says Donald Culross Peattie of Gilbert

White in *The Road of a Naturalist.* "He is, with admirable modern spirit, taking up the larger problems of biology as they occur in his experience and on a small scale – migration, hibernation, instinct, habitat, adaptation, distribution, life histories, and animal psychology." It is pedestrian, and lacks poetic altitude. It is the sort of book, had Thoreau been so inclined, he might have written to Louis Agassiz, as from one scientific naturalist to another. *Walden,* unlike *Selborne,* is directed to the general reader who is interested in discussions of books, people, house-building, work, ethics, and economics interspersed with talks of trees, birds, bean-fields, pickerel, and the Pond.

3

In the little world he knew around Coate, Wiltshire – the world of hedgerow, copse, and stream – Richard Jefferies was the *genius loci.* When a farmer inquired, "See'd ye owt on the Downs?" the usual reply was, "Nobbut Dick Jefferies moonin' about." Thick-thatched Wick Farm, with its cottage, carthouse, sheds, rickyard, garden, and water meadows, was the centre of a world whose periphery touched Bucks on the east, Sussex on the south, Devon and Somersetshire on the west, and Oxfordshire and Berks on the north. In his nature essays and books we fall in stride with the tall, silent, solitary, self-contained Jefferies and ramble over heath and common, through copse and forest, along sheep-walk and towing-path, by meadows and hop-fields. We are now on some headland looking toward the Severn Sea, now in the Quantocks, or now on Beachy Head overlooking the Channel shipping. We see haymakers in the fields, gaze at gypsies in their encampments, study Torre steps on a Somersetshire bridge, glimpse rickyards where the granaries stand on stone staddles, listen to midsummer hum, wander along a wild green lane, loll in August heat.

So Jefferies went forth over the arable earth, calling the turns of nature, following the water brooks, treading the chalk hills, stopping by dew ponds shallowly cupped in the upper breadths of the downland, and always he was alive to light, color, shape, and sound. Since his appetite for natural things was insatiable, there is little that he missed; he had hungry eyes, avid for a multitude of intimate natural details. Absorptive he was and full of fervor and sensuous in the pleasures that quickened his senses. He had, too, the writer's gift of expression, and he describes naturally and skilfully what he looked upon. While reading Jefferies one feels the frost locking bare, leafless land, sees a million million purple heath bells, hears the high-singing lark, snuffs the fragrant bean-fields, tastes the rain and the white, sun-impacted dust. The abundance in Jefferies is overpowering: the gold-flecked furze; the blue line of down; a little crumble of mould; heavily massed trees; the silence of the fields; the rainy scud; the delicate-veined petals of wood sorrel; the black shadow of trout in the stream; the green hedges; the wild free hawk and "the throw of his pinions"; red-tipped hawthorn buds; the pheasant dusting-beds; rabbit runs and buries; and birds no end — corncrakes, field-fares, chaffinches, rooks, wood pigeons, cuckoos, redwings. Indeed, as Robert Bridges says,

> The very names of things belov'd are dear,
> And sounds will gather beauty from their sense.

In Jefferies there is the sense of place — of foremeads and home fields, tall yew hedges, fir plantations and filbert walks, downland and market town. There is the sense of people in the background: of cottagers, gamekeepers, poachers, shepherds, rickmakers, mowers, farmers, thatchers, simple rustics. There is the sense of time suggested by the ancient green track running across the chalk ridge of the downland, once trod by Danes and before them by Saxons and before them by Romans and before them by Britons. "A summer's day is not long enough to trace it to the end." And there were the tumuli where rabbits drilled into the tombs of long-unknown warriors, or the solid crust of the earth which was composed of an infinite number of tiny white-shelled snails. "These tiny shells have had millions of ancestors . . . " There is the sense of mortality — of the brief tenantry of earthly life — suggested by the bleached skull of a hare which lay lightly in the palm of the hand "with the bright sunshine falling on it, and a shadowy darkness in the vacant orbits of the eyes."

Strong in Jefferies was the simple, eye-opening wonder before the natural environment. Even as to Whitman, the press of his foot to the earth sprung a hundred affections. What he looked upon he saw with a poet's eye accurately as well as imaginatively. Like Thoreau, he possessed stamina without great physical strength and, like the Concorder, he, too, was early cut down. Similarly, he was a solitary, was self-absorbed, lacked social gifts, and even there the similarities do not end. When the *Wandertrieb* was upon Jefferies, he walked in a southerly direction, and Thoreau we remember walked toward the southwest, along the old Marlborough road. The linkage between the two men extended beyond temperament to creative expression. Occasionally Jefferies struck off ringing suggestive sentences the like of which so characterize Thoreau's work. He wrote about nature in a way Thoreau might have written. "I will sit here on the turf and the scarlet-dotted flies shall pass over me, as if I too were but a grass. I will not think, I will be unconscious, I will live."

Breadth of outlook was common to both, and in their way of life they were more alike than unlike. Each outgrew the early sportsman viewpoint and became sympathetic lovers of nature. Both opposed dissection, classification, monographic tomes on nature. Of the two, Thoreau was the tougher, the gnarlier. The width of their interests and the range of their ideas was about the same, yet in the expression of them Thoreau is the stronger writer; he is sharper, more trenchant. The profusion of detail in Jefferies brings one to a halt. It is a little like trying to advance through a bramble thicket. Now Thoreau preferred to go head-first through a shrub-oak thicket, but when he wrote about it he didn't make you go through it with him. Further, Jefferies is the more animated, abandoned lover of nature; Thoreau, the more restrained, the more searching. Jefferies is gentler and more sentimental; Thoreau is more bristling and combative. There was no anti-slavery movement to arouse Jefferies, but there was struggle against poverty and misery and day-dogging illness.

The viewpoint of Richard Jefferies helps us the better to understand Thoreau. The latter would have accepted the former's view that "only by walking hand in hand with nature, only by a reverent and loving study of the mysteries for ever around us, is it possible to disabuse the mind of the narrow view, the contracted belief that time is now and eternity tomorrow." What the Concorder called "the absolute view of things," the Wiltshireman called the "higher terrace." As with Thoreau so with Jefferies, for each sought to experience life in nature on the "higher terrace." "The moment the eye of the mind is filled with the beauty of things natural an equal freedom and width of view come to it." So Jefferies thought as he lay out on an English down and looked toward the blue hill line, and up at the sky, and off toward the sea, and upon the flower at hand, snatching from "inevitable time" the beauty of the moment.

This higher view Thoreau also experienced when, on an early dark November day, he saw the scarlet oaks from a pasture on the northeast of Fair Haven Cliff. By their very brilliance, they surpassed in splendor even the maples, and imparted warmth to the November view. From the hilltop they looked like "great oak roses." "I admire these roses three or four miles off in the horizon. Comparatively, our gardening is on a petty scale, the gardener still nursing a few asters amid dead weeds, ignorant of the gigantic asters and roses which, as it were, overshadow him and ask for none of his care. . . . Why not take more elevated and broader views, walk in the greater garden? . . . However, you will not see these splendors, whether you stand on the hilltop or in the hollow, unless you are prepared to see them. The gardener can see only the gardener's garden, wherever he goes. The beauty of the earth answers exactly to your demand and appreciation." While observing the intense red of the oaks, he, too, snatched moments of beauty from "inevitable time." He walked then as in a greater garden and experienced a more elevated and broader view, where the beauty of the earth answered exactly to his demand and appreciation.

Each went down to nature, in Jefferies' fine phrase, "with considering eye." Each knew what it meant to watch "the slow fulfilment of the flowers." They were like the humble-bee. "Humble he is, but wild; always in the field, the wood; always by the banks and thickets; always wild and humming to his flowers." Neither wasted regret on the day that had been. Each would sooner fight "in the foremost ranks of Time." That is where you will find them so long as nature writers are read. The very titles of Jefferies' three most characteristic nature books – *An Amateur Poacher, A Game-keeper at Home,* and *Wild Life in a Southern County* – indicate the difference between the Concord saunterer and the Wiltshire stalker. The way of life of the English poacher and gamekeeper is in them, and if they are less intense than *The Story of My Heart,* they are also closer to the fields and hedgerows. The dominant characteristics of the English naturalist's books are intensity and sentience and a knack of coming close to the ways of nature's small creatures. He was, indeed, a close observer of what took place in the arable fields.

4

John Burroughs, a Roxbury, New York, farmer's son, knew what it was to do a boyhood stint on a Catskill dairy farm summer and winter. This background influenced his love of nature, for we recall how, while working at a desk in Washington, the memory of fields and woods came to him with such vigor that he felt compelled to write of them. As he developed, Emerson's *Essays* nourished his self-belief, Whitman's poetry stimulated an enthusiastic wonder about life, and Audubon's drawings whetted an interest in avifauna. A field-and-woods man like Thoreau, he leaned more toward the scientific side of nature study as *Fresh Fields, Signs and Seasons,* and *Riverby* indicate, but in *Wake-Robin, Locusts and Wild Honey,* and *Pepacton* — books by which he is best known — Burroughs shows what a keen birdman he was. His country was in the Catskills, where one finds the Hardscrabble, Rondout, Esopus, Neversink, Pepacton, and Beaver Kill. Consequently, it is the eastern land bird that he knows best. What the water-ouzel and crested quail were to John Muir, the hummingbird to De Crèvecoeur, the sandhill crane to Audubon, the wood thrush to Thoreau, the golden plover to Hudson, the warblers, vireos, flycatchers, thrushes, finches, and especially the vesper sparrow of the Catskill region were to John Burroughs. He had discovered the nest of the black-throated blue warbler; he had seen eagles; he could distinguish between the song-thrushes, and between oven-bird and water thrush. He corrected Audubon's description of the female yellow-bellied woodpecker. And so on and on. As a self-trained observer he tested his observations by the most rigorous discipline — accuracy. He worked at his bird study, learning directly from nature, not from books. Of ornithology he said, "The satisfaction is in learning it from nature." In his classification and analysis of birds, he was a far keener scientist than Thoreau.

He sated his hunger for wilderness areas by tramping in the Adirondacks, or in the Laurentian Mountains. He traversed deep woods, roamed high, wild-wooded mountain areas, lingered along the upper reaches of boulder-strewn trout streams, picked blackberries in old bark clearings. Unlike Thoreau, he used a gun in securing bird specimens;

with no signs of squeamishness he killed and ate a woodchuck; he jacked deer at an Adirondack lake without contrition; he took a nip or two of whiskey to revive a fatigued body.

As nature-prosemen there is a considerable difference between the Catskiller and the Concorder. Burroughs' talent expressed a friendly, even-tempered personality. He is more orderly, accurate, and economical than Thoreau and Jefferies, but far less the poet, far less exciting and stimulating. Though slow-pulsed, he is not nerveless. If his writing does not contain a leavening wit like Thoreau's, nor rise in fervid exaltation as in the pages of John Muir's wind-chastened journals, still it never loses the qualities of plainness, freshness, and friendliness, which wear hardily. Thoreau's tangy prose induces a chokecherry pucker while Burroughs' writing is balsamic like a fir forest. You breathe it deeply upon entrance and then proceed to forget its fineness, but once you have got back home, your hands and clothes still retain the good woodsy smell.

The reader takes a homely satisfaction in Burroughs' descriptions. They are a genuine invitation to the unacquainted and a satisfying representation to the initiated. His description of the song of the vesper sparrow is a good example of his prose ability:

> Have you heard the song of the field sparrow? If you have lived in a pastoral country with broad upland pastures, you could hardly have missed him. Wilson, I believe, calls him the grass finch, and was evidently unacquainted with his powers of song. The two white lateral quills in his tail, and his habit of running and skulking a few yards in advance of you as you walk through the fields, are sufficient to identify him. Not in meadows or orchards, but in high,

breezy pasture-grounds, will you look for him. His song is most noticeable after sundown, when other birds are silent; for which reason he has been aptly called the vesper sparrow. The farmer following his team from the field at dusk catches his sweetest strain. His song is not so brisk and varied as that of the song sparrow, being softer and wilder, sweeter and more plaintive. Add the best parts of the lay of the latter to the sweet vibrating chant of the wood sparrow, and you have the evening hymn of the vesper-bird, — the poet of the plain, unadorned pastures. Go to those broad, smooth, uplying fields where the cattle and sheep are grazing, and sit down in the twilight on one of those warm, clean stones, and listen to this song. On every side, near and remote, from out the short grass which the herds are cropping, the strain rises. Two or three long, silver notes of peace and rest, ending in some subdued trills and quavers, constitute each separate song. Often you will catch only one or two of the bars, the breeze having blown the minor part away. Such unambitious, quiet, unconscious melody! It is one of the most characteristic sounds in nature. The grass, the stones, the stubble, the furrow, the quiet herds, and the warm twilight among the hills, are all subtly expressed in this song; this is what they are at last capable of.

Burroughs' quality is his own. He quotes Thoreau constantly, yet not so much in corroboration as in literary allusiveness. He remembers Thoreau after his own discovery. It is not Thoreau who says this and that, but a phrase or distinction which intensifies the point Burroughs is making which is recalled and used. This suggests the limitation and the strength of Thoreau: the fact that he was mainly the poet, not the scientific naturalist. Thoreau is quoted to set off a point, not to decide it. In his own right,

Burroughs described very ably the song of the gnatcatcher or what it seemed like to listen to the lays of the wood sparrow or what a field sparrow looked like or how a partridge drummed. He surpassed the "compleat angler" in his counsel on trout-fishing. He caught in a memorable phrase the little trout lake which the mountain carried high on its hip "like a soldier's canteen." We never forget how he called the Merrimac and the Connecticut and the Passumpsic "dusky, squaw-colored streams," or how savorily he described the strawberry with its "delicate, fine-grained expression." His keen observation comes through in his description of how nature concentrated its energy on the wing of the partridge chick, "making the safety of the bird a point to be looked after first," hence the wing-quills unfold on the down-covered young before signs of feathers are visible. His humor is quiet and gentle and pertinent; it is redolent of his life and way. When he heard the saucy wren wagging its tongue at some bluebirds, he stopped to muse: "I have no doubt that if it [the wren's chatter] could have been interpreted, it would have proven the rankest and most voluble Billingsgate ever uttered." He lacks Thoreau's tartness, but not his strenuous love of the wild. He was like those bees of whom he wrote in *Locusts and Wild Honey* which were actually wild bees – as are all bees – and truly incapable of domestication, for the instinct to go back to nature and "take up again their wild abodes in the trees is," as he said, "never eradicated."

Burroughs' special quality as a naturalist consists in the diligence with which he cultivated the habit of accurate observation; he was a deliberate observer, a decisive one. Like Thoreau, he thought there must be some intention of the eye. "The eye must have purpose and aim. No one ever yet found the walking fern who did not have the walking fern in his mind." He trained himself to describe exactly what he looked at — the specific features of natural objects. So he watched nature's objects carefully until he could describe how, for example, the wax-making bees filled themselves with honey and then retired into their chamber for private meditation. "It is," he writes, "like some solemn religious rite, they take hold of hands, or hook themselves together in long lines that hang in festoons from the top of the hive, and wait for the miracle to transpire." It is difficult not to see the bees at their meditation. Burroughs, too, was earth-wise, nature-wise, and the best of his writing reports his "original experience with the birds."

5

What the thin, sandy, Concord terrain was to Thoreau, and what the Catskill region was to Burroughs, the terrain of the High Sierra was to John Muir. This ardent Scots mountaineer, who emigrated to the Wisconsin frontier from Dunbar, Scotland, in 1849 when he was eleven, became the *genius loci* of the High Sierras. He stalked their spines, gazed from their granite shoulders, lay in their meadowy laps, penetrated the reaches of their canyons and streams, was on terms of intimate acquaintance with hemlock, towering sequoias, woodchuck, the "curious" pika, Douglas squirrel — "this brave little voice crying in the wilderness" — and water-ouzel, who made "a summer any time of year." Further, he was chiefly responsible for the establishment of the theory of glacial origin of the Sierra region by showing how a vast ice-sheet which once covered the Sierra slowly retreated, leaving the multiform domes, canyons, peaks, meadows, and crevasses. By tracing a bit of gray mud to its source in a high remote lair in the Black Mountain Glacier, he proved conclusively that Yosemite was the product of glacial action.

An interest in wilderness creatures had early been awakened in him by Alexander Wilson's descriptions of the fish hawk and the bald eagle. The new country was a paradise to his exploratory instinct. The first memorable discovery was the blue jay's nest with its beautiful green eggs. Afterward there were thrushes, whip-poor-wills, bull-bats, prairie chickens, and wild ducks in the rice marshes along the Fox River. He was enkindled by the glowing cumulae, wild strawberries, moccasin-flowers, the drumming of partridges, the love-song of the jacksnipe, and in the arrival of the passenger pigeons at the Muir farm.

He knew, too, what the feel of the American earth was like. He helped his father break the stiff wild sod mat composed of the roots of perennial grasses interwoven with century-old oak and hickory tap-roots on a quarter-section. Muir is generally associated with the far western country, although at heart he was a nomad, an earth-wanderer. On the fly-leaf of one of his journals, he inscribed his address: "John Muir, Earth-Planet, Universe." What he knew best, because he loved it best, was the Yosemite region at the headquarters of the Tuolumne and Merced Rivers. He revelled in its storm-beaten sky gardens amid domes and peaks, and in its crevasses and coniferous forests. With a bundle of bread, and a notebook tied to his belt, the tall, lean, sinewy Muir worked his way into its most remote reaches. Certainly his pack did not weight him down. He described it as "unsubstantial as a squirrel's tail." His flair for the tonic upland was immense. He was exhilarated by its bracing air, rocked ecstatically by its wild gales, listened raptly to catch the varying tones from its wind-tossed trees, and on the highest ridge climbed a tree in order to hear the music of "its topmost needles," clinging "with muscles firm braced, like a bobolink on a reed."

His enthusiasm for the wild does not perhaps transcend Thoreau's, but in the actual direct participation with the wild he outdistances the New-Englander. In the essay entitled "The Allegash and East Branch" in *The Maine Woods*, Thoreau described the wild country on the carry to Mud Pond which contained a mossy swamp ready "to echo the growl of a bear, the howl of a wolf, or the scream of a panther." Ready, mind you! In "Ktaadn," another essay in the same book, he describes the primeval wilderness of the Maine forest, not without a feeling of awe. I cannot imagine John Muir standing in awe of these wilderness aspects of nature. There are degrees in one's love of the wild, and I think if you measured Muir's love for the wild by a clinical thermometer, it would be about fever-pitch – ecstatic. He not only revelled in cloud-tossed skies, storm-swept seas, rocky canyons, towering mountain peaks, and flaming aurora borealises, but also in spouting geysers, fire-spitting volcanoes, thunderous avalanches, and an earthquake was positively "noble." Dryly, he once wrote: "If you are not very strong, try to climb Electric Peak [in Yellowstone National Park] when a big bossy, well-charged thunder-cloud is on it, to breathe the ozone set free, and get yourself kindly shaken and shocked. You are sure to be lost in wonder and praise, and every hair of your head will stand up and hum and sing like an enthusiastic congregation."

His "method of study" bears a close resemblance to Thoreau's during the last ten years of the latter's life:

> This was my "method": I drifted about from rock to rock, from stream to stream, from grove to grove. Where night found me, there I camped. When I discovered a new plant, I sat down beside it for a minute or a day, to make its acquaintance and try to hear what it had to say. When I came to moraines, or ice-scratches upon the rocks, I traced them. . . . I asked the boulders I met whence they came and whither they are going. I followed to their fountains the various soils upon which the forests and meadows are planted; and when I discovered a mountain or rock of marked form and structure, I climbed about it, comparing it with its neighbors, marking its relations to the forces that had acted upon it, glaciers, streams, avalanches, etc., in seeking to account for its form, finish, position, and general characters.

His discovery of the cassiope, in *My First Summer in the Sierra,* reminds us of Thoreau's search for and discovery of Indian hemp:

> September 2.
>
> Ever since I was allowed entrance into these mountains I have been looking for cassiope, said to be the most beautiful and best loved of the heathworts, but, strange to say, I have not yet found it. On my high mountain walks I keep muttering, "Cassiope, cassiope." This name, as Calvinists say, is driven in upon me, notwithstanding the glorious host of plants that come about me uncalled as soon as I show myself. Cassiope seems the highest name of all the small mountain-heath people, and as if conscious of her worth, keeps out of my way. I must find her soon, if at all this year.
>
> September 7.
>
> Left camp at daybreak and made direct for Cathedral

Peak. . . . And lo, here at last in front of the Cathedral is blessed cassiope, ringing her thousands of sweet-toned bells, the sweetest church music I ever enjoyed.

The vein of natural piety is strong in Muir's writings. Undoubtedly John Muir was a "transcendental mystic," as Vernon Louis Parrington, in *Main Currents in American Thought,* used that term in referring to Roger Williams; as one who discovered "an indwelling God of Love in a world of material things. . . ." He quested chiefly to find the beauty of God made manifest in the wilderness. He tried to be "like a flake of glass through which the light passes," but the purpose beyond this selfless impersonal attitude was to draw people nature-ward. "I care," he said, "to live only to entice people to look at Nature's loveliness." On another occasion he wrote: "Heaven knows that John Baptist was not more eager to get all his fellow sinners into the Jordan than I to baptize all of mine in the beauty of God's mountains."

Some readers will feel that Muir's success is partial. His writings are difficult at times, not because they lack lucidity (he is not esoteric), or charm (he is immensely charming), but because his raptuous temperament is like sun-glare on a glacier. He blinds by the dazzle of ineffability. Burroughs is positively nerveless and opaque by comparison. When Muir is at his best, the light is like alpenglow. There is more of nature's profusion in Jefferies than in Muir, but fully as much ecstasy in Muir as in Jefferies, and there is a wind-swept chasteness in Muir not to be found in any other literary naturalist, not excepting Thoreau.

His descriptive skill is sometimes brilliant and poetic, as, for example, his thumbnail description of the Douglas squirrel. "The Douglas [squirrel] is a firm, emphatic bolt of life, fiery, pungent, full of brag and show and fight, and his movements have none of the elegant deliberation of the gray [squirrel]." Another more extended example is his description of the water-ouzel. Thoreau also would have rejoiced in the companionship of the self-contained, self-possessed water-ouzel, which, in his long tramps, John Muir found high up on the Upper Merced by small glacial lakes, and which he observed in its sub-aquatic flight against the force of the heavy rapids in the Merced River. It was a kin spirit to him, this "joyous and lovable little fellow" who in form was "about as smoothly plump and compact as a pebble that has been whirled in a pot-hole." It represented splendidly the ideal of form fitting function, what with its strong feet and bill, its up-slanted wren-like tail and its down-slanting wings. It was the bird of the mountain stream, traced its windings exactly in its solid, impetuous flight over the stream-bed, built its extraordinary moss-woven hut-like nest on a rock-shelf close to the water-flow, laid eggs "white like foam-bubbles," fed on the larvae of mosquitoes attached to pebbles at the water's edge, and continuously broke into sweet, fluty strains — "perfect arabesques of melody."

> One stormy morning in winter, when the Merced River was blue and green with unmelted snow, I observed one of my ouzels perched on a snag out in the midst of a swift-rushing rapid singing cheerily, as if everything was just to his mind; and while I stood on the bank admiring him, he suddenly plunged into the sludgy current, leaving his song abruptly broken off. After feeding a minute or two at the bottom, and when one would suppose that he must inevitably be swept far down stream, he emerged just where he went down, alighted on the same snag, showered the water-beads

> from his feathers, and continued his unfinished song, seemingly in tranquil ease as if it had suffered no interruption. . . . The ouzel alone of all the birds dares to enter a white torrent.

Thoreau's writing is more various – contemplative, ironical, witty, whimsical – although hardly more lyrical or dramatic than Muir's. At the top of his skill, Thoreau's writing is muscular and sinewy. He was a writer of substantial sentences. He uttered no impotent thoughts with their stingers drawn. His prose has the twang of bow-thongs, an edge like that of a whetted blade, and, as in the John Brown address, a bayonet's stab. No book of Burroughs' or Muir's can top *Walden* in sheer prose craftsmanship.

6

For fifty years Jean-Henri Fabre studied assiduously and rewardingly in their natural state the insects he found close to hand in the depleted waste land at Sérignan in Provence. His laboratory was a dreary stretch where once a fine shady forest stood, now laid waste because covetous husbandmen cut down the forest to plant vine-stocks. When the vine-stocks perished from Phylloxera, the green tableland was left barren. The sum of Fabre's observations and studies of the instincts and habits of wasps, wild bees, gnats, flies, beetles, caterpillars, and spiders were recorded in the now famous *Souvenirs entomologiques.*

Fabre was a devoted scientist. Infinite patience, insatiable curiosity, constant questioning, characterize his method of study. His study of spiders was brilliant and illuminates

his general methods. He examined patiently the art of the silky epeira, which excelled at weaving big hunting-webs. Once having trapped its victims, it spun rapidly a silken winding-sheet until the victim was so tightly bound it had no longer power of motion. The torpid victim was paralyzed by the epeira, which then proceeded to feed upon it at leisure. Another spider, the fat-bellied banded epeira, excelled in the art of nest-building. To Fabre, the tiny, pear-shaped satin bag which formed the nest of the latter was a marvel of gracefulness.

> Its neck ends in a concave mouthpiece closed with a lid, also of satin. Brown ribbons, in fanciful meridian waves, adorn the object from pole to pole.
>
> Open the nest. . . . Under the outer wrapper, which is as stout as our woven stuffs and, moreover, perfectly water-proof, is a russet eiderdown of exquisite delicacy, a silky fluff resembling driven smoke. Nowhere does mother-love prepare a softer bed.
>
> In the middle of this downy mass hangs a fine, silk, thimble-shaped purse, closed with a movable lid. This contains the eggs, of a pretty orange-yellow and about five hundred in number.

Yet what incredible news it was to learn that when the bag had been carefully woven and suspended ready for the precious eggs to be deposited in it, the spider, apparently disturbed at the moment of discharging them, dropped them on the floor. And instead of abandoning the nest, the stupid spider persevered and sealed the empty bag. "You speak to me, in your own fashion," reflects Fabre, "of strange psychology which is able to reconcile the wonders of a master-craftsmanship with aberrations due to unfathomable stupidity."

Time and again Fabre fascinates us with his discoveries and experiments, whether it is the exciting methods by which he arouses the black-bellied tarantulas to seize and kill their victims, or studies the sturdy carpenter bees, or observes the stoical vigilance of the lycosa at its burrow-mouth waiting for its quarry, or detects the web-marks by which the epeirae initial their webs like painters signing their oils or watercolors. (The banded epeira signed her web with a zigzag opaque ribbon, extending from the lower part of the web, from centre to circumference.) The alert Fabre detected the sticky matter on the spiral thread that lined the quarry caught in the epeira's web, noted the telephone wire which connected the web with the leg of the spider when she hid at a distance from her web. "Clutching her telephone wire with a toe, the spider listens with her leg; she perceives the innermost vibrations; she distinguishes between the vibration proceeding from a prisoner and the mere shaking caused by the wind." He watched the Narbonne lycosa, or black-bellied tarantula, terminate her nuptials by devouring her mate. He watched her incubate her eggs in the sun. He found how a spider's web was extracted, not emitted. He studied the exodus of spiders flying through the air on tenuous thread. "The South-American Indians are said to cross the abysses of the Cordilleras in travelling-cradles made of twisted creepers; the little spider passes through space on the invisible and the imponderable." He proves, contrary to public opinion, that the garden spider cannot mend the severed meshes of its web. Each day the epeira swallowed its old web and each night it renewed it, but it did not mend the broken threads. "In spite of her thoughtful appearance, the epeira is incapable of the modicum of reflection required to insert a piece into an accidental gap."

Fabre is truly amazing. He never dispenses with the conscientious observer's scruples; he never inflates the bladder of theory. He stalks, searches diligently, studies, and finally records naturally, simply, distinctively, the results of his findings. Like the nest-building and hunting-net weaving spiders, he too is a master-craftsman. His writings are crystal-clear, orderly, economical, and fascinating. There are few other instances in the history of natural study where such a healthy, explorative, questing mind closely observed the habits and psychology of the insects as Fabre did with such communicable success in his Sérignan harmas. If he is not a greater writer than Maurice Maeterlinck (*The Bee* and *The White Ant*), he is at least fully as interesting. He was no classifier like Charles Linnaeus, but more the observer like Réaumur, who noted the marriage flight of ants, and like Auguste Forel and François Huber and Lubbock. Among the literary nature writers, Fabre is an authentic scientist. Thoreau's observations, analyses, and nature experiments appear tentative and inconsequential beside the full-length efforts of the Sérignan "insects' Homer."

7

W. H. Hudson is by many remembered chiefly as the author of *Green Mansions* and *The Purple Land.* For others, it is Hudson the field naturalist, especially the birdman, who is most interesting. The latter group find *Far Away and Long Ago* and *A Naturalist in La Plata* enkindling books. Certainly the autobiographical book has a peculiarly radiant clarity as of nimbused memories. Since it is as a literary naturalist that Hudson mainly concerns us, it will be important to learn something about his environment and those aspects which differentiate it from the environment of Thoreau or White or Jefferies or Fabre. What was Hudson's personal attitude toward it? What interested him in it? What was his method of approaching its flora, fauna, and avifauna? As a writer how does he present it? In sum, in what relationship did he stand to nature?

Hudson was born on the pampas and lived there for thirty-three years. When he left the level green world for England, it was with the feeling that his life ended. As a boy he roved the pampas with a wild joy and delight in nature that intensified with the years. We celebrate him now as the natural historian of the region south of La Plata, extending over two hundred thousand square miles of humid, grassy country, halfway from the Atlantic Ocean and the Plata and Parana Rivers to the Andes. Stretching westward, the country of head-high, feathery-spiked, stately pampa grass gradually gave way before a sandy, barren, igneous country of dry, harsh, arborescent vegetation. This extensive pampean country was the wide angle of his vision, the focus of which was the undulant part ringed by the blue horizon surrounding the plantations where he lived as boy and man.

Early and late he haunted the great pampas, and usually as a rider, rarely as a walker. He was constantly on the go – riding, shooting, fishing, studying bird-life, visiting old Gaucho friends at their ranches, attending cattle-markings, dances, and gatherings. Although he delighted in what he saw, he considered the pampas as the poorest in species of flora of any fertile district on the globe. Its wild natural life seemed limited to him. In spite of his disclaimer that nature on La Pampa was neither exuberant nor grand, in certain ways it was both grand and exuberant. Its grandeur was not that of the Yellowstone or the Grand Canyon and its fertility was not that of the prolific growth in a tropical jungle, but compared with the Concord country or with the downland country of Jefferies' Wiltshire, it was unusually interesting terrain. Its breadth inspired a feeling of grandness, but Hudson thought that because of a pervasive silence, the paucity of life on it, and its generally monotonous aspect, the feeling which it inspired was one of melancholy. Nor is it quite exact to describe a region that contained pumas, rheas, hairy armadillos, huanchos, vizcachas, storks, opossums, and flamingos as merely drab, uninteresting, and lifeless. Hudson doesn't make this mistake, because for him the avifauna, which was relatively richer than the mammalian life, entirely compensated for other omissions in flora and fauna. There were eighteen species in the heron group, twenty species of ducks, twenty-five species of the aquatic order of curlew and snipe, ten or twelve species of ralline birds, and about forty species of land birds, among which were the eagle-sized carrion-hawks, like the lordly carancho, the violent-tempered tyrant birds, and the grave-looking burrowing owls. If there were few resident land birds, it was only because of the scarcity of food and because the trees were few. Most characteristic of the pampean country was the rufous tinamou, or partridge, whose flute-like evening call-note charmed the wanderer on the pampas. The largest of the avians was the grand archaic South American ostrich – the big bluish-gray rhea – a bird often hunted with the bolas.

Not far from the plantation on which Hudson lived were

four shallow lagunas, or lakelets, several hundred acres in size, and in the dense beds of green sedges, reeds, and bulrushes were the breeding-places of egret and night heron, stork and wood ibis, marsh hawk and roseate spoonbill, grebe and coot. Among the many birds frequenting the region those which interested him most were the ypecaha rails, who danced in small, level, rush-hemmed assembling places, the brilliant wing-displaying jacanas, and the crested screamers, or chakars, the clarion note of whose long, clear, jubilant cry descended from a great height as the birds soared the upper sky above the pampas. Innumerable times Hudson heard the chakars "counting the hours," as the Gauchos say, that is, singing without rising; the first song coming at nine o'clock, the second at midnight, and the third just before the dawn. Once he heard the mighty song of thousands of chakars break from a marsh and resound in the night over the dark, lonely plain. Once, too, he saw a couple of chakars soar directly and fearlessly into a thundercloud, singing resoundingly as they soared, and in their flighting disappear into the cloud which muffled their voices. A few minutes later the notes sounded loud and clear as the chakars ascended out of the surcharged cloud.

What moved him most deeply were the wild, beautiful cries of the golden plover as the flocks descended upon the great plain in their annual migrations. He tells us, in a poignant passage in *Far Away and Long Ago*, how when the solitary plover was in migration he would lie in bed and gaze out upon the earth and sky on still moonlight nights, ever listening

> . . . to the three-syllable call-note of the upland or solitary plover, as the birds went past, each bird alone far up in the dim sky, winging his way to the north. It was a strange

vigil I kept, stirred by strange thoughts and feelings, in that moonlit earth that was strange too, albeit familiar, for never before had the sense of the supernatural in Nature been stronger. And the bird I listened to, that same solitary plover I had known and admired from my earliest years, the most graceful of birds, beautiful to see and hear when it would spring up before my horse with its prolonged wild bubbling cry of alarm and go away with swift, swallow-like flight — what intensity and gladness of life was in it, what a wonderful inherited knowledge in its brain, and what an inexhaustible vigour in its slender frame to enable it to perform that annual journey of upwards of ten thousand miles!

Whether rich or poor in wild life, Hudson's environment was fascinating. He did not feel properly alive when out of sight of natural things — growing grass, birds' voices, rural sounds, the scent of moist earth on a river-bank. His interest in nature was expansive, not contractile; it included the black acacias, red willows, and especially the poplars, which he liked because they seemed to feel the sunshine and expressed it in their fragrance the way the peach tree did with its flowers. It included lakelets with yellow camaloté plants, and the Lágrimas de la Virgen, with its tough-stalked tussocks of velvety green leaves and its sensitive yellow blossoms. It included the batrachian *Ceratophrys ornata*, a big venomous toad which preyed on common toads. It included crepuscular bats and luminous insects, aeronautic spiders and gossamer spiders, raptorial birds and umbelliferous flowers. The primitive world of the great naked pampa was not greater than his sympathetic joy in and understanding of it.

But what really was his attitude toward nature, what was

his method of studying it, and how did he present his findings?

As a boy he was moved by animistic impulses. He is careful to define this animistic impulse as "the sense and apprehension of an intelligence like our own but more powerful in all visible things." This "*sense of the supernatural in the natural*" persisted, and, beginning with tentative youthful intimations, it strengthened into the nature mysticism of his maturity. His first experience of all natural things was purely physical. While riding along the plain, he would throw himself from his pony at the sight of scarlet verbenas in full bloom and lie on the turf among them enraptured by the sight of their brilliant color. When he was about eight, he became conscious of some other element in nature. This further awareness was more poignant and often frightened him. Sometimes a grand sunset was beyond his endurance and he wished to hide. When the animistic sense was stimulated by the sight of a small and beautiful or singular object, like a flower, the sole effect was an intensification of the object's loveliness. Some flowers later on failed to produce this intensity; others magically never failed. The emotion for the latter accompanying the first impression endured throughout his lifetime, and of these he said, "I would gladly travel many miles any day to look again at any of them." His feelings were evoked more strongly in the presence of trees on moonlight nights. Time and place and the appearance of the locust or white acacia trees had much to do with the intensity of the supernatural feeling. "The loose feathery foliage on moonlight nights had a peculiar hoary aspect that made this tree [or trees] seem more intensely alive than the others, more conscious of my presence and watchful of me." Sometimes the sense of mystery altered sharply from delight to fear, so intensely, in fact, that to recover the sense of actuality he had to escape indoors from the moonlight night.

Like Jefferies and Thoreau, Hudson was a nature mystic. At times he felt lifted out of himself by surges of feeling for the "earth life." The poignant moods in which he caught "the long unheard familiar call-note of some newly-returned migrant" or had a "first sight of some flower in spring" were interpierced equally by joy and pain. As a nature mystic he came to accept Darwin after first rejecting him, but long before the acceptance Hudson shows his inclination to study nature with the avidity of a true and tried field naturalist.

In *A Naturalist in La Plata,* the scientific aspect of Hudson's study appears. For example, although greatly interested in the flora and fauna in and for itself, frequently he speculates on the general problems which their behavior suggests. His method of study still remains personal — that is, there is a vivid personal interest in the object he studies; but — and this is very important as distinguishing his nature study from Thoreau's — he takes an objective viewpoint and investigates such problems as the instinct of fear in birds, mimicry and warning colors in grasshoppers, the use of the firefly's light, the death-feigning instinct of certain fauna, the unusual behavior of the puma toward man, and the huanaco's strange dying instinct. Independent observation convinced him that spiders were attracted by musical instruments; that nothing compared in all organic nature with the wasted energy of the mosquito's elaborate blood-pumping apparatus and instincts for bood; that the unsocial flea is the mental equal of the ant, and so on. The following passage reveals Hudson's method of studying nature — by direct authority. He had been studying the problem of music and dancing in nature. The problem was whether or not the dancing performance in birds was related to conscious sexual selection.

> But I am convinced that any student of the subject who will cast aside his books . . . and go directly to nature to note the actions of animals for himself . . . the result of such independent investigation will be a conviction that conscious sexual selection on the part of the female is not the cause of music and dancing performances in birds, nor of the brighter colours and ornaments that distinguish the male. It is true that the females of some species, both in the vertebrate and insect kingdoms, do exercise a preference; but in a vast majority of species the male takes the female he finds, or that he is able to win from other competitors; . . . and if we go to the insect class, we find that in butterflies, which surpass all creatures in their glorious beauty, the female gives herself up to the embrace of the first male that appears, or else is captured by the strongest male, just as she might be by a mantis or some other rapacious insect.

Hudson was more the independent investigator than Thoreau. He has more to tell us about nature than has the Concorder, but he does not draw us closer to it. Both were acquainted with unusual things in nature, and each makes us feel the impactive wonder that is in natural things. For instance, there was the curious flight of the dragonflies, always in advance of the violent, dry, cold pampero or southwest wind which Hudson often saw on the pampas. The mystery in the flight, he thought, consisted in the fact that the dragonflies flew before the wind and always in the same direction with it.

What the Concord background was for Thoreau, the background of the pampas and the interesting sights were for Hudson.

> Riding on the pampas one dark evening an hour after sunset, and passing from high ground overgrown with giant thistles to a low plain covered with long grass, bordering a stream of water, I found it all ablaze with myriads of fireflies. I noticed that all the insects gave out an exceptionally large, brilliant light, which shone almost steadily. The long grass was thickly studded with them, while they literally swarmed in the air, all moving up the valley with a singularly slow and languid flight. When I galloped down into this river of phosphorescent fire, my horse plunged and snorted with alarm. I succeeded at length in quieting him, and then rode slowly through, compelled to keep my mouth and eyes closed, so thickly did the insects rain onto my face. The air was laden with the sickening phosphorous smell they emit, but when I had once got free of the broad fiery zone, stretching away on either hand for miles along the moist valley, I stood still and gazed back for some time on a scene the most wonderful and enchanting I have ever witnessed.

Environmentally Hudson seems to have the edge, but the joy that he takes in the flight of the crested screamer is hardly more than the emotion felt by Thoreau in the song of the hermit thrush. And so it goes, balanced perhaps equally, significantly, complementary: Indian grass (*Sorghum nutans*) and stately pampa grass (*Gynerium argenteum*); woodchuck and vizcacha; green bittern and glossy ibis; flight of ephemerae and dragonflies winging before the pampas; drumming of partridges and dancing of the rupicola, or cock-of-the-walk; nighthawk and peregrine falcon; tanager and *Phaithornis splendens,* a marvellously beautiful hummingbird; wood frog and wrestling frog. Thoreau holds the partridge chick in his hand and Hudson holds the incubating egg of the jacana through which the young bird leaped and fell into the water. While Thoreau's precocious partridge chick when placed on the ground rests in exactly the position it is placed, Hudson's newborn jacana, dropping into the water, puts out its neck and, like a wounded bird trying to escape detection, swims to a little tussock where it conceals itself.

Both assailed with feeling the extermination of species of wild life. Hudson defended from extermination the rhea, rufous tinamou, flamingo, crested screamer, and swans, either directly by gun or indirectly by the destruction of environmental habitat. Charmed as he was by things "as they exist in the unconquered provinces of Nature's dominions," he lamented altering the earth's surface by cultivation and domestication. The disappearance of many noble and beautiful forms of life both animal and vegetable was his despair. What he liked was the grace and spirit which freedom and wildness gave nature's phenomena. In his time, not only New Zealand nor Australia nor North America, but, as well, the pampas were also suffering from the encroachment of sheep-ranchers and wheat-farmers.

Hudson impresses us not as an egg-blowing naturalist, nor a classifier of size, form, coloration, voice, and habits, but rather as a lover of nature in all forms, one who was familiar with the Gauchos – a kind of Gaucho-naturalist, riding horseback, often with gun in hand, over the dense growth of cardoon thistles and wild artichokes of the pampas, stirred deeply by the ethereal tints of the feathery-spiked grass, absorbing sights and sounds. Nature was a presence which encompassed him widely; it ringed his horizon and filled his days and nights. Before this presence he was reverently humble and not abject, because he recognized the emotion which he felt for exactly what it really was – the sense of the supernatural in nature. Like Thoreau, he, too, possessed an informing intelligence. Nature was not so much the medium of an intelligence greater than his own as it was the medium of an intelligence which corresponded to his own. Nature and he met on equal terms, and his capacity for feeling was pampas-broad. The feeling for place was in him like the feeling for a personality. "His heart was," as Cunninghame Graham said, "an old Gaucho of the plains."

Of the literary nature-lovers discussed, Gilbert White, John Burroughs, Jean-Henri Fabre, John Muir, and W. H. Hudson were the most scientifically inclined; Jefferies and Thoreau the most poetically inclined. In reaction to nature each has a memorable quality: Walton is buoyant; White sensible; Thoreau intense; Jefferies rapturous; Muir fervid; Burroughs equable; Fabre clairvoyant; Hudson expectant. The effect of their work upon the reader is another matter. Walton is beguiling; White instructive; Thoreau provocative; Jefferies reanimating; Muir infectious; Burroughs informative; Fabre fascinating; Hudson exhilarating.

In view of the attitudes and temperaments of other nature-lovers, it can hardly be said that Thoreau felt nature in a new way — that is, in the poetic. For the same could be said of many other men before and since Lucretius. He has not, therefore, contributed a new sensibility to the world in his attitude toward nature. But he does reflect a very intense refinement and application of sensibility. He exemplifies the functional capacity for use and enjoyment which the human sensibility possesses. His sensibility was more expansive; it was more receptive, more intense, so far as man's relationship to nature is concerned. A close reading of *Walden* or the *Journal* makes most nature writers appear limited — an eye or an ear or a taste or a touch; but in Thoreau the senses are integrated and focussed.

III

Nature and Natural Men

I am not only grateful because Veias, and Homer, and Christ, and Shakespeare have lived, but I am grateful for Minott, and Rice, and Melvin, and Goodwin, and Puffer even.

JOURNAL, December 3, 1856

THE CRITICS who take Thoreau to task somewhat harshly for turning away from man and toward nature should first examine closely his attitude toward man. He stated his position clearly enough when he said: "Nature and man; some prefer the one, others the other; but that is all *de gustibus*. It makes no odds at what well you drink, provided it be a well-head." One might better respect the disparagement of Thoreau's preference of nature to man *if* — and this is the crux of the matter — *if* he really did reject man for nature. On the contrary, he contended that the lover of nature was preëminently the lover of man. On the twenty-fifth of October, 1859, Thoreau saw a remarkable sunset that reached from west to east. "But it was hard for me to see its beauty then," he said, "when my mind was filled with Captain Brown. So great a wrong as his fate implied over-shadowed all beauty in the world." So absorbed was he in John Brown's fate that he was surprised to detect the old routine running still and people going about their affairs indifferent to it. "It appeared strange to me," he wrote, "that the little dipper should be still diving in the river as of yore; and this suggested that this grebe might be diving here when Concord shall be no more. Any affecting human event may blind our eyes to natural objects." Surely, in this test case, Thoreau's abiding sentiment for man mastered even the commanding sentiment for nature.

Thoreau believed it was man's capacity for love which humanized nature and made it possible to enjoy her scenes. "Nature must be viewed humanly to be viewed at all; that is, her scenes must be associated with humane affections, such as are associated with one's native place, for instance. She is most significant to a lover. A lover of Nature is preëminently a lover of man. If I have no friend, what is Nature to me? She ceases to be morally significant." Two months earlier, in April, 1852, he had recorded in the *Journal*: "It appears to be a law that you cannot have a deep sympathy with both man and nature. Those qualities which bring you near to the one estrange you from the other." As his sympathy deepened toward nature, he felt that he sacrificed an intensification of human fellowship, and this sacrifice worried him. The tension which he felt between nature and man had a parallel in a similar tension between science and poetry to be discussed later.

Thoreau's reaction shows us that in human development the two forces – one social (the relationship to one's fellowman) and the other natural (the relationship to the world of natural phenomena) – are not always evenly balanced. Thoreau did not explore the world of social relationships, in which one comes into intimate association with one's fellowmen, with the same assiduity that he explored the world of natural phenomena. He was never out of himself. As Whitman said, "He couldn't put his life into any other life — realize why one man was so and another man was not so." He did lack the capacity to project himself into the life and actions of other human beings, but he never lacked the imagination to understand sympathetically the life of the creatures of the fields and woods.

The reason for his preference for nature is significant. "I love nature partly *because* she is not man, but a retreat from him. None of his institutions control or pervade her." This is certainly a definite declaration. Since nature represented freedom to enjoy an "absolute view of things," he turned from what he considered to be the piddling, narrow society of his fellow human beings and their ugly, gross, institutionalized existence. When he invited an intellectual neighbor to go into the woods with him, he found that it was impossible for the neighbor "to empty clean out of his thoughts all institutions of men and start again." Most men failed usually to take extended views; they saw only the shallow foreground; they had no vista, no vantage-point. "Most with whom you endeavor to talk soon come to a stand against some institution in which they appear to hold stock — that is, some particular, not universal, way of viewing things."

The grave limitation of most men was their inability to free themselves from institutionalized existence. "I do not value any view of the universe into which man and the institutions of man enter very largely and absorb much of the attention. Man is but the place where I stand, and the prospect hence is infinite. It is not a chamber of mirrors which reflect me. When I reflect, I find that there is other than me. Man is a past phenomenon to philosophy. The universe is larger than enough for man's abode. Some rarely go outdoors, most are always at home at night, very few indeed have stayed out all night once in their lives, fewer still have gone behind the world of humanity, seen its institutions like toadstools by the wayside." Advocating the higher view, he condemned the pettiness and egotism of those who saw life narrowly, concerned with only themselves and their trivial affairs. To be a citizen of the universe, to live ever in the great taskmaster's eye, not in the eye of one's fellow-citizen, represented the greater view.

Thoreau rejoiced personally in a landscape so immense that man and his affairs of school, trade, church, state, agriculture, manufacturing, and politics occupied no greater margin of notoriety than a woodchuck's burrow. No matter how trivial man's institution-ridden life might be, the life in nature was not trivial but "holy and heroic." Walking through shrub-oak stands and pine woods, away from the village, with mountain vistas before him, he thought he might pass his life there because it would be so "simple, and true and natural." He turned to nature, then, partly because he was drawn by an intensely passionate interest in the phenomena of the physical universe, and partly because he found it possible to realize in nature a sense of freedom which the institutionalized life of man thwarted.

Thoreau's preference for the solitary way of life, so necessary to the saunterer in nature, did not reflect an aversion to all men. It reflected an aversion to some men and to the institutions of man. He was hardly motivated by a reason similar to Robinson Jeffers who asserts:

> It would be better for men
> To be few and live far apart, where none could infect
> another; then slowly the sanity of field and mountain
> And the cold ocean and glittering stars might enter
> their minds.

Fear of infection from his fellow-men did not influence Thoreau's preference for the footpath that led away from the village. A man might be a merry companion or fellow-pilgrim for a short way, but usually parted from him at the first turn in the road, for, as he said, none was travelling *one* road as far as himself. Usually, when accompanied by a companion on his walk, he felt alienated from direct communion with nature. How rare was the companion who could sympathize with one's present mood, whose presence was not an interruption, who walked side by side in one's thoughts, who heard the other's silence! So he exulted like an early settler in the retirement and solitude of a locality where he did not meet as many men as he should have three centuries before, when the Indians roamed the Concord woods.

He felt imposed upon when people — certainly not his chosen friends — were so inconsiderate as to ask to walk or sail with him regularly every day. One August afternoon, as he started to go by boat to Hubbard's Bath Swamp, a fancy-free man sat by the shore waiting to be invited into his boat, but he would have none of him. "He thinks I could merely take him into my boat and then not mind him. He does not realize that I should by the same act take him into my mind, where there is no room for him, and my bark would surely founder in such a voyage as I was contemplating." He was anxious to put distance between the man and himself. "I have come on purpose to sail," he added, "to paddle away from such as you, and you have waylaid me at the shore." When he excused himself from taking self-invited parties on excursions, he was thought rude and unaccommodating. He explained: "They do not consider that the wood-path and the boat are my studio, where I maintain a sacred solitude and cannot admit promiscuous company. I will see them occasionally in an evening or at the table, however. They do not think of taking a child away from its school to go a-huckleberrying with them. Why should not I, then, have my school and school hours to be respected? Ask me for a certain number of dollars if you will, but do not ask me for my afternoons." Such occasions arose frequently as his reputation widened. No matter how politely he excused himself, one can imagine how those denied access to his company would talk or gossip. In their obtuseness they could not escape the sting of Blake's proverb in *The Marriage of Heaven and Hell*: "He who has suffer'd you to impose on him knows you."

One can live for oneself – a self-centred egocentric life; by oneself – the solitary life; and from oneself – the inward life. In order to realize the last, Thoreau turned to the second. He throve best on solitude. It compounded his experiences in nature. The company of men tended to dissipate the value of his days, and, like the Eskimos of Smith's Strait in North Greenland who laughed when Kane told them they might be utterly exterminated by the encroaching ice "unless they attempted in season to cross the glacier southward," so he laughed when one pointed out the danger of impoverishing himself through isolation. "It is here," he said, "that the walrus and the seal, and the white bear, and the eider ducks and auks on which I batten, most abound." Wishing to avoid the meanness, narrowness, and triviality of society-bound men and their ways, he sought the solitary places, spending a considerable part of his days where the problems of existence were simplified. He was not satisfied with ordinary windows; he needed the true *sky light*. He preferred solitude, but he did not either defiantly or with bravado maintain that all men must or ought always stand alone.

Thoreau's inclination toward solitude was hardly the result of social gaucherie. He was uninhibited by any sense of social inferiority. He never felt like the barefoot boy before the gentry in the big house on Beacon Hill. He met the upper-crust Concord Hoars or Emersons on equal terms. His social equality sprang in part from the family background on his mother's side – the well-bred Dunbars and the well-born Joneses. But he also had a practical ascendency. After all, he wasn't a subaltern; he captained huckleberry parties; his time was for hire on his own terms.

Sociables and town-and-country farmers' clubs simply bored Thoreau. Parties where young women abounded were his despair. He thought that certain young women described as pretty were simply light and flighty. Their company was unprofitable to him. At a party where he was introduced to two young women in a small, warm, and noisy room crowded with people, one of the women seemed lively and loquacious as a chickadee. Accustomed as she was to the society of watering-places, she got no refreshment out of his dryness. The other, said to be pretty, could scarcely be heard in the inordinate din. "Why, this afternoon, even, I did better," explained the incorrigible bachelor. "There was old Mr. Joseph Hosmer and I ate our luncheon of cracker and cheese together in the woods. I heard all he said, though it was not much, to be sure, and he could hear me. And then he talked out of such a glorious repose, taking a leisurely bite at the cracker and cheese between his words; and so some of him was communicated to me, and some of me to him, I trust." "These parties," he dryly surmised, "I think, are part of the machinery of modern society, that young people may be brought together to form marriage connections." One can imagine his stiffening when he first detected the hidden intent.

The outdoors was his club, and it met in turn at Well Meadow Field or Brown's scrub-oak lot or at Fair Haven Cliff. "It is as if I always met in those places some grand, serene, immortal, infinitely encouraging, though invisible, companion, and walked with him. There at last my nerves are steadied, my senses and my mind do their office." His society was, perversely enough, in the fields and woods and along the river. No caucus, meeting-house, lyceum, or club-room provided such experience. Outdoors he felt in his element "as when a fish is put back into the water." During his temporary sojourn at Walden Pond, he strolled into the village every day or two to learn the gossip of the Mill Dam. After a bout with the village worthies and after running the gantlet of the village vitals – grocery, bar-room, post-office, and bank – he bolted suddenly from a village parlor or lecture-room and, with a bag of rye or Indian meal slung over his shoulder, set out for his snug harbor in the woods, there to renew his adventuring on life.

2

In exactly what relation did Thoreau stand to his fellow-man? He did not assume that the character of the man he met was already inflexibly shaped. Each contributed directly to the other's character development. Each must have capacity for growth. In each man he believed there was a capacity for giving as well as for receiving, and a sharing of mutual growth depended neither upon an exchange of words nor upon heroic acts; the relationship itself sufficed. The thought of potential growth between men kindled his expectation. He said that he approached a great nature with infinite expectation and uncertainty as if it lay before him broad and unexplored like "a scraggy hillside or pasture."

For Thoreau, relationships between men were based neither on respect for excellencies of mind nor on physical attractiveness; they were based on a mutual sympathy, physical attractiveness and mental excellencies notwithstanding. Spontaneity, sincerity, and especially naturalness in his fellow-men gave a tone to the relationship and aroused his sympathy. In a man's discourse he wanted sincerity – to hear something as steady and cheering as the creak of the cricket. What is natural must also be present. The woods, as he said, must be relieved against the sky. And as for spontaneity, the "flux of sparkling streams" should animate the relationship. He demanded the flower and fruit of a man, "that some fragrance be wafted over from him to me, and some ripeness flavor our intercourse. His goodness must not be a partial and transitory act, but a constant superfluity, which costs him nothing and of which he is unconscious."

In the chapter in *Walden* entitled "Visitors," Thoreau enumerated the kind of people who came to visit him at the Pond. Some were objects of charity, not guests. Others had one idea, "like a hen with one chicken, and that a duckling." Some had a thousand ideas, "like those hens which are made to take charge of a hundred chickens, all in pursuit of one bug, a score lost in every morning's dew"; men of ideas, "instead of legs, a sort of intellectual centipede that made you crawl all over." There were girls, boys, business men, farmers, doctors, lawyers, uneasy housekeepers, gossips, restless committed men "whose time was all taken up in getting a living or keeping it," ministers "who spoke of God as if they enjoyed a monopoly of the subject," the old, infirm, and timid of both sexes, and self-styled reformers, "the greatest bores of all." He became acquainted with the different types without ever leaving his doorstoop. Perhaps he did not thus see them at their best, but he got a fair view. He saw them as they wanted to be taken.

He met some who, without doing or saying anything, excited expectation, "like fine-edged tools gradually becoming rusty in a shop-window." What he preferred was a piece of steel or iron "out of which many such tools will be made, or the bushwhack in a man's hand." He preferred serviceable men who could carry immortal errands, and who could take their place in the world and acquit themselves worthily.

He found it difficult to talk with those who recognized no principles. They were the opportunists, and though, like gentlemen, they listened to a rational argument and seemed to be seeing the light, soon shrank hopelessly within their narrowness. Occasionally he encountered one of the offensive kind of men who jests coarsely about the sexual relation. How could a chaste-minded man lay the foundation of any mutual friendship with another so perverted in the fundamental quality of clean-mindedness!

He found the majority of men superficial – men of society, whose interests were transient and fleeting, who used policy, and made up for want of matter with an overdose of manner. They measured success by wealth and by the approbation of other men. They were worldly; that is, took counsel from the world and considered the enterprises of society as final. They were, at best, pompous and ridiculously stately, creatures of circumstance who had no knowledge of truth. Such he referred to as "puffballs filled with dust and ashes."

Thoreau made his observations from direct experience. He talked with an old fellow about the winter snow, thinking the man might be able to tell him of past winters. Instead the old codger asserted that he had never seen snow so deep between his house and his neighbor's. "Very few men take a wide survey; their knowledge is very limited and particular," he decided. As a matter of fact, the knowledge of most men lacked reference to a wide, high perspective. If this lack persisted in their intimate relations to particular phenomena, how much more so was the lack felt in their less gross relationship to spiritual laws! People foolishly apologized for talking or attending to small things outside their ordinary business, "When, if the truth were known, their ordinary business was the small thing, and almost their whole lives were misspent, but they were such fools as not to know it." The farmer, while hoeing, saw someone paddling a boat on the river, or even sitting a half-day motionless in the boat, and cast a look of withering scorn toward the boatman. He failed to see that the object of his own labor was merely to add another dollar to his heap. Contact with the world of business made Thoreau feel chagrined, as though he had done some wrong. He thought if the contact with the materialistic world of business were long continued, men became thoroughly prosaic, hard and coarse. "But the longest intercourse with Nature, though in her rudest moods, does not thus harden and make coarse. A hard, insensible man whom we liken to a rock is indeed much harder than a rock. From hard, coarse, insensible men with whom I have no sympathy, I go to commune with the rocks, whose hearts are comparatively soft."

He saw a kind of activity, or restlessness, apparent in most men, a busy-ness and adventuresomeness, but always as in someone else's employ. Intense and emphatic enterprise was noticeably lacking, for these busy people did little on their own account. Was this the result of gregariousness and unimaginative termitic activity? Many men, if not most, were a sort of natural mummy, exactly like the snipe he heard about that, though neither plucked nor drawn, underwent no change, but dried up naturally. "So some men, though all true life was long ago extinct in them, wear this deceitful semblance of life. They seem to *live* on, without salt or season, from mere toughness or dryness or some antiseptic quality in their fibre." How to live the real life – without mummifying – this is the question. If the real life could be lived in association with man, all right, or if it could be lived only by turning from society, take that turn. The only question is whether or not life is to be lived – truly, richly, and deeply.

3

Thoreau praised man, even as he so severely criticized him. If man was at times frivolous and insignificant, there was also something divine about him. "I think," he said, "that we are not commonly aware that man is our contemporary, – that in this strange, outlandish world, so barren, so prosaic, fit not to live in but merely to pass through, that even here so divine a creature as man does actually live." He recognized a disparity between men. Some were only fit to serve a low use, while others were intended for high uses. "Undoubtedly," he thought, "all men are not equally fit subjects for civilization, and because the majority, like dogs and sheep, are tame by inherited disposition, is no reason why the others should have their natures broken, that they may be reduced to the same level." There are two kinds of strength. The first is produced by working together—by solidarity. This is Walt Whitman's message in *Leaves of Grass*. This is the strength of the social man. The second kind of strength results from standing alone. This is the single strength. It is the individualist's strength and Thoreau is one of its exponents.

When one criticizes man it makes a difference from what point of vantage one offers testimony. Is man merely a tiny lump of impure carbon and water, crawling about on a microscopic planet of the solar system, which itself is an infinitesimal speck in the Milky Way, or is he "a mechanism, undevised and uncreated, and a badly and carelessly driven one at that," as Theodore Dreiser has contended? Or is he the paragon of all virtues and a creature in all respects divine? What Thoreau has to say about man generally has its basis in particular specific events. He was not scornful of man's plight. On the contrary, he was sympathetic toward the situation in which man found himself, and he stood ready to help him out of untoward circumstances by either thought or deed. After he had fetched fuel from the river for his own home, he was quite willing to fetch wood for his neighbors. "I feel disposed . . . to do the getting a living and the living for any three or four of my neighbors who really want the fuel and will appreciate the act, now that I have supplied myself."

Could human beings actually become free and emancipated? Wasn't their normal state a kind of slavery of either mind or body? "Some men," he declared, "are bedridden; all, world-ridden." No doubt man derived some benefit from his institutions, but when human beings cried out in desperation, it was time to pause and reflect. He was stopped by one farmer who said that his hill farm was poor stuff and "only fit to hold the world together." The farmer envied his neighbor's fertile land. Thoreau thought the farmer missed the point, forgetting how his lean soil sharpened his wits and how he could see the heavens at a lesser angle from the hill than from the vale, two advantages to offset the disadvantages. The poetic way of life gave one the most favorable angle.

To an unhappy man, inquiring whether or not some of his neighbors were as happy as anybody, the "poet-naturalist" replied to the man's condition. "Why! . . . the stones are happy, Concord River is happy, and I am happy too. When I took up a fragment of a walnut-shell this morning, I saw by its very grain and composition, its form and color, etc., that it was made for happiness. The most brutish and inanimate objects that are made suggest an everlasting and thorough satisfaction; they are the homes of content. . . ." Wasn't happiness a condition of the mind, a matter of imagination and understanding? There was a man he saw fishing, a man "run down," as they say, who has failed, lost his self-respect, and who ended up by going fishing. What was the outcome of his private misfortune? Only a mellowing and toning of the man, making him more human. "Perhaps he begins to perceive more clearly that the object of life is something else than acquiring property, and he really stands in a truer relation to his fellow-men than when he commanded a false respect of them. There he stands at length, perchance better employed than ever, holding communion with nature and himself and coming to understand his real position and relation to men in this world. It is better than a poor debtor's prison, better than most successful money-getting." While misfortune had perhaps saved this man, who now fished from the river-bank, look closely at what caused misfortune in the first place — the lack of clear thinking and originality and imagination. How many poor immortal souls had Thoreau encountered creeping down the road of life, pushing before them barns seventy-five feet by forty and one hundred acres of land, tillage, mowing, pasture, and woodlot!

Others in as sorry a plight did not realize it. What an army of non-producers society produced! — the coupon-clippers, those flushed and swollen maggots who battened on unearned increment, and who thought themselves well-employed as dispensers of charitable gifts bequeathed to them! Those also of luxurious habits, who avariciously wanted the most, and who vociferated longest and loudest when denied their desires, were "literally paupers maintained at the public expense" and "the most importunate and insatiable beggars." "They cling," as Thoreau said vigorously, "like the glutton to a living man and suck his vitals up." Great wonder Thoreau should have as much regard for his fellow-men as he had. There were the unimaginative, acquisitive, world-ridden, institutionalized creatures who, like Sisyphus, pushed the rock of despair up insurmountable promontories. Perhaps sorriest of all was the army of non-producers, the creatures of fate, boasting of their success but doomed, nevertheless, like Ixion bound to the revolving wheel in Tartarus, to repeat endlessly a stultifying routine.

Obviously some men, perhaps most, were indifferent toward nature. In the broad fields and in the extensive woods and along the curving river he rarely met a walker. Why, there was the booming of the snipe, and he estimated that hardly one in a hundred heard it. Were men inherently artificial and trivial and frivolous? He recorded plaintively in his *Journal*: "I should be pleased to meet man in the woods. I wish he were to be encountered like wild caribous and moose." On occasion man did respond to nature's beauty. During the winter of 1859 there were several days of beautiful frost-work in January and both a miller and a farmer remarked to Thoreau upon the beauty, the farmer even thinking that he had never seen anything so beautiful in all his life. However, such natural and sincere responses were unusual.

When man's relationship with nature lacked virtue, it appeared as reprehensible to Thoreau as the institutionalized life within society. It was equally gross, mercenary, and stupid. In *A Week* he commented on how men, in the name of the corporation, interfered with the life of the Merrimack shad by damming all the streams in order to secure power to turn more mill wheels. If he had lived to the present day, he might have included among man's major depredations destruction of the passenger pigeon, the heath hen, and the buffalo, and, as well, the northwest forests and the fertile prairie land. And what, also, of the Labrador duck, the great auk, the sea mink, Townsend's bunting, and the Eskimo curlew? John Muir gives a vivid account of the incontinent slaughter of the passenger pigeon in his autobiography, *My Boyhood and My Youth.* In *The Oregon Trail* we find Francis Parkman, a Harvard Phi Beta Kappa, along the Arkansas River, in the middle of the nineteenth century, ruthlessly annihilating buffalo bulls because he believed them too ugly to live. Books like Stuart Chase's *The*

New Western Front and *Rich Land, Poor Land,* Paul Sears's *Deserts on the March* and *This Is Our World,* and R. D. Whyte and G. V. Jacks's *Vanishing Lands* present close-up pictures of the devastation of man's rich natural land heritage. And partly through pictures and partly through poetry, Archibald MacLeish makes this devastation poignant in *The Land of the Free.*

Thoreau found the farmer often not only mercenary but insensible. He ignored the handsome grasses in the August fields, which prompted the poet-naturalist to declare, "Heaven, or paradise, might be defined as the place which men avoid," and, very culpably, a certain farmer he knew permitted Irish workmen, equipped with axe and bushwhack, to go out and cut off the natural hedges of sumach, Roxbury waxwork, and grapes, along the walls of the hill farm "in order," Thoreau punned satirically, "that his cows may get a little more green." These same hirelings – the bog-trotting Irish laborers – witlessly cut down the very rare celtis tree, which the botanist and lover of nature had discovered and blessed, since it was the sole representative of its kind in Concord. If some people were prosecuted for abusing children, why weren't others prosecuted for maltreating nature? Most men spared the birds only because they devoured the insect life, or because they ate more crabs than cherries. Most men did not seem to be interested in nature because of its beauty or because of its cheering influence. He found the only account man published on the insects was entitled *Insects Injurious to Vegetation.* "We too admit both a good and a bad spirit," he commented, "but we worship chiefly the bad spirit, whom we fear. We do not think first of the good but of the harm things will do us."

He detected particular examples of stupidity on the part

of some so-called agriculturists. When he visited a farmer's dense white-pine lot which was cut off during the winter and in which the little oaks were seeding in, what was his surprise and chagrin to find that the owner had burned it all over and sowed winter rye. He commented acidly: "He, no doubt, means to let it grow up again in a year or two, but he thought it would be clear gain if he could extract a little rye from it in the meanwhile. What a fool! Here nature had got everything ready for this emergency, and kept them ready for many years, — oaks half a dozen years old or more, with fusiform roots full charged and tops already pointing skyward, only waiting to be touched off by the sun, — and he thought he knew better, and would get a little rye out of it first, which he could feel at once between his fingers, and so he burned it, and dragged his harrow over it. As if oaks would bide *his* time or come at his bidding." Such an agriculturist should have a guardian or forest-warden placed over him; "overseers," as he suggested, "of poor husbandmen."

Thoreau saw that most men did not really care for nature. They would readily sell their share in all her beauty "for a stated sum." Because his own attachment to nature was such a passionate one, it was difficult for him to realize that a similar passion in others had to be acquired. Notwithstanding Thoreau's contention, doubtless most men do care for nature, but their interest is a matter of degree. Few are as passionately attached to nature as he was and few, indeed, combine as he did the interests of herbalist, entomologist, geologist, meteorologist, agrologist, and ornithologist. Knowledge of some phase of natural phenomena generates interest in other phases, and the true nature-lover advances deliberately in his quest of knowledge. An interest in herbs may extend to an interest in insects. An interest in the formation of the earth sometimes advances to an interest in climatic conditions. An interest in grasses can conceivably lead to an interest in birds. Each interest requires cultivation, but most men are too preoccupied with what they term "business affairs" to give the necessary time to nature-study. Only the "natural men" have time to cultivate their relationship to nature.

4

Countrymen like George Melvin, Alek Therien, John Goodwin, George Minott, Edmund Hosmer, and Reuben Rice were thoroughly naturalized in the Concord briar patch. Because they had more "of the wind and rain and meadow muck in their composition" and because, "compared with ordinary men, they grow like a Rohan potato beside a Lady's-Finger," Thoreau cultivated their acquaintance. They were adept; they whittled their own axe-helves. What they wore suited them, like the huntsman George Melvin's russet clothes. Their knowledge Thoreau liked best because it had so much humanity in it.

Civility and manners and dress and habits, which prevented most men from participating directly with nature, did not stand in their way. Attracted by a common interest, Thoreau probed their natural lore. In their way of life events took place which the trained naturalist might wait years to see in vain. Once George Minott had seen a muskrat resting under the ice a long way from its cabin on the bank. When it stopped, a bubble issued from its mouth and fluttered out against the ice. It remained for half a minute with its mouth in the bubble, then drew it in and went on its way. Jacob Farmer spent a Sunday afternoon watching republican swallows feed their young. "There were five young, and he was curious to know how each received its share; and as often as the bird came with a fly, the one at the door (or opening) took it, and then they all hitched round one notch, so that a new one was presented at the door, who received the next fly; and this was the invariable order, the same one never receiving two flies in succession." Such incidents as Minott and Farmer observed would have enkindled Izaak Walton and Gilbert White, even as they did Thoreau. Humphrey Buttrick's unique way of catching ruffed grouse also impressed him. Finding the young birds, Buttrick lay down on them and passed his hand back and forth under his body until he felt one which he grasped, not by the feathers, but by the leg or head. If he raised his body, the chicks squeezed out. Somewhat of a champion at grouse-catching, Buttrick had caught as many as a dozen in his hands. He had seen them drum – sometimes for an hour – as he thought striking their body with their wings, but actually they beat their wings on the air. He also knew where to find woodcock's eggs and the nests of wood ducks and goshawks.

On his walks, Thoreau met countrymen, like old Joseph Hosmer, who told him much that he had not known, or, like Pratt, who brought things that might interest him. The former had detected a difference between two kinds of white oak because one kind, which was finer-grained and heavier than the common, stained his axe-blade steel-blue in the spring when the sap was running. The latter, a man of rare naïveté who believed in the efficacy of eyestones and in the appearance of human skeletons twenty feet in length, brought for dissection wings of sparrow hawks and the nests of chimney swallows. But it was Witherell who solved for Thoreau the mystery of the stone heaps which he detected at the bottom of Walden Pond. When Thoreau asked Witherell what made them, he answered readily that it was the lamprey eel, for he had seen one piling up the stones.

Among the natural men whom Thoreau celebrated were the fishermen and the hunters. An expert fisherman, he had outclassed the bog-trotting Irishman, John Field, in fishing skill at Fair Haven Pond. While camping in the Maine Woods, at the mouth of the Aboljacknagesic, where he had wakened from his sleep dreaming of fish, he picked up his birch pole, went to the bank and fished until moonlight faded into daylight, the fish he caught describing bright arcs on the dark side of Ktaadn as he pulled them in. Then he stopped and sharpened sticks four feet in length and spitted the well-salted trout over the morning campfire. He eyed with approval an old brown-coated Walton of the Musketaquid who, come winter, fished through the ice for Walden's dazzling and transcendent pickerel; the fish-spearers — "dusky, fuliginous figures, half enveloped in smoke" — their lurid, reddish blaze of pitch-pine roots kindling by the riverside; bibulous Luke Dodge, with a nutmeg-grater voice who in his eighty-third year fished the river; and two such piscatorial nonpareils as Sudbury Haines, of the Joseph's coat-of-many-colors, who, when a sudden shower fell, took down his pole and hastened to the river, and short, square-bodied, broad-shouldered, blue-frocked, one-eyed John Goodwin, the fishing genius of the Concord streams.

An order of natural men similar to the fishermen were the hunters. On his river tramps, Thoreau saw the weather-beaten muskrat hunters — the gods of the river — supplied with powder and shot, pushing up the Musketaquid, their eyes sharp-set and their minds dreaming piles of dead rats. The sound of their guns exhilarated him, and he celebrated their seasonal advent with a fanfare. "As a mother loves to see her child imbibe nourishment and expand, so God loves to see his children thrive on the nutriment he has furnished them. . . . These aboriginal men cannot be repressed, but under some guise or other they survive and reappear continually."

Thoreau thanked his stars for "awkward, gawky, loose-hung" George Melvin, the chief Concord hunter, who was such a trial to his mother. To Thoreau, who encountered the hunter dressed in a russet suit and accompanied by a lank, bluish-white, black-spotted hound as he made his way home from a day's venture in the woods, Melvin was agreeable "as a tinge of russet on the hillside." A world separated them, but he was still a neighbor and a contemporary. "He is one tribe, I am another, and we are not at war." Melvin represented a level of activity which he had transcended. When a man understood the relationship of the animals to their natural environment, he renounced killing them. "No humane being, past the thoughtless age of boyhood, will wantonly murder any creature which holds its life by the same tenure that he does. . . . He goes thither at first as a hunter and fisher, until at last, if he has the seeds of a better life in him, he distinguishes his proper objects, as a poet or naturalist it may be, and leaves the gun and fish-pole behind."

Equally interesting as the the fishermen and hunters were men like old Bill Wheeler — supposedly love-cracked — whom he met once in every five years and who slept in the woods by the Great Meadows in a kind of woodman's shelter which consisted of meadow-hay thrown over a rude frame; or cheery old Brooks Clark, bent like a bow and padding along the old Carlisle road on bare feet, "like an old squirrel shuffling to his hole with a nut," his shoes full of knurly apples held in one hand, an axe gripped in the other. In the Maine Woods, he had discovered the incomparable Penobscot watermen, "Uncle George" McCauslin and Tom Fowler, who, like voyageurs, exhibited the cunning of their craft in the waterways as at Passamagamet. When "Uncle George" sat in the stern and Tom crouched in the bow, clutching twelve-foot, iron-shod spruce poles, both poling on the same side, the thirty-foot batteau shot up the rapids "like a salmon, the water rushing and roaring around."

Down on Cape Cod, he met a merry old Panurge of an oysterman at Wellfleet. The eighty-eight-year-old man remembered having seen George Washington ride his horse along the streets of Boston and he had heard the guns fired at Bunker Hill. In spite of being under "petticoat government," he was brimful of life and curiosity. He tapped Thoreau eagerly for information and in return generously divulged sea lore. Thoreau and a companion remained under the old man's roof for a night, and, as they left next morning, the old oysterman plied the former with inquiries to the gate.

Perhaps the best specimen of the natural men was Alek Therien, a skilful young Canadian wood-chopper and post-maker. "A more simple and natural man it would be hard to find." In physical appearance, he was stout, thick-necked, bushy-haired, and dull-eyed. But his sluggish temperament was offset by an ingratiating good nature. He had never been educated by the Catholic priests of Canada to the degree of consciousness, only to the degree of trust. In him the animal man was chiefly developed while the intellectual or spiritual side slumbered. Yet he was a primitive, rudimentary intellectual thinker in whom Thoreau delighted, since "he could defend many institutions better than any philosopher, because, in describing them as they concerned him, he gave the true reason for their prevalence, and speculation had not suggested to him any other." Therien was so primitive Thoreau could never manoeuvre him into a position from whence he would take a spiritual view. He was, indeed, an elemental man, who set out to work soon after sunup of a cold winter's morning with a lunch of cold woodchuck and coffee in a stone bottle, and throughout the day, while the ice whooped on Flint's Pond, skilfully cut his tree close to the ground, because, as he noted, the sprouts that came from such stumps were better. To the reflective Thoreau such an elemental man "suggested that there might be men of genius in the lowest grades of life, however permanently humble and illiterate, who take their own view always, or do not pretend to see at all, who are as bottomless even as Walden Pond was thought to be, though they may be dark and muddy."

The most satisfying natural men were the Concord husbandmen – George Minott, Edmund Hosmer, and Reuben Rice. George Minott, for example, was one of the most poetical farmers of whom he knew. His speech was full of good old English words; his husbandry was skilful; and his way of life was simple, economical, unhurried, satisfying. He did nothing in haste nor with an eye incessantly cocked on the main chance; he was repaid wholly by "the constant satisfaction" which his labor yielded him. Unharassed by more land than he could handle or more work than he could do or more hired labor than he could direct, he lived a free man.

His small, square, one-storied, weather-stained house, with hipped roof and dormer-window, was snugly and picturesquely lodged, a third the way down the south side of a long hill, perfectly harmonious with its surroundings. Although there were no gravelled walks or side fences or flower plots about it, only a sloping bank, yet it had position, afforded warmth, shelter, dryness, and prospect. It overlooked the brook, meadow, road, neighboring houses, and revealed the distant woods. Spring came earlier to its dooryard and summer lingered longest.

When Thoreau found its owner sitting in the corner behind the door, close to the stove, his hat on and a cat by his side, he was usually full of humor and gusty stories that were faithful to the minutest detail. While narrating hunting stories, he always emphasized the kind of gun he used – a "half-stocked" piece or "a cocking piece" or flint-lock, although it was doubtful if he had more than two guns in his life. His word for finishing off his game was "gave him gavel." When Thoreau walked with him, he found Minott had a story for every woodland path; he had hunted in all of them. He was a man wise in the ways of natural things; he heard with infallible accuracy the notes of the migrating birds; he got most out of his garnered corn by placing the cut stalks to dry over braces in his barn when they were fresh and fullest of nutritive strength; he had heard the stake-driver or bittern, which he called "belcher-squelcher," make its noise "*slug-toot, slug-toot, slug-toot*"; and he had caught ruffed grouse by the wing. In speaking of foxes he told Thoreau: "As soon as the nights get to be cool, if you step outdoors at nine or ten o'clock when all is still, you'll hear them bark out on the flat behind the houses, half a mile off, or sometimes *whistle* through their noses. I can tell 'em. I know what that means. I know all about that. They are out after something to eat, I suppose." Here was an indigenous man after Thoreau's own heart who loved to hear the goldfinches sing on the hemp which grew near his gate, and who loved to walk in a swamp in windy weather to hear the wind groan through the pines.

The second of the triumvirate of unusual husbandmen was the long-headed farmer, Edmund Hosmer, whose farm was on a part of Governor Winthrop's old manor. Less poetic than George Minott but very shrewd, Thoreau wondered why Hosmer had never been invited to lecture at the Lyceum. Hosmer, one of the most intelligent farmers in Concord "and perchance in Middlesex," disappointed him a little because with all his property he was so perpetually employed with the work of his hands. "He has not even planned an essentially better life." He was resourceful; he could whittle his own axe-helves out of white oak, but he was not essentially hopeful. Although he lived in a house under the elms on the sunniest of green slopes that looked "like a terrestrial paradise, the abode of peace and domestic happiness," yet he wondered despairingly what life was for. Thoreau, fresh from reading in Columella, considered that "human life may be transitory and full of trouble, but the perennial mind, whose survey extends from that spring to this, from Columella to Hosmer, is superior to change. I will identify myself with that which did not die with Columella and will not die with Hosmer."

The third of the triumvirate was Reuben Rice, who lived a successful poetic life related to primitive nature on his Sudbury and Concord farms. He was one of "the saving remnant" who had learned the rare art of living. He got more out of his enterprises than his neighbors because he was prepared to enjoy whatever pleasures there were in store for him in them. Hearing Thoreau complain of the want of tools, he reproved him, saying that he ought to have a chest. When Thoreau replied that he wouldn't use them enough to pay for them, Rice rejoined, "You would use them more, if you had them." Discovering the need of certain tools when he came to do a piece of work, Rice set about making each tool as he needed it and thus secured a kit of valuable tools. A man of good sense and calculation, he acquired riches through careful investment and had property in the city as well as in the country. By practicing a neat economy it cost him less to live and he got more out of it. "To get his living, or keep it, is not a hasty or disagreeable toil. He works slowly but surely, enjoying the sweet of it," declared Thoreau. He had observed the ways of the birds, especially the bold robber cuckoo and the frog hawk, and the creatures of the field, as well; for example, how the muskrats make a corral to keep the water from freezing or how foxes caught meadow mice by jumping up and down on tussocks and so scared the mice into their grasp. Rice had also taken time to participate in nature. Thoreau joined him on very satisfying bee-hunts.

Wherever an independent way of life was expressed through natural craft or lore, Thoreau's appreciation and respect responded. As interesting as the husbandman was the blacksmith who performed simply and easily by fire and rude tools work which "would have surpassed the skill of a tribe of savages," and the wood-chopper — "who has written the history of his day?" — who, "now that the Indian is gone, stands nearest to nature," and the stonemason, who, with hammer, chisels, wedges, shims, and iron spoons, plied with patience and skill the stubborn task of splitting durable granite.

Because he discovered that "the habit of looking at men in the gross makes their lives have less of human interest for us," Thoreau has something really important to say to us. He penetrated successfully beneath the surface and suggested the "little epic life" which the laborer each day led, whether that laborer was the stonemason, or George Minott, or Alek Therien. The poetic life represented the unrepressed, self-dependent, craftsman-like life, the life of replenishable energy, renewable enthusiasm, and personal skill. As Whitman chanted:

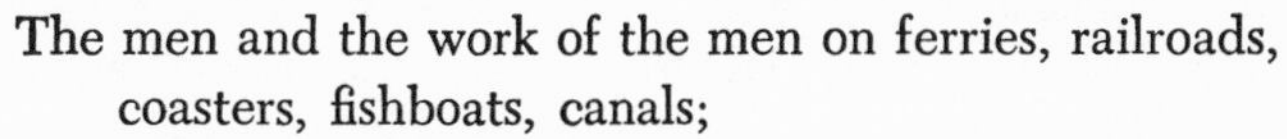

> The men and the work of the men on ferries, railroads,
> coasters, fishboats, canals;
> The hourly routine of your own or any man's life, the
> shop, yard, store, or factory . . .
>
> . . . .
>
> In them realities for you and me, in them poems for you
> and me.

IV

An Indian Memory

For Indian deeds there must be an Indian memory;
the white man will remember only his own.
The First and Last Journeys of Thoreau

A YEARNING FOR WILDNESS drew Thoreau directly to the Indian, and Concord was as fertile a spot as any in New England to study an Indian domain now abandoned. The first white settlers at Concord bought their land from Tahatawan, an Algonquin sachem whose fishing and hunting lodge had been pitched on Nawshawtuct (now Lee's) Hill. Traces of the red man's occupation were abundant. Thoreau found gouges on Dennis Hill, beak-like pestles in Hosmer's field, an Indian creel or eel-pot constructed of wattled wickerwork in the sluiceway of Pole Brook, and rude ornamental soapstone pottery washed out on Clamshell Hill by the heavy spring rains. There were flints, hoes, mortars, spearheads, stone hatchets, arrowheads galore. And a meandering footpath, which must have been worn there by Indian hunters, encircled Walden Pond.

So keen was Thoreau's interest in the Indian, he kept special notebooks – eleven in number containing twenty-eight hundred pages and approximately a half-million words — which would doubtless have formed the basis for a study of the Indian. His references to the Indian and his way of life are frequent in *A Week*, *Walden*, *The Maine Woods*, and, of course, in the *Journal*. When he died on May 15, 1862, five years after the fourth trip into the Maine Woods, his last words were said to have been "moose" and "Indian," which is revelatory of the tenacity with which the red man gripped his imagination.

What really concerns us is why he studied the red men so sedulously. Was it because he found in their lore a measure by which he might determine the progress of his own approach to nature? He was pleased certainly when he discovered how the yellowish-green shoots of the young soft white pine indicated the east, since it confirmed a fact in the red man's lore. He was stimulated, too, when he found that the white man had absorbed into the almanac the natural lore of the Indian. There were, for example, the Indian observations that one should not look for winter until the springs were full and the saying that an abundance of acorns and the unusual thickening of corn-husks in the summer augured a hard winter.

He was excited as well by the arrowheads — "the mind-print of the oldest men" — which were sown over the earth like a kind of stone fruit. One of his regular pursuits in the fall was to observe where some farmer turned a sandy field or ploughed a meadow knoll, and in the spring, as soon as the earth began to dry, he made his way to field or knoll lately washed by the spring freshet, to harvest a crop of arrowheads. These Indian arrowheads were "fossil thoughts" which forever reminded him of the mind that shaped them. "I would fain know," he said, "that I am treading in the tracks of human game, – that I am on the trail of mind, – and these little reminders never fail to set me right. When I see these signs I know that the subtle spirits that made them are not far off, into whatever form transmuted." He trailed the mind of the indigenous man of America from whom he thought much might be learned. He wanted to know what the Indian was like, and how he lived.

In 1850 he visited the Indians still living in their tents on the outskirts of Concord. They talked about the use of moosehorns, the making of clothes, spears, sleds, canoes, cradles, birch-bark vessels, snowshoes, traps, and of spitting food to cook. A far more intimate knowledge of the Indian came from his acquaintance with his Indian guides on journeys in the Maine woods. Of four trips to the Maine woods – the first in 1838, the second to Ktaadn in 1846, the third to Chesuncook in 1853, and the fourth to the headwaters of the Penobscot in 1857 – the last two were the most rewarding.

On the trip to Chesuncook in September, 1853, his Indian guide, Joe Aitteon, was a member of the Penobscot tribe. Aitteon was short, stout, broad-faced; a good-looking Indian who wore a red flannel shirt, woolen pants, and a black hat, just like a lumberman. At the head of Moosehead Lake they went over a "carry" or portage to the Penobscot River and set out in a nineteen-foot birch canoe for Chesuncook Lake. At nightfall they camped wherever they happened to be, and in the moonlight hunted unsuccessfully for moose. With his fifteen-inch birch horn, Aitteon frequently made the moose call, but to no avail.

They had more success at Pine Stream Deadwater. When Thoreau glimpsed a cow moose with her calf standing at the edge of the stream, he thought they resembled "great frightened rabbits, with their long ears and half-inquisitive, half-frightened looks." His cousin, Mr. Thatcher of Bangor, shot and wounded the cow moose. At once Aitteon started in pursuit of the wounded quarry. Proceeding with a "peculiar, elastic, noiseless, and stealthy tread, looking to right and left on the ground," he trailed the bloody spoor, but without recovering the moose as immediately as Thoreau thought an Indian should. Eventually Thoreau and Aitteon returned to the canoe and while paddling up Pine Stream came upon the body of the cow moose lying dead and quite warm in the middle of the stream. "No doubt," Thoreau remarked pointedly, "a better hunter would have tracked it to this spot at once." Joe Aitteon did not "prove up" unqualifiedly as a hunter in his eyes.

On the return up the Penobscot toward the Moosehorn, they camped with some of Aitteon's Indian friends, who were busy smoking moose meat and curing the skins of twenty-two moose, killed within the last two months. "Altogether," Thoreau noted, "it was about as savage a sight as was ever witnessed, and I was carried back at once three hundred years." Lying there in the camp among the wild Indian hunters, he felt "as near to the primitive man of America, that night, as any of its discoverers ever did."

His last trip to the Maine woods was made in July, 1857. In company with Edward Hoar and an Indian guide he set out on July twentieth for a journey of three hundred and twenty-five miles. The party travelled to the headwaters of the Kennebec, Penobscot, and St. John Rivers, by Moosehead Lake to the Allegash lakes, and returned by the East Branch of the Penobscot on August seventh.

On this trip Thoreau was anxious to get a real Indian guide, one, at least, who surpassed the youthful and not very informative Joe Aitteon. "We wanted to get one who was temperate and reliable, an older man than we had before, well skilled in Indian lore," he said. "I was warned not to employ an Indian on account of their obstinacy and the difficulty of understanding one another, and on account of their dirty habits in cooking, etc., but it was partly the Indian, such as he was, that I had come to see. The difficulty is to find one who will not get drunk and detain you where-ever liquor is to be had."

More fortunate this time in his selection of an Indian guide, he secured the services of Joe Polis, the chief man of the Penobscot tribe of Indians. Joe, about forty-eight years old, was a rugged man, above middle height, with a broad face and characteristic Indian features and complexion. By his fellows he was regarded as a man of property and means. Thoreau found Joe busy before his door dressing a deer skin. A skilful dresser of moose hides, he averaged seven or eight dollars a hide. Some days he made as much as fifty or sixty dollars. As a hunter he had killed as many as ten moose in one day.

Since Joe Polis exhibited the chief characteristics of the Indian temperament, Thoreau observed him narrowly. As a matter of fact, his study of Joe Polis during this trip was the chief source of his information regarding the characteristics peculiar to the Indian nature. Trying to plumb secrets subtler than the natural phenomena of the wild Maine forests, he warily struck his psychological probe into Joe Polis, a man as strange in his way as the extensive Maine spruces were different from Emerson's familiar stand of white pine on the edge of Walden Pond. He noticed how vague Joe made his answers, "vague as a puff of smoke, suggesting no responsibility." In traversing portages, Joe made no effort to let his companions know where he was waiting for them. "Indians," Joe told Thoreau, "like to get along with the least possible communication and ado." When he did not at once reveal his whereabouts, Joe thought he was actually paying his companion a compliment.

While Joe's reserve was rather tantalizing, his wood lore was inexhaustible and generously shared. He pointed to the red osier bark as good as a substitute for tobacco. He informed his companions that a light noise which he heard was a snake, and upon request whistled a low note in imitation. He gathered thread from the black-spruce root, which he grubbed from the ground without glancing at any of the trees overhead. He made a candle in a minute from a piece of birch-bark, which he rolled hard into a match-like beam, fifteen inches long, and he stuck this in a split stick three feet high. He constructed a pipe out of birch-bark in a few moments. There was no end to his skill in applying natural lore to practical utilities. So wide, too, was his botanical knowledge that for every plant pointed out he named some medicinal use. Ingeniously he transported his canoe over the carries by an arrangement of cords so that the weight was distributed more evenly over his shoulders, chest, and forehead. Though Thoreau, carrying the pack, beat him when they raced over one of the carries, Joe, with the canoe over his head, gave him a good race. Polis demonstrated his skill as a boatman when he navigated Webster Stream, a feat which was "somewhat like navigating a thunder-spout." Joe's knowledge of the woods was both comprehensive and accurate. He could find his way anywhere, living off the land; for, as Thoreau explained, "he does not carry things in his head, nor remember the routes exactly, like a white man, but relies on himself at the moment." Joe retraced his steps through difficult ways totally unmindful of his previous passage. Such instinctive *rapport* with nature filled Thoreau with restrained admiration.

Twice only did Joe appear uncommonly like the white man, and both times were disillusioning to Thoreau. Once, as he shot at a moose, Joe appeared as agitated and nervous as a small boy with buck-fever. A more damaging blow to Indian stoicism occurred when Joe was taken with the colic. Thoreau, amazed at the deficiency of Indian impassivity and fortitude, declared, "It seemed to me that, like the Irish, he made a greater ado about his sickness than a Yankee does. and was more alarmed about himself." However, these two exceptions to the generally accepted picture of the Indian temperament would not go far toward undermining the Indian's racial reputation. The preponderance of evidence was in the Indian's favor wherever an intimate relationship with nature was to be considered. Perhaps, too, the Indian might well have explained his reactions from a different viewpoint. We have only the white man's indefatigable and intelligent scrutiny for evidence.

Throughout the trip Thoreau tried to catch "the scent" of Joe; tried to penetrate to the essence of strangeness and difference which separated the red man from the white man. When they arrived back in Bangor, the secret was still safe. Thoreau never discovered the inner secret or mystery; at best, he remained the more acutely aware of it. Once, on the trip, when Joe, making "a curious squeaking, wiry sound with his lips," called the muskrat, Thoreau thought that at last he was in the deepest thickets of the wilderness with an indigene. "I did not know," he commented of Joe Polis and the muskrat, "which of the two was the strangest to me."

To Thoreau, the Indian stood "free and unconstrained in

Nature." He was not like a guest in the great house of Nature but an inhabitant. In contrast, the white man had only the habits of the house. He was not free and unconstrained in nature, but moved about as though he were oppressed and confined, all the time holding up his arms as though the walls of his prison-house would fall in and crush him. His muscles were taut. He was an anxious, impatient, restless, dogged creature. "We talk of civilizing the Indian, but that is not the name for his improvement. By the wary independence and aloofness of his dim forest life he preserves his intercourse with his native gods, and is admitted from time to time to a rare and peculiar society with Nature. . . . The Indian's intercourse with Nature is at least such as admits of the greatest independence of each. . . . If we could listen but for an instant to the chant of the Indian muse, we should understand why he will not exchange his savageness for civilization. Nations are not whimsical. Steel and blankets are strong temptations; but the Indian does well to continue Indian." Apparently the position could be reversed, and the Indian could teach the white man, who was pathetically involved in his self-created civilization, the necessity of a more congenial *rapport* with a natural environment. The white man had learned from the red man the use of corn and how to plant it; the red man had taught the paleface how to dry whortleberries for winter use, shown how to make baskets, and added many edible berries and domesticated plants to the white man's larder.

In studying a dictionary of the Abenaki language, Thoreau learned that whatever the Indians had a word for they had a thing for. Their words were direct evidence of what they knew. He caught the "bow-arrow tang" in the unsubdued accent of a Chippeway Indian from whom he learned that the red men traced their origin to Asia, and who, because of the similarity of customs, thought they might be Jews. He inspected some Indian ornaments, and especially, a cradle. He deprecated scientific names of things which conveyed only partial information when the Indians' knowledge was ampler.

> How little I know of the *arbor-vitae* when I have learned only what science can tell me! It is but a word. It is not a *tree of life*. But there are twenty words for the tree and its different parts which the Indian gave, which are not in our botanies, which imply a more practical and vital science. He used it every day. He was well acquainted with its wood, and its bark, and its leaves . . . how much more conversant was the Indian with any wild animal or plant than we are, and in his language is implied all that intimacy, as much as ours is expressed in our language. How many words in his language about a moose, or birch bark, and the like! The Indian stood nearer to wild nature than we. The wildest and noblest quadrupeds, even the largest fresh-water fishes, some of the wildest and noblest birds and the fairest flowers have actually receded as *we* advanced, and we have but the most distant knowledge of them. . . . It was a new light when my guide gave me Indian names for things for which I had only scientific ones before. In proportion as I understood the language, I saw them from a new point of view.
>
> A dictionary of the Indian language reveals another and wholly new life to us. Look at the word "canoe," and see what a story it tells of outdoor life, with the names of all its parts and modes of using it, as our words describing the different parts and seats of a coach, — with the difference in practical knowledge between him who rides and him who walks; or at the word "wigwam," and see how close it brings

> you to the ground; or "Indian corn," and see which race was most familiar with it. It reveals to me a life within a life, or rather a life without a life, as it were threading the woods between our towns still, and yet we can never tread in its trail. The Indian's earthly life was as far off from us as heaven is.

Among the Indian relics he found in Concord was a pestle whose handle resembled the beak of a bird. To him it indicated how the Indian sometimes carried his art a step beyond arrowheads, and incidentally a step beyond pure utility. Here was evinced taste and fancy.

> It is a great step to find a pestle whose handle is ornamented with a bird's-head knob. It brings the maker still nearer to the races which so ornament their umbrella and cane handles. I have, then, evidence in stone that men lived here who had fancies to be pleased, and in whom the first steps toward a complete culture were taken. It implies so many more thoughts such as I have. The arrowhead, too, suggests a bird, but a relation to it not in the least godlike. But here an Indian has patiently sat and fashioned a stone into the likeness of a bird, and added some pure beauty to that pure utility, and so far begun to leave behind him war, and even hunting, and to redeem himself from the savage state. In this he was leaving off to be savage. Enough of this would have saved him from extermination.

Well, and what of the Indian's fate? To Thoreau the Indian was not only fated, but was already a member of a vanishing race. The history of the white man represented improvement; the history of the Indian represented only fixed habits of stagnation. Only the persevering poet had not forgotten the red man entirely. The white man had begun a new era. Like a race who had exhausted the secrets of nature, the Indian moved on. The plough replaced the bow-and-arrow, and an agricultural civilization replaced a hunting age, in the history of this continent. His fate says sternly to him, "Forsake the hunter's life and enter into the agricultural, the second, state of man. Root yourselves a little deeper in the soil, if you would continue to be the occupants of the country." Though Thoreau sympathized with the Indian hunters, the supremacy of the agricultural way of life over the more primitive was apparent to him. "A race of hunters can never withstand the inroads of a race of husbandmen." As for the game, "the rifle alone would never exterminate it, but the plow is a more fatal weapon; it wins the country inch by inch and holds all it gets." What of the Negro? Why should he endure and not the red man? "The African will survive, for he is docile, and is patiently learning his trade and dancing at his labor; but the Indian does not often dance, unless it be the war dance."

2

In a rather memorable discussion between Alcott and Thoreau at Emerson's home after a lecture on "Barbarism and Civilization," delivered by Higginson on the evening of January 24, 1860, Alcott maintained that civilization represented "the ascendency of sentiment over brute force, the sway of ideas over animalism, of mind over matter. . . . The barbarian has no society; this begins in sympathy. . . ." Thoreau, meanwhile, defended the Indians' right not to be exterminated because he held a place between civilized man and nature. Alcott, a staunch defender of civilization, unwilling to give any quarter in the discussion, asserted: "I say that he goes along with the woods and the beasts, who retreat before and are superseded by man, and the planting of orchards and gardens. The savage succumbs to the superiority of the white man. . . . Man's victory over nature and himself is to overcome the brute beast in him." The difference between two attitudes is here sharply focussed, and yet who will say that Thoreau, the cultivator of bean-fields, was no planter of gardens? Is it not fair to admit with Thoreau that the Indian experienced "a rare and peculiar society with Nature" which the inhabitants of drawing-rooms never enjoyed? Thoreau was not unmindful of "the innocent pleasures of country life." He found it pleasant "to make the earth yield her increase, and gather the fruits in their season," yet he thought the heroic spirit did not fail "to dream of remoter retirements and more rugged paths." He explained: "We would not always be soothing and taming Nature, breaking the horse and the ox, but sometimes ride the horse wild and chase the buffalo. The Indian's intercourse with Nature is at least such as admits of the greatest independence of each. If he is somewhat of a stranger in her midst, the gardener is too much of a familiar. There is something vulgar and foul in the latter's closeness to his mistress, something noble and cleanly in the former's distance."

The difference in attitude toward nature of Alcott and Thoreau is quite illuminating. In *Pedlar's Progress,* Mr. Odell Shepard shows clearly how Bronson Alcott's attitude toward nature was a humanistic one while Thoreau's was a naturalistic one. Alcott himself distinguished between his own attitude and Thoreau's acutely: "He [Thoreau] is an observer of Nature pure, and I discover her as exalted and mingled in Man." To Bronson Alcott, the gardener and husbandman and conscious artist, it was "a pleasure to add something to the landscape, completing in some sort the design of nature. . . . The country, indeed, as discriminated from the wilderness, is purely of man's creation. His improvements are the country. The savage has none. . . ." Humanistic in his attitude, Alcott sought to humanize the landscape by meliorating the wild asperities of nature. He preferred the partnership between man and nature which produced the garden or the orchard and the old-time New England village.

The most enlightening clarification of man's relationship to nature with which I am acquainted appears in the Prolegomena to Thomas Henry Huxley's Romanes Lecture of 1893 on *Evolution and Ethics*. Huxley shows that although man is the product of an evolutionary, or, as he terms it, cosmic process, man stands in opposition to it; for, by virtue of the power of reasoning, man's aims and achievements now differ from those of the original process. Huxley clarifies his viewpoint in an extended metaphor. A gardener, desiring to plant a garden, extirpates all native vegetation within a small area. After he clears the turf of all extraneous vegetation, he imports a colony of strange plants and sets them out in the garden. The plants are, of course, sustained by and dependent upon the gardener's supervision, and he is constantly occupied in protecting them from the antagonistic influences of the general cosmic process — i.e., weathering, quadrupedal or bipedal invasion, birds, insects, blight, mildew, weeds. When the garden flourishes, it represents a victory for the art of the gardener over the cosmic powers at work in the state of nature.

In applying Huxley's metaphor, man's position in nature is

that of the gardener; his civilization is like the garden. The gardener and the garden are dissociated parts of the cosmic process. The cosmic process which produced man is now distinct from him, and the civilization which he has cultivated and which he tries to preserve can be preserved from the implacable opposition of the cosmic process only by exercising the utmost vigilance.

What I glean from Huxley's metaphor is positive enough. It is as though he said: Of course the natural forces do not voluntarily co-operate with man. They are not predisposed to help *him*. He must at all times watch warily the inorganic forces of wind and water, sun and storm, and the organic forces of pestilence and wild beasts, and in his personally supervised garden of civilization, he must also keep an eye on the human forces — personal or natural enemies from within or without. He exercises his intelligence purposively, not when he invokes or placates these natural forces, but when he finds a way of mastering and controlling them to his own ends. Neither by imitating nor by evading the cosmic process will man progress, but only by confronting it. "Social progress," summarizes Huxley, "means a checking of the cosmic process at every step and the substitution for it of another, which may be called the ethical process; the end of which is not the survival of those who may happen to be the fittest, in respect of the whole of the conditions which obtain, but of those who are ethically the best." When the cosmic process is thus checked, it may well be said of man that "in virtue of his intelligence, the dwarf bends the Titan to his will."

Undoubtedly Thoreau was closer in spirit to the Indian than to the gardener in his relationship to nature. Thoreau, like the Indian, did not try to assert his domination over nature; he simply acclimatized himself in nature. Others, like Franklin and Fulton and Morse and Edison, and the builders of transcontinental railroads and cities and power dams, might seek to control natural forces, or, like Alcott, others might seek to improve nature – to beat back the wilderness stretches and open the earth and sow the fertile fields and plant the hillside orchards; but Thoreau, neither a power-avid controller of mines, quarries, waterfalls, or forests, nor an ardent improver and utilizer of wilderness spaces, sought to become naturalized. Who, one wonders, is really the more valid humanist, the man who seeks to control nature by creating from the wilderness area gardens and pastures, or the one who seeks to understand nature with a subtle responsive sympathy and who succeeds in living with, rather than simply on, the natural earth? Undoubtedly these two viewpoints are not antithetic but complementary: the latter precedes the former in a valid relationship.

Undoubtedly the one who achieves the most valid relationship to nature is not the one who loses himself in the landscape nor yet the one who dominates it ruthlessly, but the one who lives harmoniously with it, understanding, interpreting, and using it wisely. The measure of the latter's mastery is as much spiritual as it is physical. Wallace Stevens suggests how this mastery is realized. In one of his poems he shifts his viewpoint from the superior position that "Man is the intelligence of his soil" to the sympathetic position – ". . . his soil is man's intelligence," which means that only by accepting and learning from his environment can man fulfil himself. There is a sense, too, in which man's much-vaunted domination of nature is more illusory than real. Count Keyserling, in *Travel Diary of a Philosopher*, asserts: "... the man of today does not rule as God, but as the spirit of the earth. Materially he dominates nature, he is not superior to it; instead of guiding it in accordance with his own ideals, he generally only does what the elements themselves demand from him. He resembles those river-gods in which the ancients believed, whose dominating will corresponded with the natural gradient."

Our contemporary attitude toward nature reflects vigorously an interaction between the human organism and its natural environment. The organism is shaped by its environment, but, in turn, it shows insurgence in its attempt to control the natural environment. If the former action represents passive compliance, the latter represents active domination through energy, skill, invention, and intellect. Nature is accepted, studied, and enjoyed, but it is not necessarily viewed as the source of moral symbols. The attitude is not so much one of conformity to, nor yet of liberation from, as it is one of integration with, nature. Thoreau's relationship to the contemporary view is clear. He was passive in the sense that he accepted his environment. He was also active in the sense that he explored the ways and means by which man might attain a far closer harmony with nature than primitive man succeeded in realizing by placative and propitiatory magic, or even than civilized man had realized, bound as the latter was by the responsibilities of an institutionalized life. To the twentieth-century thinker nature is impersonal and mysterious – sometimes alien and hostile, but nevertheless not wholly unknowable. Thoreau's contribution consists in the fact that he made nature less unknowable to us. He showed us the way to a harmony with it as well as the effect of such a harmony upon the human spirit.

Yet Mr. Odell Shepard finds Thoreau no bold way-breaker, but "a quite conventional follower along old and beaten paths." Meanwhile, Alcott, who neither exalted the pantheistic deification of nature nor yielded to primitivistic dreams, looked forward in imagination to the time when the American landscape should be mastered, controlled, and humanized. Mr. Shepard thinks Thoreau looked backward to the time before the white man came, and, as "a panegyrist of the wild," represented the romantically sentimental view "that has laid the American wilderness open for game-slaughterers, stream-stiflers, converters of forest into match-sticks, and the common horde of vulgarians generally, to trample and crush and almost destroy." How Thoreau's attitude prepared the way for these nature-despoilers baffles me. He deprecated game-slaughterers, and in *Walden* indicated the valid use of firearms. (The activities of the National Wildlife Federation in correcting abuses would have appeared slightly tardy to him.) In *A Week* he struck out against Massachusetts' stream-stiflers who set up the myriad mill-dams that thwarted the migrant shad. (The salmon elevators at Bonneville Dam would have amused him!) In *The Maine Woods* he denounced the wholesale destruction of our forests in order to convert virgin timber into match-sticks, and in the same essay – and long before John Muir began his insistent campaign – Thoreau with foresight advocated National Parks in which to preserve the game and save the forests. The depredation of a virgin continent is every citizen's responsibility. This responsibility has been met in part by setting aside wilderness areas, by reforestation in the Shelter Belt, by intensive irrigation, by flood and erosion control, and by contour ploughing and strip cropping.

It was a desire to test his doctrine of the wild that impelled Thoreau to study the Indian. Since the doctrine held that in order to become revitalized it was necessary for civilization to retain direct contact with the source of its vitality in primitive nature, he found that the Indian, who lived in *rapport* with primitive nature, had attained a relationship which might benefit the white man. Certainly an unconstrained relationship with nature can strengthen man's physical well-being, increase his hardiness and stamina, and so help counterbalance an unnatural existence in a highly mechanized society.

The white man's attitude toward nature has been mainly one of aggression and exploitation. Nature has been held in bondage by mechanical means, like the garden plot in Huxley's metaphor. To the Indian, who did not regard nature in terms of personal domination but in terms of personal association, nature was to be neither coerced nor dominated; it was to be lived with. Writing about the Southwest Indians in *Death Comes for the Archbishop,* Willa Cather says: "They seemed to have none of the European desire to 'master' nature, to arrange and re-create. They spent their ingenuity in the other direction; in accommodating themselves to the scene in which they found themselves." If Willa Cather's statement of the Indian ingenuity is correct, then it embodies an imaginative understanding of nature which the white man has not yet shown. To the champion of material progress, the Indian ingenuity is either gravely or wilfully limited. Either the Indian was intellectually unable to take advantage of the opportunities for material progress latent in nature, or he repudiated them.

Thoreau did not suggest that the white man renounce civilization and return to the Indian's primitive way of life. He did very definitely challenge the so-called benefits of industrial and mechanized civilization. By replacing an agrarian way of life with an urban, by developing our industries at top speed, and by ever-increasing standardized products to satisfy the insatiable appetite of man for things, have we concomitantly increased the happiness of man? The question really is whether, in order to be free and happy, it is not necessary for man to understand in what life and living consist, the kind and degree of freedom desired, and the tokens by which happiness can be ascertained and evaluated.

V

The Machine Age and Man

Let your life be a counter-friction to stop the machine.
Civil Disobedience

IN THE SUMMER OF 1837, two weeks before Ralph Waldo Emerson delivered a compelling address on *The American Scholar* at the exercises of the Phi Beta Kappa Society in Cambridge, Henry Thoreau took part in what was termed "a conference" in the Commencement exercises at Harvard. Speaking on "The Commercial Spirit" of the times, he contended that the accelerated tempo of life brought with it new problems which required strenuous thought and intelligent action. The young nation was surging westward, fulfilling a "manifest destiny." Its temper expressed freedom of thought and action. Independence and restlessness intensified a nascent commercial spirit, the origin and sustention of which he thought was "a blind and unmanly love of wealth." The universal spirit of freedom which characterized the age he did not deprecate. Instead, he hailed this spirit of freedom as a source of glory, and he indicated that man would not always be the slave of matter. But "the commercial spirit" was a virus infecting the age with poison. Men, confounded by a materialistic lure, made riches the end of existence, and so they failed, or so he thought, "to lead manly and independent lives." The antidotes to the commercial spirit were the cultivation of the moral affections, the subordination of riches, and a sympathetic understanding and admiration of the world.

In November, 1843, six years after delivering his Commencement Address, Thoreau published an essay in the *Democratic Review* on J. A. Etzler's "The Paradise within the Reach of all Men, without Labor, by Powers of Nature and Machinery," entitled "Paradise (to be) Regained." In a utopian essay Etzler promised "to show the means of creating a paradise within ten years, where everything desirable for human life may be had by every man in superabundance, without labor, and without pay." Etzler's conception of a new world, where mankind might live on a far higher plane of material happiness, drew from Thoreau neither the pouncing enthusiasm of a volatile temperament nor the supercilious disparagement of the croaker. He admitted, honestly enough, that he arose from reading Etzler's book with enlarged ideas and grander conceptions of one's duties in the world. "It did," as he admitted, "expand us a little." He, too, dreamed that man might yet become "the lord of creation" by making his will the law of the physical world, and Etzler's objective, to revitalize man's interest in the paradise that lay before him, renewed this dream. Etzler's book reminded man of the immense unimproved powers existing in nature that awaited understanding, control, and guidance "for generous and universal ends." In a sequel called "The Mechanical System" Etzler indicated the possible application of a few of the familiar powers, such as the wind, tides, waves, and sunshine.

Although Thoreau felt enlarged and expanded by Etzler's scheme, he did not miss either its limitations or its virtues. He examined closely Etzler's application of tides and sun, waves and wind, and, while agreeing with Etzler on the incalculable power at man's disposal, under searching scrutiny he questioned the use which was made of them; it was frequently trifling, slight, and irregular. What poor compliments man paid his indefatigable and energetic servants! How little man did to make his relationship to animated nature nobler and finer! He exclaimed: "O ye millwrights, ye engineers, ye operatives and speculators of every class, never again complain of a want of power: it is the grossest form of infidelity. The question is, not how we shall execute, but what. Let us not use in a niggardly manner what is thus generously offered."

He refused to be imposed upon by the vast application of forces. He could appreciate the dream of inhabiting a crystal palace in a place the most eligible of any in space where mankind would be served by a servitor beyond comparison. But he could not imagine the possibility of a new heaven and a new earth – a paradise almost beyond the ken of man – coming to pass without industry. Etzler assumed that the people in their utopian homes might satisfy their daily needs "by a short turn of some crank." Thoreau readily agreed that there must be a crank – "the crank within," as he termed it. Nevertheless, the prime mover in all machinery was, as he knew, "a certain divine energy in every man." It was necessary to give that crank a turn. A slight motion of the hand would hardly do. "We believe," he said, "that most things will have to be accomplished still by the application called Industry." Once aroused, the force of this divine energy would be irresistible.

He thought it a serious objection to Etzler's scheme that it required time, men, and money. "Three very superfluous and inconvenient things for an honest and well-disposed man to deal with," he rejoined dryly. "There is far too much hurry and bustle, and too little patience and privacy, in all our methods, as if something were to be accomplished in centuries." In short, if man was ready, paradise began at once. Nor was money a necessity to the real paradise. One's virtue didn't live on the interest of one's money. Nor was Thoreau in agreement with Etzler's assertion that "Nothing great, for the improvement of his own condition, or that of his fellow-men, can ever be effected by individual enterprise." Characteristically he countered with the assertion: "Nothing can be effected but by one man. He who wants help wants everything. True, this is the condition of our weakness, but it can never be the means of our recovery. We must first succeed alone, that we may enjoy our success together."

In "The Mechanical System" Thoreau detected two main difficulties. First, the Mechanical System was plainly theoretical; the successful application of the powers of nature by machinery had yet to be proved. What was even more important, because it was harder, was the application of man to the work by faith. "Faith, indeed, is all the reform that is needed; it is itself a reform," he contended.

Etzler was not, like Franklin, Eli Whitney, Fulton, Morse, McCormick, and Edison, "one of the enlightened practical men," nor was he one of the "pioneers of the actual" who move with the "slow deliberate tread of science, conserving the world." But he did, indeed, impart faith. His defect lay in a failure to build his castles lofty enough. He aimed to secure the greatest degree of gross comfort and pleasure merely. Was it not more to the point that we reform our inner life first, thus superseding the necessity of reforming the outer? "Undoubtedly," Thoreau maintained, "if we were to reform this outward life truly and thoroughly, we should find no duty of the inner omitted. . . . But a moral reform must take place first, and then the necessity of the other will be superseded, and we shall sail and plough by its force alone."

Constructively Thoreau suggested how paradise might be regained. To him the Mechanical System was not the important thing. He was interested, not in the horsepower of the wind or tide, but in how many horsepower the force of love blowing on every square foot of man's soul would equal. By the application of love to man's inner needs, thus superseding the application of the forces of nature to man's physical needs, he thought paradise could be regained. The way was through love — a transcendentalism in ethics rather than a transcendentalism in mechanics.

> Love is the wind, the tide, the waves, the sunshine. Its power is incalculable; it is many horse-power. It never ceases it never slacks; it can move the globe without a resting-place; it can warm without fire; it can feed without meat; it can clothe without garments; it can shelter without roof; it can make a paradise within which will dispense with a paradise without. But though the wisest men in all ages have labored to publish this force, and every human heart is, sooner or later, more or less, made to feel it, yet how little is actually applied to social ends. True, it is the motive power of all successful social machinery; but, as in physics we have made the elements do only a little drudgery for us, steam to take the place of a few horses, wind of a few oars, water of a few cranks and hand-mills; as the mechanical

> forces have not yet been generously and largely applied to make the physical world answer to the ideal, so the power of love has been but meanly and sparingly applied, as yet.

In his Commencement Address Thoreau had deprecated the growing commercial spirit, and in his essay on Etzler's book he had evaluated and found wanting the idea that a paradise might be reached by man, without labor, simply by harnessing the powers of nature through machinery. Deliberating on material progress through mechanical instrumentalism in *Walden* (1854), he questioned the so-called modern mechanical improvements. Invention fostered the introduction of new machines, but weren't inventions only "improved means to an unimproved end"? Further, he doubted whether the factory system which inventions made possible was the best mode by which man obtained, among other things, his clothing. Then, too, trade cursed everything with which it was associated. It increased artificiality and complexity.

To Thoreau the point was whether with all his speed and busy-ness man attained a full measure of happiness. He thought man failed to realize his goal because he lived an unnatural life and tried to solve his problem in an unnatural way. Nor did he believe that it was the descendants of tradesmen who kept the state alive. Rather it was the descendants of simple yeomen and laborers. One-eyed John Goodwin, who wrested his livelihood directly from nature, who secured his fuel from driftwood in the river, who got his dinner from a mess of fish caught in the river, succeeded in living a simple and natural life. The merchant succeeded in living only a complex and unnatural life supported by profits from tape-selling, and usually he spent his allotted time after boyhood in accomplishing a particular design, without taking time to look around and appreciate the phenomenon of his existence.

There was something wrong, Thoreau thought, when men focussed their energies on the acquisition of material things. A pecuniary capitalistic system which abetted money-grubbing notably failed. The insidious desire for money worked subtly upon the people of a country through public opinion, so subtly in fact that the community tended to commend one as industrious and hard-working, simply because that person was selfishly attempting to derive profits. If a man like Thoreau chose to devote his time and energy to interests which yielded no actual pecuniary profits, public opinion, or what he termed so aptly "the police of meaningless labor," accused him of squandering time. Because Thoreau had no cash to show for his walking and contemplation and recording of notes in private journals, his behavior was regarded with some disapprobation. Because he refused to capitulate to conventional standards, he was considered an idler. The man who walked in the woods for love of them was called a loafer, while the one who cut down forests was considered industrious and enterprising. Thoreau's leisure was, however, never "conspicuous" in the Veblenian sense. It was enjoyed for its own sake and not indulged as a show of idleness.

In an era when America was becoming increasingly acquisitive-minded, Thoreau examined closely the philosophy of getting-on. He saw that material abundance and physical satiety counted for little unless one had gained moral and intellectual freedom, for was there not a kind of slavery to things? Only for want of intelligent discrimination were the real values of life indistinctly glimpsed. Almost without exception, he found the ways of acquiring money led downward. To work for money merely was to him equivalent to idleness and perhaps worse, since it tended to corrupt the man by curtailing purposeful efforts. Shouldn't the laborer realize something more than cash? Shouldn't he have so much enjoyed his task that the money would represent a bonus above the stipulated contract? Thoreau offered the employer this advice, "Do not hire a man who does your work for money, but him who does it for love of it."

Seeking independence, he reduced his obligations to society. He observed that when his wants were increased, his industry to supply those wants was taxed and became sheer drudgery. Any increase in obligations curtailed his freedom. If he sold both forenoons and afternoons, what leisure remained in which to expand? So he aimed to make *getting* a living not only "honest and honorable" but also "inviting and glorious." Certainly the wise men of the day should be the men who possessed not only knowledge but an understanding of how better to live than other men. The sorry thing is not the enormity of our ignorance; it is the realization that our acquired knowledge is not accompanied by wisdom.

2

One reason for Thoreau's experiment in living at Walden Pond, from July 4, 1845, until September 6, 1847, was that he thought society with all its arts had done little to solve the most important of all practical problems: how to make getting one's living poetic. What counsel could one expect either from those who were plainly disgusted with their own existence or from those who apathetically resigned themselves to the common modes of existence?

Another group — a minority, to be sure — conceived of life as a condition neither to be resisted nor accepted with complaisance, but rather to be shaped by an inward vision. Thoreau belonged to this group. He held the vision of a poetic life in the shelter of his inward sight. He resisted with characteristic defiance the exercise of all conventional coercion that asserted he *must* conform to the inflexible pattern of institutionalized society. And he rejected with scorn the ingratiating ethical reformers who said he *ought* to live his life thus and so. The only counsel which he accepted was the inward one that showed him the life a man *could* live. He would have agreed that one of the chief disgraces was to make one's life an apology or an apostasy rather than a dare.

Implicit in the problem of how to make getting one's living poetic was learning what life had to teach when one confronted only its essential facts. When he came to die, Thoreau did not want to discover that he had not lived. "I wanted to live deep and suck out all the marrow of life," he asserted, "to live so sturdily and Spartan-like as to put to rout all that was not life. . . ." Further, he wanted to find out whether life was really sublime or essentially mean, "and, if it proved to be mean, why then to get the whole and genuine meanness of it, and publish its meanness to the world; or if it were sublime, to know it by experience, and be able to give a true account of it in my next excursion." He knew also that by thinking too much of what we should be, we can lose the sense of what we are.

In society he encountered formidable deterrents to living. Where was the man who truly possessed the freedom to satisfy his inmost appetencies? Who, indeed, realized his most deeply imbedded potentialities? Some were ignorant of the good life; others inexpertly chose mistaken ends. Many lives were frittered away by preoccupation with details. Some capitulated to factitious cares; others surrendered to the superfluous coarse labors of life. Most men in fact lived lives of "quiet desperation." Unwilling to compromise with society, the intransigent Thoreau detached himself from society temporarily by removal to Walden Pond. He contended: "It will not be worth the while to accumulate property; what would be sure to go again. You must hire or squat somewhere, and raise but a small crop, and eat that soon. You must live within yourself, and depend upon yourself always tucked up and ready for a start, and not have many affairs."

He was no rebel who had drawn the wrath of society upon his head and who in bitter scorn withdrew to Walden Pond until he secreted sufficient venom to renew an insidious attack upon it. There was no animus in his action; nor is there any spleen in his record. The basis of his experiment rested on the belief that society existed for the individual, not the individual for society. Since he wanted to live the kind of life which provided the greatest freedom, independence, and leisure for association with nature, the source of his inspiration and the materials of his writing, he had to find a way which prevented the exactions of society from encroaching on his time and frustrating his opportunities. He had no idea of reforming society; he would reform himself. By exploring himself thoroughly, by balancing his needs and resources, he thought he could find a way to arrange his life and make it impossible for the institutionalized life of society to interfere with him. This was the substance of his experiment, which was, I should say, less a "one-man revolution" than a one-man reformation.

The Walden experiment was, therefore, not a rejection of society. The hut at the Pond was a retreat; but, like the slopeside burrow of Robert Frost's drumlin woodchuck in *A Further Range,* it was "a strategic retreat," where a man might rally his forces to meet life's problems more earnestly.

Thoreau once remarked, "I see men with infinite pains endeavoring to realize to their bodies, what I, with at least equal pains, would realize to my imagination, – its capacities; for certainly there is a life of the mind above the wants of the body and independent of it." This was what he sought to do: to live the life of the mind by realizing the capacities of his imagination. When insight is the eye of the mind at work, the idealist is mainly intent on realizing the capacities of his imagination. He uses his senses only as a means to a sympathetic relationship with the phenomena of the natural universe. Allied "to the powers that rule the universe," he seeks to relate himself for mind and body's health "to a universal fact." Greater than any near and gross mundane end is "a new and absolute view of things." Man's failure lies in the fact that he does not take sufficiently "elevated and broader views."

Thoreau was avowedly an idealist, but a practical one who saw that in order to experience fully the life of the mind, he had first to find a method. He was personally fortunate. He had "as many trades as fingers," and, moreover, he made his greatest skill to want but little. To determine what the gross necessaries of life were, he went to Walden Pond where he lived a primitive, frontier life, and pursued without hindrance the bent of his genius, which was "a very crooked one." The freedom to enjoy the life of the mind was, however, not a bestowal. It had to be wrested from circumstances by securing economic independence. Consequently the Walden experiment commends itself to those who acknowledge that freedom is an act of the human spirit, not a bestowal of divine justice.

Thoreau manoeuvred, first of all, to the vantage-ground of "voluntary poverty." The synonym for poverty in his economy of real values was simplicity of life. "By poverty, i.e. simplicity of life and fewness of incidents, I am solidified and crystalized, as a vapor or liquid by cold. It is a singular concentration of strength and energy and flavor. . . . By simplicity, commonly called poverty, my life is concentrated and so becomes organized. . . . " The virtuous man sheds the unnecessary, and Thoreau is the classic example of the virtuous man who successfully avoids a cluttered life. Even the three pieces of limestone on his desk in the hut must go because they required daily dusting when, as he said, "the furniture of my mind was all undusted still."

Simplicity, basic in his economy of *real* values, was the core of a method that freed the equation of existence of all encumbrances by reducing it to its simplest terms. Emphatic as he was in insisting on simplicity, he was just as emphatic in his denial of having any scheme for living that could be universally applied. He had a deeper insight. Simplicity was only the means, a clearing of the ground so that a man might live more worthily and profitably. "To what end do I lead a simple life at all, pray? That I may teach others to simplify their lives? – and so all our lives be *simplified* merely, like an algebraic formula? Or not, rather, that I may make use of the ground I have cleared, to live more worthily and profitably? I would fain lay the most stress forever on that which is the most important, – imports the most to me, – though it were only (what it is likely to be) a vibration in the air. As a preacher, I should be prompted to tell men, not so much how to get their wheatbread cheaper, as of the bread of life compared with which *that* is bran. Let a man only taste these loaves, and he becomes a skillful economist at once. He'll not waste much time in earning those. . . ." Give a man something worth struggling for, and he will find a means by which to realize his desires. Only let the objective be an ideal – the bread of life – and already one's life takes on an aspect of valor.

By reducing existence to its necessaries, and by intelligently supplying his wants, Thoreau found that it was possible to secure shelter, food, fuel, and clothing annually with a maximum of six weeks' effort. Certainly a *reductio ad parvum.* It is thus apparent that his experiment at Walden was no attempt to dodge the practical problems of life. It was simply the reactions of a fox who had whiffed the bait in the trap. Although he did not stand up defiantly in the market-place and oppose the assaults of life shock by shock, nor yet endure life meekly with Christian resignation, it was mainly because he never got himself in the position where he had to do one or the other. Nor did he seek to escape from personal responsibility like Paul Gauguin in his flight to Tahiti, or retreat permanently into a cloister like Cardinal Newman, or seek immurement in a cork-lined room like Marcel Proust.

The Walden experiment was not a Rousseauistic Arcadia. It was not the heaven of a man's imagining, as the "incredible splendor" of the holy city of Byzantium was to Yeats. "I think if I could be given a month of Antiquity and learn to spend it where I chose," said Yeats, "I would spend it in Byzantium, a little before Justinian opened St. Sophia and closed the Academy of Plato. I think I could find in some little wineshop some philosophical worker in mosaic who could answer all my questions, the supernatural descending nearer to him than to Plotinus even." Nor was the Walden experiment the embodiment of a sublimated vision similar to the one Henry Adams experienced in the choir loft at Chartres. Thoreau did not turn from the multiplicity of a modern world of mechanics, electricity, and radium, to look backward wistfully toward the age of faith in the Middle Ages, symbolized for Adams by the Virgin. Thoreau's experiment was neither an imaginative escape like Yeats's, nor a mental rebellion from a less charitable present to a more cherishable past like Henry Adams's! Nor is the Walden country a mythical never-never realm like Branch Cabell's Poictesme, "bounded by Avalon and Phaeacia and Sea-coast Bohemia, and the contiguous forests of Arden and Broceliande, and on the west of course by the Hesperides." The setting of Walden is a geographical present, bounded on the east by Lincoln Woods, on the west by Conantum and Fair Haven Cliff, on the south by Baker Farm, and on the north by Emerson's woodlot.

Thoreau left Walden Pond and became once more a sojourner in civilized life because, as he said, he "had several more lives to live, and could not spare any more time for that one." He had penetrated the problem of his relationship to society which otherwise he might never have realized. He had tried out the transcendental doctrine of plain living and high thinking at Walden Pond, and he had found that though its realization by all was problematic — for example, questionable as a social scheme at Brook Farm — nevertheless it worked admirably individually. By exploring his own higher latitudes he discovered that "new, universal, and more liberal laws" established themselves around and within him, and thenceforth he lived as "with the license of a higher order of beings."

The measure of his mastery over society was essentially self-mastery. By mastering his needs and desires, he freed himself from fettering possessions. He found that he could so order his affairs that society didn't make it impossible for him to live as he chose. He was, then, no anarchist, deliberately rejecting society and its benefits; he was its critic. He did not conform to it – did not accept its values as his values – but through insight succeeded in living a life free of class pride, hypocrisy, or conformity to the suspect social conventions of an institutionalized life.

He also made a very direct answer to the question how much civilization was necessary. If civilization were constantly growing more and more complex, it was necessary that one prevent its encroachment upon one's private life. By determining how much civilization was necessary – that is, how many of the so-called modern appliances one required – he learned that through simplification it was possible to reduce life to its lowest terms. His method of a planned economy was certainly not a rationalization of improvidence. Something, surely, can be said for his shrewdness in outsmarting the bread-and-butter aspect of necessity. He is a solitary symbol of the vanishing tribe of mankind who have not been worn down by the economic attrition of existence. It is very important to note that what he did was entirely within – not without – the normal pattern of the economic system. He squatted on another man's land, it is true, and he converted another man's acres into a bean-field, but from there on he played according to the rules. The bookkeeping figures – with the favorable balance – in the first chapter of *Walden* indicate a reassuring honesty.

He learned, too, that if he pursued the life he imagined, he would meet with a success unexpected in common hours;

for, as he also discovered, "the laws of the universe are not indifferent, but are forever on the side of the most sensitive." He found out what it meant to live the life of the poet, and after exploring his own higher latitudes, and after becoming expert in "home-cosmography," he returned to society, not jaded, but full of vigor, eagerness, trust, his interest in life whetted. He summed up: "In short, I am convinced, both by faith and experience, that to maintain one's self on this earth is not a hardship but a pastime, if we will live simply and wisely; as the pursuits of the simpler nations are still the sports of the more artificial. It is not necessary that a man should earn his living by the sweat of his brow, unless he sweats easier than I do." The product of Benjamin Franklin's economy of industry, frugality, and prudence is, in Henry Adams's phrase, "economic thinking machines." The product of Thoreau's economy of voluntary poverty is an improved individual.

The strongest defense of any thinker is the potential application of his ideas and principles. Thoreau's problem was every man's problem, though all men neither could nor should answer it in the same way. He remarked: "One young man of my acquaintance, who has inherited some acres, told me that he thought he should live as I did, *if he had the means.* I would not have any one adopt *my* mode of living on any account; for, beside that before he has fairly learned it I may have found out another for myself, I desire that there may be as many different persons in the world as possible; but I would have each one be very careful to find out and pursue *his own* way, and not his father's or his mother's or his neighbor's instead." This statement should be sufficiently informative and clarifying for all those who think Thoreau was trying to win converts to his way of life. He took out no patent; he had no magic formula; he practised no legerdemain; he applied no thaumaturgy. He advocated no infallible system by which life could be always successful. Least of all was he messianic or apocalyptic. There was not one way only, but "as many ways as there can be drawn radii from one centre"; yet he was quite sure that his problem was in most respects every man's problem. He counselled simply: find your own way and be sure it is the one that suits you best. Common sense will show how wise the choice has been. His choice was the higher one. That most men chose the lower one and lived lives of "quiet desperation" was not so much to be condemned as regretted, since there was always a deliverance for the honorable brave.

3

To the highly specialized society of an air-and-atom-minded world the first half of the nineteenth century seems remote, and the vista of Thoreau, the man of Concord and Walden, appears circumscribed. Nevertheless, from his limited vantage-point Thoreau realized the general effect upon man implicit in the advent of the machine. In at least four different ways he was distrustful of a technological civilization. He was skeptical of an artificial urbanized environment. He foresaw that a constant depletion of vital human energy would inevitably produce sterility, mental or physical, or both, if the tempo of urbanized existence was continuously geared to an excessive voltage. Secondly, he opposed machine servility. Thirdly, he considered division of labor suspect. Lastly, he rebelled against standardization in any form. He would have found the standardization of life resulting from the widespread application of the machine technique invidious in the development of the human personality.

Thoreau was a counter-friction to the machine age. An artificial urbanized environment was curbing, for if man failed to keep direct associational relationship with nature, he separated himself from the sources of physical health, mental stimulation, and moral energy. "There may be," he declared shrewdly, "an excess of cultivation as well as anything else, until civilization becomes pathetic." The plight of urbanized man, insulated through rubber, glass, cellophane, wood, cement, and cottonwool from the sanative and exhilarative effect of a regenerative natural environment, has grown grimmer with the passing decades. To Wallace Stevens

> The sun no longer shares our works
> And the earth is alive with creeping men,
> Mechanized beetles never quite warm.

Come summer, and the conscious or unconscious sense of dissociation from the natural environment impels the mechanical beetle to hasten to seaside or mountain trail or woodland lake or river-reach, where, with self-conscious strenuousness, he attempts to identify himself with "primal sanities."

What Thoreau thought of the worker's relationship to the advancing machine age is apparent from a notation that he set down in his *Journal* after visiting Sam Barrett's cobwebby mill, where an apprentice – not a factory "hand" – made wooden chopping trays of black birch and of red maple for the housewife. Pleased at the sight of the simple hand tools with which these trays were made, he was reminded of the contrast between Sam Barrett's mill and the pail-factory.

> They may make equally good pails, and cheaper as well as faster, at the pail-factory with the home-made ones, but that interests me less, because the man is turned partly into a machine there himself. In this case, the workman's relation to his work is more poetic, he also shows more dexterity and is more of a man. You come away from the great factory saddened, as if the chief end of man were to make pails; but, in the case of the countryman who makes a few by hand, rainy days, the relative importance of human life and of pails is preserved, and you come away thinking of the simple and helpful life of the man . . . and would fain go to making pails yourself. . . . When labor is reduced to turning a crank it is no longer amusing nor truly profitable; but let this business become very profitable in a pecuniary sense, and so be "driven," as the phrase is, and carried on on a large scale, and the man is sunk in it, while only the pail or tray floats; we are interested in it only in the same way as the proprietor or company is.

The contrast between the mechanized pail-factory and the craftsman at Sam Barrett's mill making wooden trays by hand is a penetrating arraignment of one major problem in the twentieth-century machine age.

In the division of labor which followed the introduction of the machine, the factory worker has often been limited in his daily task to the routine of repeating interminably a given operation. Consequently there has been no resultant sense of mastery of man over the machine, but rather a subserviency to the machine which deprives the workman of self-respecting individualism. Forced to serve the oppressive and monotonous rhythm of the machine, the workman becomes one of many servile attendants on an assembly-line. Dissociated from an organic natural rhythm and imposed upon by a mechanical rhythm, he becomes numb. In Sam Barrett's mill the workman met time as an equal not as a servant, and the wooden trays which were produced represented something of each workman's personality.

Since Thoreau defended the craftsman, whether stoneworker, farmer, woodsman, or maker of wooden trays, he would have assailed directly the relentless conveyor-belt idea in an age of large-scale production and standardized parts – in an age of Fordissimus! The cost in human devitalization would have affected him in exactly the same way that the slavery issue passed like iron into his soul and aroused his caustic denunciation.

It was not enough to escape the servility of the assembly-line. There was also a danger in division of labor. In a provocative passage in *Walden,* Thoreau tells about building one's house with one's own hands. This he did, but he never found another in all his walks who was similarly engaged. The surrender of our independence provokes him to conclude: "We belong to the community. It is not the tailor alone who is the ninth part of a man; it is as much the preacher, and the merchant, and the farmer." He inquires critically: "Where is this division of labor to end? and what object does it finally serve? No doubt another *may* also think for me; but it is not therefore desirable that he should do so to the exclusion of my thinking for myself." Excessive development of any human faculty leads to overspecialization with its concomitant liability: the inability to take a broad general viewpoint.

Thoreau would probably have recognized in the machine a possible means of gaining greater leisure and independence for more people. He did acknowledge that the Iron Horse increased punctuality and enterprise. Yet he would have agreed, I think, with Hawthorne's criticism of progress in *The Marble Faun*:

> The entire system of man's affairs, as at present established, is built up purposely to exclude the careless and happy soul. The very children would upbraid the wretched individual who should endeavor to take life and the world as — what we might naturally suppose them meant for — a place and opportunity for enjoyment.
>
> It is the iron rule in our day to require an object and a purpose in life. It makes us all parts of a complicated scheme of progress, which can only result in our arrival at a colder and drearier region than we were born in. It insists upon everybody's adding somewhat — a mite, perhaps, but earned by incessant effort — to an accumulated pile of usefulness, of which the only use will be, to burden our posterity with even heavier thoughts and more inordinate labor than our own. No life now wanders like an unfettered stream; there is a mill-wheel for the tiniest rivulet to turn. We go all wrong, by too strenuous a resolution to go all right.

Twentieth-century America would be a colder and drearier region to Thoreau than his own day, and he would reject the strenuous Franklin-like feverish accumulation of "a pile of usefulness." Simplicity was one of his touchstones, another was naturalness, and so also was wisdom. Indeed, he might have written, "We go all wrong, by too strenuous a resolution to go all right." The sentence has his tone and temper and edge.

The best evidence of what Thoreau's reaction would have been in our time is his way of life. His life makes us doubt the power of the machine by itself to make man essentially happier. If one could be supremely happy – physically and intellectually and spiritually – without benefit of the machine, what, then, has the machine given us that we *really* need? is the question Thoreau would have asked. Having achieved an inner harmony, the machine could, of course, increase our outer happiness by producing material comforts. If we have not achieved inner happiness, is there any way in which the machine could sustain our spirits? Thoreau would have argued that inward harmony must precede true outer happiness. He shows us that man's relationship to the machine is not the important thing. The machine's relationship to man as a means of liberation from physical drudgery, in order that one's spiritual enjoyments may be increased, is the important thing. "Let us not obstruct ourselves, for that is the greatest friction," he counselled. Isn't this the key of the answer to man's victory over the machine, a victory that is mainly won by self-understanding and self-discipline?

Even if Thoreau had no ready answer by which man could extricate himself from the domination of the machine, at least he succeeded in issuing some very important caveats. Beware, he tells us first of all, of an artificial urbanized environment. Beware, too, of machine servility. Beware of the division of labor and overspecialization. Finally, beware of standardizing tendencies which produce a mechanized routine. These were his caveats. He did not sound the tocsin of revolt but the tocsin of vigilance. He wished to protect freedom as an inestimable human value. How could man lay any claim to physical freedom when he served a machine like a helot? How could man exercise mental freedom when his individual opinion was dominated by standardized sources of human expression? How could man realize spiritual freedom when the means to experience it were denied him?

Thoreauvianism embodies two co-ordinate beliefs: the belief that an abiding happiness flows from an inalienable relationship to one's native soil, and the belief in the independence, dignity, and supremacy of the human spirit. Since the industrialization of society tended to render violence to both of these beliefs, Thoreau's vigilance was aroused, and, determined to be heard, he spoke out clearly and thoughtfully. He is one of the voices heard in the American continent raised in defence of the freedom of the human spirit wherever and whenever it is challenged. Thoreauvian idealism bays the moon, but also bites the thief.

VI

Nature Mysticism

The ears were made, not for such trivial uses as men are wont to suppose, but to hear celestial sounds. The eyes were not made for such grovelling uses as they are now put to and worn out by, but to behold beauty now invisible. May we not see God? . . . When the common man looks into the sky, which he has not so much profaned, he thinks it less gross than the earth, and with reverence speaks of "the heavens," but the seer will in the same sense speak of "the Earths," and his Father who is in them.
A Week on the Concord and Merrimack Rivers

THE COMMON TENDENCY of the ordinary rustic in close relationship with nature is to vegetate like a dusty weed in fat soil. Neither is that relationship completely fruitful where the countryman isolates himself from all neighborly intercourse and seeks to live wholly independent of his fellowmen. When Emerson heard of a man in Maine who chose to live forty-five miles from his neighbors, he recorded in his *Journals*: "I hear the account of the man who lives in the wilderness of Maine with respect, but with despair. . . . Perhaps he has found it foolish and wasteful to spend a tenth or a twentieth of his active life with a muskrat and fried fishes. I tell him [Thoreau] that a man was not made to live in a swamp, but a frog. If God meant him to live in a swamp, he would have made him a frog." When the individual gains perspective on his relationship to nature, he becomes the *conscious* natural man. Henry Thoreau went beyond the long-headed farmer Edmund Hosmer, and one-eyed John Goodwin, the fisherman; beyond Joe Polis, the Indian guide, and Alek Therien, the Canadian wood-chopper; beyond George Melvin, the Concord huntsman, and George Minott, the poetical farmer. He aimed to be a natural man *wholly* conscious of the implications in his association with nature. He was not absorbed by the landscape; he kept his identity inviolate. He did not, like Walt Whitman, think he could turn and live with the animals because they were so placid and self-contained. Nature was indeed beautiful to him, but only because consciously he had resolved on a beautiful life. "Nature," he asserted, "is beautiful only as a place where a life is to be lived." In his experience he exhibited the beauty of man's relationship to the world of natural phenomena, *as a part of it*. He did not seek the wilderness "to find in mountain forms the substantive of abstract beauty," but, as in *N by E*, where Rockwell Kent describes his own relationship, "to renew through solitude the consciousness of being." Because his attitude was more humanistic than materialistic, he represents the cultivation of the human spirit through feeling for nature.

A further relationship between man and nature sometimes arises. Frequently the tendency is to intellectualize nature or theorize about it self-consciously. The association becomes as warped as that of the simple man who, lacking the imagination to conceive of nature's possibilities, becomes stunted rather than strengthened in his development. In the main Thoreau did not make the mistake of intellectualizing nature into an abstraction. When he lapsed it is apparent, for then we have passages of self-conscious theorizing, the defects of any human being who tries to take nature into his head and dominate it rather than attune himself inwardly to its seasonal rhythms.

The motives for Thoreau's attachment to nature were strong ones. Freedom from the institutionalized life of society, physical well-being, intellectual stimulation, and moral energy were among the strongest. He turned to the rugged outdoor life as the source of physical health, deriving the vigor, stamina, and strength necessary to balance the hard indoor work of writing. The solitude and wildness of nature acted like a kind of thoroughwort or boneset to his intellect. He felt as if he always met in nature "some grand, serene, immortal, infinitely encouraging, though invisible, companion, and walked with him." Nature was exhilarative and restorative. It was like the remedial touch of the hand on the troubled waters of Bethesda. He exhorted: "Live in each season as it passes; breathe the air, drink the drink, taste the fruit, and resign yourself to the influences of each. Let them be your only diet drink and botanical medicines. . . . Open all your pores and bathe in all the tides of Nature, in all her streams and oceans, at all seasons. . . . She exists for no other end. Do not resist her. . . . Why, 'nature' is but another name for health, and the seasons are but different states of health." When sickness occurred, man lost his *rapport* with nature. Sympathy with nature indicated perfect health, but to insure health Thoreau saw that one's relationship with nature must be very tender, personal, and friendly. His own relationship to it was friendly and strenuous, but not, I think, as Lowell supposed, a search for the doctor. He responded with a genuinely palatable zest for cloud and sky and field and weather. He could truthfully say, "I go and come with a strange liberty in Nature, a part of herself," because his association was generally direct, companionable, and intimate.

Thoreau cherished a *rapport* with nature's forces that was like a bird's instinctive use of the wind currents in its flight or a salmon's response to the weight and pressure of the ocean densities and currents. He was moved by the sound of the approaching rain as it beat on the forest leaves a quarter-mile distant. The scent of the south wind blowing over the naked ground in January invigorated him. He rejoiced when the white oaks bore an abundant crop in October. When, from Fair Haven Cliff, he noticed how the needles of the pine trees shone as with a subdued but clear ethereal light, he exclaimed, "At sight of this my spirit is like a lit tree." The normal product of his participation was serenity as well as exhilaration, and he thought that neither the discipline of the schools nor business could impart such serenity to the mind as the observation of natural phenomena.

The second motive for his attachment to nature was the intellectual stimulation that originated in the contemplation of natural forms and aspects. "I may be either the driftwood in the stream, or Indra in the sky looking down on it," he said. Not wholly involved in nature, he could withdraw at will and contemplate it objectively from a point of vantage. He was not solely a saunterer in the fields; in the Emersonian sense, he was Man Sauntering. His sympathetic association with nature was counterpoised by contemplative detachment. He asks continually, What does this particular phenomenon mean to me? "The intellect is a cleaver"; he said, "it discerns and rifts its way into the secret of things." Natural phenomena as various as snowflakes, migrating sparrows, arrowheads, dwarf andromeda, hibernating dormice, lichens, the arching reeds and rushes with their sheaf-like tops, sun sparkles, the fringed orchis, muskrat cabins, phosphorescent wood, or drops of dew on pontederia leaves, quickened his thought and served as the source material of his writing. He made it his business to extract whatever nutriment nature could furnish him, "though," as he was fully conscious, "at the risk of endless iteration." While abroad in the fields or on the streams or mid the woods, he thought ovipositors planted seeds in him.

A sensibilitist with an agile mind, he was not only receptive but seminal. Yet he was a seer before he was an expresser. Writing was only his talent; his genius was his way of looking at and understanding life. He found his reality here and now in what the concrete suggested of the abstract, the particular of the general, the relative of the absolute, the microcosm of the macrocosm, Concord of the world. But he did not force the association. "Let me not be in haste to detect the *universal law;* let me see more clearly a particular instance of it," he remarked. Thoreau started with the earth closest to him; Concord was his Rosetta Stone. When he could read that, he imagined he could read the rest of the world. The secrets were not behind the stars; they were within the mind of man.

When he saw sand and clay thawing in a bank along the railroad track, he was mentally stimulated. The shelving bankside, twenty to forty feet high and extending for a quarter of a mile, was called the Deep Cut, and sometimes he passed through it on his way to the village from Walden Pond. When the frost thawed in the spring, the sand flowed freely down its slopes. Little streams interlaced and overlapped, following the laws of currents and those of vegetation. The luxuriant foliage was the creation of an hour, and he felt as though he stood in the laboratory of the Artist who made the world and himself. "You find thus in the very sands an anticipation of the vegetable leaf. No wonder that the earth expresses itself outwardly in leaves, it so labors with the idea inwardly. . . . The Maker of this earth but patented a leaf. . . ." Here was no dead earth but a living organic earth! "This phenomenon," he exclaimed, "is more exhilarating to me than the luxuriance and fertility of vineyards."

Nature was flint to his steel; it sparked his thought. A sunset glimpsed from a river's bank thrust him into the reaches of his own thought. One very serene evening, after pitching camp during the voyage on the Concord and Merrimack Rivers, his brother John and he sat on the bank eating supper and enjoying the sunset. Light from the west fell aslant the eastern trees and was reflected in the water before them. It reminded Henry mainly of how generally deceived he was when he considered there were but a few degrees of sublimity. Were there not yet sublimer visions before which all others paled? In his mind's eye formed a vision of transcendent beauty — a vision of the higher laws to which he was related in the most direct and intimate way.

> For the most part we think that there are few degrees of sublimity, and that the highest is but little higher than that which we now behold; but we are always deceived. Sublimer visions appear, and the former pale and fade away. We are grateful when we are reminded by interior evidence of the permanence of universal laws; for our faith is but faintly remembered, indeed, is not a remembered assur-

> ance, but a use and enjoyment of knowledge. It is when we do not have to believe, but come into actual contact with Truth, and are related to her in the most direct and intimate way. Waves of serener life pass over us from time to time, like flakes of sunlight over the fields in cloudy weather.

Natural phenomena, whether bean-fields or thawing sand or the depth of a pond or evening light reflected on trees and water, touched off his mind in imaginative musing, in transcendental speculation, and often in muscular thinking.

A further motive for his attachment to nature was the apprehension of a moral association in natural phenomena. Of the two chief ways of viewing the relationship of man and nature – *either* the subjective way, where nature is reflected and illuminated by the mind of man, *or* the objective way, where man is revealed as the product of the working of the forces of natural law – Thoreau's viewpoint was definitely the former. He was an importer, not an exporter, of moral value in nature. In Thomas Mann's *The Magic Mountain,* Settembrini remarked of his counter-disputant, Herr Naphta: "Like St. Catherine of Siena he thinks of the wounds of Christ when he sees a red primula in the spring." As Naphta: so Thoreau. The latter tended to do the very thing he deprecated. "The moral aspect of nature," he once set down in his *Journal,* "is a jaundice reflected from man." Although he did not ignore the objective importance of natural phenomena, he did exalt their subjective meaning. One of his major preoccupations seems to have been finding and naming the possible correspondences between nature and himself. Since nature was the source of moral energy, he turned to its natural phenomena to find joy and delight, peace and serenity, aspiration and moral courage.

The ripened purple poke exemplified a successful life.

The liquid coolness of the wood thrush's strain gave assurance of the forest's immortal beauty and vigor. It made him take higher views of things. The white water-lily was emblematic of purity. The owl represented "stark, twilight, unsatisfied thoughts." The cricket's creaking suggested a mature wisdom above all temporal considerations. Invariably the sounds of the birds' songs, as part of nature's language, were moral symbols of his thought. He detected messages in their songs. The cackles or trills of the tree sparrow made him think that even in the wildest scenes an air of domesticity and homeliness was imported into them. While he was busy planting beans in his garden just after sundown on a May day, he heard the note of the bay-wing from across the fields, "*Come here here there there quick quick quick or I'm gone.*" Instantly he felt transported from the sphere of his work. "The spirit of its earth-song, of its serene and true philosophy, was breathed into me, and I saw the world as through a glass, as it lies eternally." The notes of the bay-wing's song suggested felicity: – summer sunsets, rambling features, farmhouses in the fields, gray rail fences, cows returning from pasture. A flock of migrating fox-colored sparrows bore messages concerning his life, and he assumed it was his task to find out what the messages were. "I see," he said, "that the sparrow cheeps and flits and sings adequately to the great design of the universe; that man does not communicate with it, understand its language, because he is not at one with nature."

There is a limit to any relationship beyond which it is not wise to trespass. Norman Foerster, in his chapter on Thoreau in *Nature in American Literature*, proposes a thoughtful inquiry. He inquires pertinently whether it is not true that man possesses traits exclusively human which cannot be studied in nature. For example, we do not detect our ethical principles in nature, do we? Isn't nature non-moral? Does nature reason or express holiness, awe, veneration, humility, self-sacrifice, shame, modesty? Doesn't man acquire these human properties through contacts with society and through the growth of reason? If this is so, then there is a limit to which man can hope to progress in his association with nature. To isolate himself from intercourse with his fellow-men in society limits the possibilities of his growth in correspondence with nature.

Thoreau was aware of these bounds. He knew that as in every relationship one of the partners is dominant, so in the relationship of man with nature. He learned that nature was not an end in itself; but it was an important means toward the realization of the higher objectives in life. When he adapted himself to his natural environment, he found that he increased his physical energy, intellectual awareness, and moral steadfastness. The result was thoroughly inspiriting — renewed strength and new perspectives.

2

"I have remembered today," William Butler Yeats recorded in his diary of 1901, "that the Brahmin Mohini said to me, 'When I was young I was happy. I thought truth was something that could be conveyed from one man's mind to another. I now know that it is a state of mind.'" For Thoreau such states of mind occurred, not when he coolly regarded some phenomenon of nature as independent of him, but when transient glimpses of natural phenomena corresponded with his moods and filled his inward life with rich incremental experience. "It is not the polypody in my pitcher or herbarium, or which I may possibly persuade to grow on a bank in my yard, or which is described in botanies, that interests me, but the one that I pass by in my walks a little distance off, when in the right mood. . . . The important fact is its effect on me." The reward of the poetic life was a transient thought, a vision, a dream, and he studied how to spend a day so that he might be rewarded by a new ray of light. Like a patient watchman, he would watch a whole year on the city's walls if he might be rewarded by feeling himself elevated for an instant upon Pisgah. His goal was that of the nature mystic. To attain a perfect correspondence between nature and himself, so that he was at home in her, was his aim. "I to be nature looking into nature with such easy sympathy as the blue-eyed grass in the meadow looks in the face of the sky."

Infinitely suggestive to him was the fact that a rare flower which he had never found grew close at hand in his own neighborhood. George Melvin, the Concord huntsman, dressed in a russet suit and trailed by a lank bluish-white and black-spotted hound, had discovered where the only bush of purple azalea, or pinxter flower, in Concord grew. He had given a large twig to Mrs. Brooks's son and to the Jarvises. So Thoreau, coveting the knowledge of the bush, went to Melvin's house, and there found the discoverer sitting bareheaded in the shade with a large pailful of freshly gathered azalea close by. George Melvin would not tell where the bush was to be found – not immediately, though Thoreau felt confident that he could wheedle the secret from him. If George would not tell, he would find it himself, since he had a clue, and then George would lose the glory of it. Finally, Melvin, taking his own time, took Thoreau across the river and pointed out the bush of *Azalea nudiflora,* now past its prime.

The discovery of the azalea was a fact lifted far above the level of the actual. It had a special significance in Thoreau's subjective philosophy. His craving to see the wildflower had nothing to do with the desire of material possession. The wealth of the poetic life was not possession but simply enjoyment and satisfaction in perceiving beauty. The finding of the azalea was like an instant's elevation upon Pisgah — a Pisgah sight that related him to the natural phenomena of Concord.

On a bare, frost-bitten November day, when he threaded the spruce swamp, noting the buds of swamp-pink and panicled andromeda and high blueberry, the forms of rabbits and the catbirds' nests, he was reminded of "the incredible phenomenon of small birds in winter." Soon he would see the lesser redpolls — "delicate crimson-tinged birds" — arriving to feed on the buds and seeds, sporting about, shaking off the powdery snow.

> What a rich contrast! tropical colors, crimson breasts, on cold white snow! Such etherealness, such delicacy in their forms, such ripeness in their colors, in this stern and barren season! It is as surprising as if you were to find a brilliant crimson flower which flourished amid snows. They greet the chopper and the hunter in their furs. Their Maker gave them the last touch and launched them forth the day of the Great Snow. He made this bitter imprisoning cold before which man quails, but He made at the same time these warm and glowing creatures to twitter and be at home in it. He said only, Let there be linnets in winter, but linnets of rich plumage and pleasing twitter, bearing summer in their

> natures. The snow will be three feet deep, the ice will be two feet thick, and last night, perchance, the mercury sank to thirty degrees below zero. All the fountains of nature seem to be sealed up. The traveller is frozen on his way. But under the edge of yonder birch wood will be a little flock of crimson-breasted lesser redpolls, busily feeding on the seeds of the birch and shaking down the powdery snow!

Such a Pisgah sight in the spruce swamp charmed as well as haunted Thoreau; for, it was only necessary "to behold thus the least fact or phenomenon, however familiar, from a point a hair's breadth aside from our habitual path or routine, to be overcome, enchanted by its beauty and significance."

3

The essential characteristic of Thoreau's mystical experience was embodied in his attitude toward reality. In a revealing letter to his friend and disciple Harrison Blake he once wrote: "My only integral experience is in my vision. I see, perchance, with more integrity than I feel." What his "terrible eyes" saw, what his "unsleeping insight" (both phrases of Emerson) perceived, was *Reality* pervading the phenomenal world. He apprehended this reality in the moments of awareness when his spirit was *en rapport* with the all-embracing presence of God made manifest in natural phenomena. As Emerson remarked, "We might say of these memorable moments of life, that we were in them, not they in us." That is, these moments of inspirative awareness represent a constant while the moods of our temperaments represent the variable. No man can be invariably "keyed up" to the receptive mood. In sum, the union or envelopment of the human spirit with the pervasive spirit of God represents the conditional factor in the mystical experience, for without union the experience is unconsummated. The intensified awareness represents the effect of the union, and the apprehension of the reality is the product of the awareness.

One cannot sensibly argue that the correspondence of man with nature is the *Ultimate Reality.* The intensified awareness which results from the correspondence with nature is only the effect whose cause is the *Ultimate Reality,* or *God.* Thoreau's consciousness was simply the inward means by which he recognized *Ultimate Reality* interpenetrating the natural world. In correspondence with nature, which consists in the harmonious relationship between the inner world of feeling, imagination, thought, and the outer world of natural phenomena, man's consciousness is intensified, his insight clarified, and his spiritual energy renewed. It is, indeed, primarily in the fact that for Thoreau the mystical correspondence led to activity and recurrent renewal of his spirit rather than to the absorption of his spirit by the God-force, with its concomitant release from the act of living into Nirvana, that he differs from the Hindu religious mystic. In his essay on Pico della Mirandola in *The Renaissance,* Walter Pater says: "The word mystic has been usually derived from a Greek word which signifies to shut, as if one shut one's lips brooding on what cannot be uttered; but the Platonists themselves derive it rather from the act of shutting the eyes, that one may see the more, inwardly." Thoreau's mysticism consisted rather in opening than closing the eyes, and in feeling inwardly *en rapport* with the outward. The object is always before him as seen in the field or on the water; it is not withdrawn from its natural frame. The relationship is something entered into actively, not something passively observed.

A further characteristic of Thoreau's nature mysticism is seen when we compare it with the Puritan's. Everywhere the Calvinistic Puritan looked, he saw the will of God exhibited. "True it is," wrote Thomas Hooker in *The Application of Redemption,* "that the Lord fills Heaven and Earth with his presence, yea, the Heaven of Heavens is not able to contain him. His infinite Being is everywhere. . . ." It was not sufficient, however, that the regenerate Puritan perceive the infinite power and the eternal glory of God in the laws of nature. It was still necessary that he act in harmony with these laws, and only God's grace gave the power to observe and keep them. In *The Sainte's Dignitie,* Hooker indicated that first there was "the Word of God set down in his book, and then reasons that goe along with it, and lastly, a spirituall work of grace, that God hath made known in those reasons. . . ." This "spirituall work of grace" was experienced by the regenerate Puritan in a feeling of ecstasy. This inspirative ecstasy, as Hooker explained in *A Comment Upon Christ's Last Prayer,* left "an impression upon the most inward motions of the soul" and filled it with a comprehensive vision of the world, a vision that "exceeds, and overflies the most Eagle-sighted Apprehensions of any Natural Man in the World."

The special infusion of God's grace was necessary for the Calvinistic Puritan. By it he was withdrawn from the state of natural depravity and regenerated. But for Thoreau man did not languish in a condition of natural depravity. He was simply unawakened. There was no "dawn" in him. The correspondences between nature and Thoreau were comparable to the Puritan influxes of grace, except that the reinvigoration which resulted from inward communion was not a special dispensation to be arrogated only by God's elect. These correspondences were really accessible to all men at any time. A further difference between the Puritan mystic and the nature mysticism of Thoreau consisted in the fact that the former focussed on a heavenly salvation while the latter focussed on a natural correspondence. Thoreau's religion was, then, a natural one as contrasted with the Calvinist's revealed religion. Spiritual reality was to be experienced in nature through one's intuition.

The experience of the English nature mystic, Richard Jefferies, whose life-span overlapped Thoreau's, throws a beam of light on the mystical relationship of man to nature. Jefferies, a tall, thin, keen-sighted shoot of old English yeoman stock, was born in 1848 and died in 1887. His book *The Story of My Heart* most memorably reveals his mystical experience.

If by mysticism we mean an insatiable desire to expand the human consciousness to higher levels of awareness in order that an ultimate reconciliation of the soul with God may be effected, Jeffries was such a mystic. Insatiably Jefferies desired "the deepest of soul-life," and he signified the soul as the aspiring inner consciousness, the source of whose life was the strong earth, the great sun burning with light, the deepest darkness of night no less than noontide brightness, sky, stars, ocean, pure air, hills, woods, grassy fields, and running brooks. The visible universe of natural phenomena was the source of his inflatus. "Under the shapely rounded elms, by the hawthorn bushes and hazel, everywhere the same deep desire for the soul-nature; to have from all green things and from the sunlight the inner meaning which was not known to them, that I might be full of light as the woods of the sun's rays." So, the crumble of earth, the blade of grass, the thyme flower, were like pores through which he absorbed until he was "breathing full of existence." The ultimate end of his desire was not sensuous enjoyment, but the inner meaning of sun and light and earth and trees and grass "translated into some growth of excellence in myself, both of body and of mind . . . that I might be higher in myself."

The points of vantage – what he called "thinking-places" – where in solitude he invited the desire of his soul, were many. One thinking-place was a hill three miles from his home upon whose summit was a fosse in the entrenchment of which he lay and looked out through a gap in the southwestern bank upon a broad plain. Another was a deep hollow on the side of a coastal hill which opened upon the sea. A third was the ancient well at Pevensey whose gray stones and thin red bricks intensified his feelings. What Jonathan Edwards' praying-booth in the swamp was to him or Fair Haven Cliff to Thoreau, the grass-grown tumulus on the hill, a clump of elms, an oak, or an aspen by the brook were to Jefferies: retreats where he found renewal of spirit.

The steps in Jefferies' progression to higher levels of awareness are not different from those experienced by Christian mystics. In *American Thought*, Woodbridge Riley summarizes these steps as follows: First, there is the purgative state which is brought about by contrition and desire of amendment of unworthiness. Secondly, there is the illuminative stage which is effected by concentration on God. And lastly, there is the intuitive or unitive stage where man beholds God face to face and joins in union with Him.

"Let my soul become enlarged," pleaded Jefferies. "I am not enough; I am little and contemptible. I desire a greatness of soul, an irradiance of mind, a deeper insight, a broader hope. Give me power of soul, so that I may actually effect by its will that which I strive for." Jefferies is both contrite and desirous of amendment, but the root of his contrition is not moral (a matter of good or evil) or ethical (a matter of conduct), but spiritual – a feeling of littleness, inferiority, and whether it is condign or undeserved Jefferies does not imply. Apparently the dignity of the human spirit meant much to him.

A passage from *The Story of My Heart* also illustrates the illuminative stage. As he lay in one of his "thinking-places," he confided: "I was utterly alone with the sun and the earth. Lying down on the grass, I spoke in my soul to the earth, the sun, the air, and the distant sea far beyond sight. I thought of the earth's firmness – I felt it bear me up; through the grassy couch there came an influence as if I could feel the great earth speaking to me." As he thought of the pureness of the wandering air, its beauty touched and gave him something of itself. Similarly, as he spoke to the sea or addressed the sun or looked into the blue heaven, in turn, he felt drawn, lifted, and illuminated by "an emotion of the soul beyond all definition." While the Christian mystics concentrated on God, he concentrated on the elementals of the physical universe. Air, water, fire, and earth enkindled him.

The third and final step, the unitive one where man beholds the object of his worship face to face and is joined in union to it, has its counterpart in Jefferies' testament.

> Sometimes on lying down on the sward I first looked up at the sky, gazing for a long time till I could see deep into the azure and my eyes were full of the colour; then I turned

> my face to the grass and thyme, placing my hands at each side of my face so as to shut out everything and hide myself. Having drunk deeply of the heaven above and felt the most glorious beauty of the day, and remembering the old, old sea, which (as it seemed to me) was but just yonder at the edge, I now became lost, and absorbed into the being or existence of the universe. I felt down deep into the earth under, and high above into the sky, and farther still to the sun and stars. Still farther beyond the stars into the hollow of space, and losing thus my separateness of being came to seem like a part of the whole. Then I whispered to the earth beneath, through the grass and thyme, deep into the depth of its ear, and again up to the starry space hid behind the blue of day.

In such a way the spirit of Jefferies was joined in union with the being of the universe.

What the Christian mystics, like Saint Augustine and Edwards, called God, Jefferies called "the being or existence of the universe." But – and this is a very significant difference – the "being" or permeative force in the natural universe of which Jefferies was aware and which emanated from natural objects of the universe was not the purest form of Idea or Mind. Jefferies did not posit a divine intelligence in nature. He concluded that "no deity has anything to do with nature." (No god dwelt in nature.) The blade of grass or oak or star only "seemed like exterior nerves and veins for the conveyance of feeling" to him. In reality, the feeling and the thought which he experienced were in himself. Nature was the means by which he realized a very personal rapture; its phenomena were the stimulating sources of his expansion.

4

A man grows in two directions. He takes root in the material necessities of existence and he thrusts heavenward toward the spiritual certainty of the unseen reality. In what relationship did Thoreau stand to God? Was God a force external to or a force within the universe? What was the effect of God upon him? Let it be clearly stated that Thoreau sought with no spiritual strenuousness to be reconciled to God. He never felt unreconciled. If this suggests a lack of humility, it might as readily indicate a congenital faith which brooked no equivocating conscience. A representative of his own day, he did not assume the deist's position, which regarded God as a force external to the universe, but he reflected the romantic attitude of "immanence," or the indwelling God, which differed from pantheism, as John Herman Randall says, in *The Making of the Modern Mind*, "in interpreting the life of the universe through the soul of man rather than through the observed course of nature." In the chapter on "Solitude" in *Walden*, Thoreau communicated the sense of living in the presence of a great immanent force which was God. It was a force experienced inwardly, consequently why should he be lonely when he was aware of this power? Solitude intensified the awareness. The effect was not as of a seizure; it was, instead, a simple, natural, friendly relationship. "Nearest to all things is that power which fashions their being. *Next* to us the grandest laws are continually being executed. *Next* to us is not the workman whom we have hired, with whom we love so well to talk, but the workman whose work we are."

Like Jefferies, he was an unorthodox religious man – a secular recusant – who favored what he called the liberal divinities of Greece. Jove, exerting an intimate and genial influence, not the Jehovah of the Hebrew testament, was to him a more gracious and catholic conception. He confided: "In my Pantheon, Pan still reigns in his pristine glory, with his ruddy face, his flowing beard, and his shaggy body, his pipe and his crook. . . . Perhaps of all the gods of New England and of ancient Greece, I am most constant at his shrine." What men commonly worshipped as God was not divine; it was only the "overwhelming authority and respectability of mankind combined." And so, "Men reverence one another, not yet God." He was well aware of the self-righteous duplicity of man who simply made God in his own image. This was the searching point that he made in his attitude toward religion: men did not conceive of God from a sufficiently elevated position.

The simple, natural piety of Thoreau is also patent, and it sometimes burst forth in a simple, sincere, and emphatic reverence for God's benevolence as made manifest in nature. ". . . Now I have occasion to be grateful for the flood of life that is flowing over me. I am not so poor: I can smell the ripening apples; the very rills are deep; the autumnal flowers, the *Trichostema dichotomum,* – not only its bright blue flower above the sand, but its strong wormwood scent which belongs to the season, – feed my spirit, endear the earth to me, make me value myself and rejoice; the quivering of pigeons' wings reminds me of the tough fibre of the air which they rend. I thank you, God. . . ." He declared himself to be "God-propped," and asserted that his profession was "to be always on the alert to find God in nature, to know his lurking-places, to attend all the oratorios, the operas, in nature." Divine mind was everywhere apparent. Even such motions as the flowing sail or the running stream or the roving wind were "the circulations of God." We know how the little striped bream, poised in Walden's glaucous water, was considered by him as another image of God. Perhaps there is no more beautiful expression in his writings of the sense of the divine mind than the one which appears in *A Week on the Concord and Merrimack Rivers*:

> I hear beyond the range of sound
> I see beyond the verge of sight, —

> I see, smell, taste, hear, feel, that everlasting Something to which we are allied, at once our maker, our abode, our destiny, our very Selves; the one historic truth, the most remarkable fact which can become the distinct and uninvited subject of our thought, the actual glory of the universe; the only fact which a human being cannot avoid recognizing, or in some way forget or dispense with.

He was a man like Job whom the hand of God had touched. Indeed, to Thoreau, the nature mystic, God declared Himself in bird-song no less than in burning bushes; *He* was Everywhere. He had seen how the foundations of the world were laid by the divine mind. He had no doubt that it would stand a good while.

Although Thoreau's *Journal* is a collection of various independent records and not a carefully synthesized account, it is as genuine a testament of mystical experience as Jefferies' *The Story of My Heart*. It is not, however, possible to say with neat finality that Thoreau's mystical experience followed the orderly progression which Woodbridge Riley summarized in *American Thought*. The following passage illustrates Thoreau's desire for amendment, and, as well, it contains the illuminative flash of life which Riley associates with the second stage of the mystical experience:

> I ordinarily plod along a sort of whitewashed prison entry, subject to some indifferent or even grovelling mood. I do not distinctly realize my destiny. I have turned down my light to the merest glimmer and am doing some task which I have set myself. I take incredibly narrow views, live on the limits, and have no recollection of absolute truth. Mushroom institutions hedge me in. But suddenly, in some fortunate moment, the voice of eternal wisdom reaches me, even in the strain of the sparrow, and liberates me, whets and clarifies my senses, makes me a competent witness.

Passages in his *Journal* representing the third or pantheistic unitive state are manifold. These will later be grouped together, showing the synchronization of Thoreau with the outer rhythm of nature.

VII

Correspondence with Nature

The perfect correspondence of Nature to man, so that he is at home in her!

JOURNAL, October 26, 1857

ONE OF THE CHIEF MEANS by which Thoreau realized correspondence with nature was his use of keen responsive senses. "The seeing depends ever on the being" he knew, but the condition of being depended upon keen sensory reactions. Certainly it was not the possession of senses which negated man's spiritual inspiration, but the blunting of them which made it impossible to receive what Thoreau described as "ineffable messages" from *Ultimate Reality.* The whole duty of man is to make oneself a perfect body, a fit companion for the soul, since the bodily senses are the channels through which we may receive ineffable messages. "Our life is but the Soul made known by its fruits, the body." Like other mystics – for example, like Blake ("Man has no body distinct from his Soul; for that call'd Body is a portion of Soul discern'd by the five Senses, the chief inlets of Soul in this age") and Whitman ("The spirit receives from the body just as much as it gives to the body, if not more") – he was no rejecter of the senses. The following passage is a characteristic example of his use of and attitude toward them: "Perhaps I may say that I have never had a deeper and more memorable experience of life in its great serenity, than when listening to the trill of a tree-sparrow among the huckleberry bushes after a shower. It is a communication to which man must attend in solitude and silence, and may never be able to tell to his brother. The least sensual life is that experienced through pure senses. . . ."

Thoreau's joy in being awake was like "a well of water springing up into everlasting life." Yet it was so only because he cherished and entertained the hours of the universe, not the time of the going and coming "of the cars." To experience these hours required a mental as well as a physical regimen. Consequently, through a self-imposed discipline he refined his senses until they reacted keenly. We are all conscious that many things we would have are possible for us – if – and, of course, this is the catch – if we will pay the price. "What will you have? quoth God; pay for it and take it," quoted Emerson in *Compensation.* Few people would voluntarily accept the rigor of his austere regimen, even though it must result in chastened physical senses capable of receiving life more abundantly. The chapter in *Walden* entitled "Higher Laws" presents sufficient evidence of the price one pays. ("One moment of life costs many hours, hours not of business but of preparation and invitation. . . .") For a tuned sensibility is no permanent acquisition; it depends upon too many delicate adjustments. As an absolute, not a relative, condition of body and mind, it depends for its equipoise upon discipline.

He kept to a wholesome Spartan diet, not only because it helped to discipline his physical nature, but also because it satisfied his imagination. Conscious as he was of an animal in us which awakens in proportion as our higher nature slumbers, he gave the reptile and sensual no advantage. He was aware of an instinct toward the higher or spiritual life and another toward the primitive and savage; he reverenced both. Sometimes, as he said, he liked to take "rank hold on life" and spend his days more as the animals do. This was not, however, either his habitual mood or his general inclination. He recognized how the spirit could pervade and control the functions of the body, transmuting the grossest sensuality into purity and devotion. "The generative energy, which, when we are loose, dissipates and makes us unclean, when we are continent invigorates and inspires us." Such continence he attained by discipline. He avoided sensuality and a sluggish habit of mind by practising moderation – even abstemiousness. The acuteness of his sensory response was not, therefore, the result of primitive instinctiveness. The fining of his senses was an acquirement, not an indulgence.

A sensate man, Thoreau was *really* as alive as Doctor Oliver Wendell Holmes actually thought *he* was. He possessed the sensibility of the experiencing nature which Henry James once described as "a kind of huge spiderweb of the finest silken threads suspended in the chamber of consciousness, and catching every airborne particle in its tissue. It is the very atmosphere of the mind; and when the mind is imaginative – much more when it happens to be that of a man of genius – it takes to itself the faintest hints of life, it converts the very pulses of the air into revelation." The world of nature was filled with a multitude of tiny impulses whose vibrations he felt when allied to the natural elements. When he found on Lee's Cliff the broken shell of a large white snail, he rejoiced: "I cannot but think it nobler, as it is rarer, to appreciate some beauty than to feel much sympathy with misfortune. The Powers are kinder to me when they permit me to enjoy this beauty than if they were to express any amount of compassion for me. I could never excuse them that." Is it not true that he enjoyed beauty simply because his senses were so finely attuned? "My body is all sentient," he asserted. "As I go here or there, I am tickled by this or that I come in contact with, as if I touched the wires of a battery." One reason for his lively sentience is the fact that he disciplined his senses in two ways: positively, through incessant use, and negatively, through abstinence from bad habits. He trained his natural sensory responses so that he might attain a relationship with the common world of phenomena which was uncommonly apperceptive of natural beauty.

What of Thoreau's auditory sense? When, on a still evening, he heard a horn blowing, he thought he perceived the meaning of the word sound. It was as if the earth spoke, and recalled other sounds – the booming of ice, early morning cock-crowing, the barking of dogs in the night. There were sounds in nature's sonorousness in which he found a health that he drank like a cordial. "The effect of the slightest tinkling in the horizon measures my own soundness," he declared. He thanked God for sounds, for as the sound mounted, so it made him mount. Such was his awareness of the essence of sound, its meaning to and effect on him and his gratefulness for it.

He fairly revelled in natural sounds: in the squeaking of the pump which sounded as necessary as the music of the spheres, in the peculiar summer trilling of the toads, in the crackling flight of the grasshopper, in the vibration of a chord. He delighted in the bird-sounds: the veery's silver clarion, the "brazen note of the impatient jay," the chickadee doling out its scanty notes, the oven-bird thrumming its sawyer-like strain, the ventriloquism of the male chewink, the penetrating and space-filling sound of drumming partridges, the hoorer-hoo of the owl like "a sound which the wood or the horizon makes," or the winnowing of the snipe circling over the meadow, which was "the most spirit-like sound in nature."

Music was the crystallization of sound; it was perpetual, and hearing was only intermittent. To hear it was to wash the dust off his life. All the romance of his youthfulest moments, he thought, was contained in music. "I could go about the world listening for the strains of music," he declared. The distant sound of his brother's flute at evening a half-mile off seemed a more beautiful communication than "the sending up of a rocket would have been." He felt expanded by a strain dying away as some passing traveller went by singing. He was overjoyed with the music-box Margaret Fuller's brother Richard gave him. He commended the effort of a man he once saw making a viol, "patiently and fondly paring the thin wood and shaping it, and when I considered the end of the work he was ennobled in my eyes." On one May day, as he sat in his boat on Walden Pond playing the flute and watching the perch hover around, he felt that nothing but the wildest imagination could conceive of the manner of life he lived. Again and again his flute awoke the echoes on the water of Walden Pond as he fingered its stops of an evening. The sound of the humming wires – his telegraph harp – was far more than a physical sensation; it was a poetical experience. He heard it in the autumn in the Deep Cut. "How this wild tree from the forest, stripped of its bark and set up here, rejoices to transmit this music! When no music proceeds from the wire, on applying my ear I hear the hum within the entrails of the wood, — the oracular tree acquiring, accumulating, the prophetic fury." He thought how much the Ancients would have made of it. So great was its vibration — it was working terribly within — he felt the ground tremble beneath his feet. He remarked that the telegraph harp had spoken to him more distinctly and effectually than any man ever did.

Far surpassing the grossest terrestrial sounds were ethereal sounds caught by the rapt ear. "There is always a kind of fine aeolian-harp music to be heard in the air," he asserted. "I hear now, as it were, the mellow sound of distant horns in the hollow mansions of the upper air, a sound to make all men divinely insane that hear it, far away overhead, subsiding into my ear. To ears that are expanded what a harp this world is!" There is something Homeric about this experience, as if Thoreau had loosened his earth-bonds to attend the music of the sirens. Even silence was audible to him at all times and in all places, for silence was only hearing inwardly, sound, hearing outwardly. He could call to mind a silence which he overheard — the stillest summer hour, in which the grasshoppers sang over the mulleins. He considered there was a valor in that time the memory of which was armor that could laugh at any blow of fortune.

His sense of touch was a further means of experiencing natural phenomena. There is a passage in *Walden,* in the chapter entitled "The Village," representative of the acuteness of his tactility. While living at the Pond, he found the darkness of the woods darker than most suppose. "I frequently had to look up at the opening between the trees above the path in order to learn my route," he tells us, "and, where there was no cart-path, to feel with my feet the faint track which I had worn. . . ." A similar sentience is illustrated in Thomas Hardy's heath-folk. Diggory Venn, Eustacia Vye, Gabriel Oak, and Clym Yeobright moved about over lonely heath and moorland in Dorsetshire as though they had a preternatural sense of feeling in the pads of their feet.

Naturally, Thoreau's tactility was most clearly defined in his hands. He liked the feel of mullein leaves. When in late October he touched them, they felt so warm that he thought he should be glad "to make my bed of them sometime." By way of contrast the radical leaves of the goldenrod felt cold and clammy to his touch. His tactility was further experienced in the feel of the wind and the sun upon him. Yet in no way does it appear that his tactility was unusual.

An inveterate taster of things, he tasted sand cherries out of compliment to nature, but never learned to love them. He tasted the white froth dripping from pitch-pine and found it savorless. He tasted the black shrivelled pyrus berries in a spruce swamp and found them sweet. He tasted ripe choke-cherries and found they furred the mouth, and the juice of these when mixed with saliva feathered like tea into which some cream had been poured. The taste of the herb Indian tobacco convinced him that there were such things as drugs which may either kill or cure.

He was surprised by some tastes. The taste of the sweet froth issuing from the sap of a walnut or hickory was always cheering to him, and he thought it was somewhat unexpected to meet in nature anything so agreeable to the human palate. It was so innocent a sweet it reminded him of the days when he used to scrape this juice off the logs of his father's wood-pile.

He characterized tastes. The chub was a soft fish that tasted like boiled brown paper salted. He knew under what circumstances a thing tasted best. Canoe-birch sap, like wild apples, must be tasted in the fields. It was slightly sweetish and acid in taste and cool as iced water. The frozen-thawed apples gathered on Annursnack were the most palatable. In early autumn they were sour, crabbed, and inedible, but with the first December frost, they filled with rich sweet cider and were "soft and luscious as a custard." He valued them more than any pineapple imported from the torrid zone. He described their ripening: "Let the frost come to freeze them first solid as stones, and then the sun or a warm winter day – for it takes but little heat – to thaw them, and they will seem to have borrowed a flavor from heaven through the medium of the air in which they hang."

He considered smell "a more primitive inquisition than the eye, more oracular and trustworthy." When he criticized his own writings, he went by scent, since that sense revealed what was concealed from the other senses. By it he detected earthiness, and that was what he was after. Apparently it was his acutest sense. Yet he could claim no infallibility in the functioning of this sense. In the spring of 1852, on May sixteenth, during an afternoon trip to Conantum, he perceived a sudden fragrance, blown to him from the newly flooded meadows. He could not place it. "Yet no flower from the Islands of the Blessed could smell sweeter." He wondered if it weren't the essence of all water-plants combined. He thought it might be the willow over his head and then thought not. A fortnight later, while at the Corner Causeway, he smelled the captivating sweetness blown from the meadows. Could it be the grape? No! Could it be the mint in the meadow? Probably not! On June ninth he caught a fleeting whiff of sweetness while he stood by the shore of Walden Pond near the railroad. And at the Cliffs, when he disturbed the foliage, again he inhaled the exquisite fragrance, but what was it and exactly where did it come from? A week later he examined the blooming grape and decided that it was not the original of the meadow fragrance. He still perceived it on the twenty-third of the month, intense as ever, on the Corner Causeway. On July fourth he wondered if it came from the purple summits of the eupatorium. A year later he scented the ineffable fragrance from the Wheeler meadow. He thought that it would surely restore all the sick, if the air always possessed such a marvellous perfume. "It would be carried off in bottles and become an article of traffic which kings would strive to monopolize. The air of Elysium cannot be more sweet." Two years passed, and then – May 6, 1855 – he perceived the unaccountable scent near Jenny Dugan's. It was like the general fragrance of the year. "I am almost afraid I shall trace it to some particular plant," he stated. Two years after – May 27, 1857 – he again scented the rare meadow fragrance. Could it be the sweet-scented vernal grass? he queried, but remained doubtful. Two years later – May 11, 1859 – he smelled the elusive fragrance that for seven years had held him thrall each season. He was still mystified by it. Nature had wonders beyond his detection but not beyond his awareness.

Though denied discovery of this particularly elusive scent, he could name and label most scents. There was the slight spicy odor of hickory buds; the scent of bruised bark and of pennyroyal; of Roman wormword in potato fields; and the scent of the bruised green leaves of sassafras – a fragrance as of lemons and a hundred spices. There was the strong rummy scent of the black cherry; the fragrance of ripening grapes – an autumnal scent; the dry, rich, sweet scent of a field of ripe corn – a peculiar dry scent he could catch a third of a mile downwind.

Actually there was no end to the innumerable odors in nature. "There are odors enough in nature to remind you of everything, if you had lost every sense but smell." The aromatic fever-bush was truly an apothecary's shop; and though he was no snuff-addict, he did stoop in his walks to strip the dry whorls of the lycopus from the stalks rising above the snow and use the spicy seeds as his smelling-bottle. From these brown clusters of dry seeds – resembling coffee berries – when stripped from the dead stems of the water horehound and rubbed between the fingers, emanated the aromatic fragrance of lemon-peel. Dry sprigs of penny-royal plucked from the wayside scented him thoroughly and reminded him of a garretful of herbs The peculiar rasp-berry scent, and especially the scent of the dicksonia fern, exhilarated him. "As when Antaeus touched the earth, so when the mountaineer scents the fern, he bounds up like a chamois, or mountain goat, with renewed strength. There is no French perfumery about it. It has not been tampered with by any perfumer to their majesties. It is the fragrance of those plants whose impressions we see on our coal. Be-ware of the cultivation that eradicates it."

No matter where we turn, following Henry Thoreau through the cycle of the seasons and the course of the years, his sense of smell for earth things was remarkably fresh and responsive. On March 18, 1853, a notation reads, "To-day first I smelled the earth," but we commonly wonder, when, indeed, did he last leave off smelling the earth and its phenomena. His sense of smell was vigorous and pristine. On February 1, 1856, he scented, three rods distant, a fox's trail in the afternoon (he had done it several times before), where he crossed the river. He looked sharp and discovered where the fox had stopped by a rise of ground. "Yet," explained Thoreau, "he [the fox] could not have passed since last night, or twelve hours before, it being near the village." This particular event might be taken as a standard of his achievement in smell – the taint of a fox's trail at least twelve hours old. What a hound on the slot he would be under Pythagorean circumstances!

Through sharpness of sight also he increased the range of natural phenomena significant to him. One November day he saw fine gossamer streaming from every fence, tree, and stubble, "though a careless observer would not notice it." He was at least forty rods off looking over the grass toward the sun at Hosmer's field beyond Lupine Hill, when he noticed the shimmering effect of the gossamer, as it seemed in the still air to cover the hill almost like a web. While paddling up the north side above the Hemlocks one August afternoon, he was attracted by the singular shadows of the white lily pads on the rich-brown muddy water. "The sun playing with a lily leaf draws the outline of a lily on the bottom with its shadow," and these slightly enhaloed shadows struck his fancy.

He was avid of all sights; the color of the white acorn – "What can be handsomer, wear better to the eye, than the color of the acorn, like the leaves on which they fall polished, or varnished?" Or the rich color of the poke, the purple wine of whose berries stained his hands when he pressed them between his fingers. So the richest flower was the one which most abounded in color. Here, he considered, nature was full of blood, heat, luxuriance. "What a triumph it appears in Nature to have produced and perfected such a plant. . . ."

In the wintertime he was pleased when in the fields and meadows he glimpsed the warm-colored osier shoots; their red and yellow rising above the snow reminded him of flames; and he thought there was no phenomenon quite like the willows shining in the spring. Another phenomenon, equally alluring to him, was the brown tints of early spring "as softly and richly fair and sufficing as the most brilliant autumnal tints." He discovered them on the side of barren lichen-clad hillsides where the sand flowed beneath, where huckleberry bushes grew, and where bright white patches of snow lingered. With the proper peculiar sky light slanting through the rain-drenched air and with the vegetation dripping wet, the browns were intensified and stood out brilliantly. So sharp were his eyes that, from a bridge, he detected water-bugs swimming briskly in the water below in the moonlight, and from an elevation bordering Walden Pond he perceived a water-bug "ceaselessly progressing over the smooth surface a quarter of a mile off. . . ." On one of his walks, while searching the January sky for rainbow-tinted clouds, to his surprise he saw a star at half-past three in the afternoon, "a mere round white dot," and he wondered if the Indians ever detected one by day.

In *The American Rhythm*, Mary Austin asserts: "It is this impersonal extension of the faculty of awareness which has brought the Indian the reputation of superior sense perception, which is not borne out by scientific tests of sense reaction. The Indian sees no better than the white man, but he sees more, registers through every sense, some of which have atrophied in us, infinitely more." Like the much-vaunted senses of the Indian, Thoreau's were no better than any other human being's. They were only more extensively productive. He simply felt, saw, smelled, tasted, and heard in nature more than the average man. But he is not defined by his senses.

2

Because the truest inward experience originated in the co-ordination of the senses and the mind, he confined "the observations of his mind as closely as possible to the experience or life of his senses." He knew that "His thought must live with and be inspired with the life of the body." After he made this relationship functional, he tried to synchronize his intellect and senses with the outer rhythm of nature. He sought to adjust and co-ordinate the personal with the impersonal, the subjective with the objective, in order to derive from nature the symbols of his thought.

In *Man the Unknown* Doctor Alexis Carrel ascribes an inner rhythm to each living being. This rhythm has a dual expression: it is both physiological and psychological. While the psychological rhythm depends upon the influence of stimuli from the outside world recorded on our consciousness, the physiological rhythm depends upon the building-up and breaking-down of tissues. The wealth of our inner life is measured by the frequency of those states of consciousness when we are *en rapport* with sources of our inspiration through the synchronization of the physiological and psychological rhythms.

Since the chief source of Thoreau's inspiration was nature,

he sought to co-ordinate his psychological and physiological rhythm with the plangent outer seasonal rhythm of nature. The wealth of his life depended upon the succession of these states of consciousness. They were his true vital statistics. That nature's pace was deliberate he had noticed when the buds swelled imperceptibly during the spring as though the short days were an eternity. Why, was not the wise man restful and patient, too! Like the really efficient laborer, the poet did not try to crowd his day with work. He sauntered to his task "surrounded by a wide halo of ease and leisure." There must be a wide margin for relaxation to his day so that he could harmonize the inner rhythm of his consciousness with the outer rhythm of nature's pace. Man's chief mistake was living too fast, and such living was coarse as well as unprofitable. "You cannot," he claimed, "perceive beauty but with a serene mind."

Consider nature! In June the tortoise buried her eggs a few inches beneath the surface of some sandy field, and throughout the succeeding months, while unusual events took place three inches above them, nature advanced steadily and serenely on its own course. "June, July, and August, – the livelong summer, – what are they with their heats and fevers but sufficient to hatch a tortoise in. Be not in haste; mind your private affairs. Consider the turtle. . . . Perchance you have worried yourself, despaired of the world, meditated the end of life, and all things seemed rushing to destruction; but nature has steadily and serenely advanced with a turtle's pace. . . . Has not the tortoise also learned the true value of time?" The point was, as Thoreau saw it, for man to keep pace with nature. He counselled, "Catch the pace of the seasons; have leisure to attend to every phenomenon of nature, and to entertain every thought that comes to you." When winter broke up outwardly, so it did inwardly, and by keeping his inward time adjusted with outer time, he felt the frost coming out of him, felt that he was heaved like the road, the ice and snow within him dissolved.

So intimate was his *rapport* with nature that at times the experience became wholly personal. "Whole weeks and months of my summer life slide away in thin volumes like mist and smoke, till at length, some warm morning, perchance, I see a sheet of mist blown down the brook to the swamp, and I float as high above the fields with it. I can recall to mind the stillest summer hours, in which the grasshopper sings over the mulleins, and there is a valor in that time the bare memory of which is armor that can laugh at any blow of fortune." When he saw the first faint tinge of spring green, he revived with nature, feeling that her victory was his. Drifting on the sluggish waters of a pond in a sluggish April day, he felt dissolved in the breeze, or he felt like a feather floating on the atmosphere with unfathomable depths on every side. The sound of Heywood's Brook falling into Fair Haven Pond was so inexpressibly refreshing to him it seemed to flow through his bones. This pantheistic identification was complete when he nodded like a rye-head in the breeze, or felt like an ear of ripening corn. He had some notion what the johnswort and life-everlasting were thinking about when the sun shone on him as on them. At times, when he closed his ears and eyes and consulted his consciousness momentarily, he floated "a subjective, heavily laden thought, in the midst of an unknown and infinite sea." While at Walden it was his wont to sit in the sunny doorway throughout the morning "rapt in a revery." In those seasons he grew "like corn in the night," and he got some idea of what the Orientals meant by contemplation. Complete, at times, as we have indicated, was his identification.

> I fain would stretch me by the highway-side,
>   To thaw and trickle with the melting snow,
> That mingled soul and body with the tide,
>   I too might through the pores of Nature flow,
>
> Might help to forward the new spring along,
>   If it were mine to choose my toil or day,
> Scouring the roads with yonder sluice-way throng,
>   And so work out my tax on *Her* highway.

His experience was far more than a submergence of his personality in a kind of pantheistic "being" or Oriental contemplation of eternity. His relationship to nature was mainly active, not passive. Nature offered the raw material of the tropes and symbols with which to describe his life. The golden willows that he saw affected him because they corresponded to the beauty and promise of some experience upon which he was entering. "If I am overflowing with life, am rich in experience for which I lack expression, then nature will be my language full of poetry, – all nature will *fable*, and every natural phenomenon be a myth." His inward responsiveness made the outward experience significant, and psychological time was measured by the successive states of consciousness arising from the correspondence of nature with him. These successive states of consciousness, when he burned with "this hard gemlike flame," were moments of real *rapport*, moments that Doctor Carrel calls "inward time," moments that Richard Jefferies described as being "snatched from inevitable Time."

Marcel Proust, whose master work is *A la Recherche du*

Temps Perdu (1913–26), was a contemplater of time. However, Thoreau's experience of time is different from Marcel Proust's remembrance of things past. Proust's refined senses, when stimulated by odor, savor, shape, color, or sound, aroused dormant memories in the exhilaration of whose remembrance he glowed lambently. Like a high priest worshipping at the altar of evocation, he lighted votive tapers to illumine the secret places of his mind. Proust's special quality was to show how the sensation of a material object, such, for example, as a morsel of cake dipped in tea, has the power to evoke the hidden past; how the taste of a crumb of madeleine soaked in tea stirred palpitant images deeply imbedded in his being recalled how, as a little boy, long ago, before church-time on Sunday mornings, he would go to his aunt's room and she would give him a crumb of madeleine, dipping it first in her lime-flower tea, and how, years later, the old gray house in which his aunt lived, the garden, the town, the square, the streets, and the country roads – the village folk, the dwellings – in effect the whole of Combray and its surroundings, appeared before him, recalled at the behest of such an evocative sensation as the tea-dipped morsel of madeleine.

Unlike Proust's recollection of things past, Thoreau's experience with time was associated with the present. As a nature mystic he sought the immediacy of experience. He lived for the frequent occurrences when he became acutely aware of the heightened and intensified relationship between the natural phenomenon and himself. A single intense sensory association enabled Proust to draw from the secret caches of time within the storehouse of his memory some sublimated remembrance of deeply submerged experience. Thoreau, on the other hand, participated directly with time.

From his interior life sprang the light which suddenly illuminated the object upon which his percipient sight focused. While Proust aroused sleeping memories, evoking them in the way one gently and seductively strokes lovely things, Thoreau enkindled natural objects of contemplation experienced here and now. Both Proust and Thoreau reveal the inward feeling of time and the sensitive registering of its effect upon their consciousness, followed by states of mind when both responded to life at the very top of their being – sensitively aware and vigilantly awake.

The wealth of Thoreau's year consisted in "a certain series and number of sensations and thoughts which have their language in nature." It was his art to speak the language of nature without accent. It was his mother tongue. He measured the development of his own life by the innumerable moments of awareness that made the correspondence between nature and himself significant: by the vibration of the telegraph harp; by the sight of the Boxboro oak woods; by the discovery of a patch of dwarf andromeda; by a remarkable echo as he called to his chain man while surveying; by "the distant drumming of a partridge"; by the wood thrush's lay ("the only bird whose note affects me like music"); by the sight of the painted tortoise beginning its hole, laying its eggs, sedulously covering them with earth, and dancing on them; by the beautiful snow crystals ("perfect little wheels with six spokes without a tire"); by the sight of a hawk sporting "with proud reliance in the fields of air." By such tokens he measured his experience, for they whetted his insight, related him to universal natural facts, and allied him, as he thought, with great powers. By such awareness he released the energies which are in the language of nature.

He spurred himself constantly in order that he might not miss these sensations and thoughts; but his doctrine of salvation by awareness was altogether different from Poor Richard's doctrine of salvation by industry. He had no idea of seeking material accomplishments. His sentience was disciplined so he might enjoy the "wise passiveness." For he knew that "Only thought which is expressed by the mind in repose — as it were, lying on its back and contemplating the heavens — is adequately and fully expressed." What Herman Melville wrote in *Moby Dick* of the harpooners who have to pull an oar, and then rise to throw the dart at the whale, is also true of the thinker and his thought. "To insure the greatest efficiency in the dart, the harpooners of this world must start to their feet from out of idleness, and not from out of toil." Thoreau's strenuousness was not physical but psychical and inward. It consisted in an inward condition of the mind and spirit. In view of this he was a votary of "a kind of Brahminical, Artesian, Inner Temple life." In *Song of Myself* Whitman exulted,

> I loafe and invite my soul,
> I lean and loafe at my ease observing a spear of
> summer grass.

The connotation in Whitman's lines is not altogether self-indulgent, but the literalist would emphasize the loafing and not the poet's intention in loafing — to invite his *soul*. Thoreau, too, was a transcendental loafer; he loafed, but mainly that he might invite his soul to receive what Vaughn, the seventeenth-century mystical poet, called "the bright shoots of everlastingness" — that is, the higher power of Reality.

He applied the quirt when he thought he might become

supine. ("No man knoweth in what hour his life may come.") But he observed that the muse visited him and beauty appeared to him usually after a period of intent labor, followed by listlessness and a tendency toward repose. ("It is from out the shadow of my toil that I look into the light. . . .") In one direction – lethargy and inanition – man's will gradually atrophied; in the other direction – vigilance – the strengthening of the will and the whetting of the sensibility in order to enjoy the more abundant life.

3

The discipline of looking always at what was to be seen depended upon trained, not untrained, senses, and such a discipline was at the core of his powers of observation. He observed in two ways: by simple perception and by insight. When he asserted that nature would bear the closest inspection, inviting us "to lay our eye level with her smallest leaf, and take an insect view of its plain," obviously he was encouraging simple perception. Natural observations are manifold in his writings: the line of beauty as a curve; how the railroad cuts made cliffs for the swallows; the mother-o'-pearl tint common to the winter sky half an hour before sundown; or, how the flowering season reached its height with the appearance of the red lilies in dry land; or how the farmers were busily planting by the time the oak leaves were "as big as a mouse's ear." He perceived that the brilliancy of autumn tints depended upon a greater or less drought of the summer. A severe drought destroyed the vitality of the leaf and deadened its color, since "to produce brilliant autumns the plant should be full of sap and vigor to the last."

Beyond simple, natural perceptions were the more penetrative insights of the poet. "The question," as he said, "is not what you look at, but what you see." His discoveries depended upon his insight, and insight depended upon the intention of his mind – the relationship of natural phenomena to the human being. "I am not interested in mere phenomena," he declared, "though it were the explosion of a planet, only as it may have lain in the experience of a human being." As a poet he lived by watching his moods, omitting the unusual, describing the ordinary and common – the obscure life, the cottage of the poor, the workdays of the world, even barren fields. All he desired was eyes with which to see the things that others possessed. His facts were only as frames to his pictures; they were perceived by the mind; they were thoughts his body thought. To the common sense they appeared falsehoods; to the poet they were a kind of mythology. There was the sucker floating on the meadow in the spring rise. It was not so much "an actual terrene fish" as "the fair symbol of a divine idea." The color, form, gills, fins, and scales were like an incident in a parable of the Great Teacher, expressing to him a perfect beauty of form fitting function. Why, here was such a form as one found sculptured on ancient monuments that would be so to the end of time.

His contention that every incident was a parable of the Great Teacher would be true if every observer were truly poetic. There were times when incidents became parables of the Great Teacher which he read like a seer. On such occasions he read the handwriting in nature's multiple phenomena.

In 1857 Thoreau journeyed to the Allegash lakes in the upper reaches of the Maine Woods. In the essay that he wrote recounting his journey he told of one memorable discovery which alone made the trip worth while.

> It was a dense and damp spruce and fir wood in which we lay, and, except for our fire, perfectly dark; and when I awoke in the night, I either heard an owl from deeper in the forest behind us, or a loon from a distance over the lake. Getting up some time after midnight to collect the scattered brands together, while my companions were sound asleep, I observed, partly in the fire, which had ceased to blaze, a perfectly regular elliptical ring of light, about five inches in its shortest diameter, six or seven in its longer, and from one eighth to one quarter of an inch wide. It was fully as bright as the fire, but not reddish or scarlet, like a coal, but a white and slumbering light, like the glowworm's. I could tell it from the fire only by its whiteness. I saw at once that it must be phosphorescent wood, which I had so often heard of, but never chanced to see. . . .
>
> I was exceedingly interested by this phenomenon, and already felt paid for my journey. It could hardly have thrilled me more if it had taken the form of letters, or of the human face. . . .
>
> . . . I was in just the frame of mind to see something wonderful, and this was a phenomenon adequate to my circumstances and expectation, and it put me on the alert to see more like it. I exulted like "a pagan suckled in a creed" that had never been worn at all, but was bran-new, and adequate to the occasion. I let science slide, and rejoiced in that light as if it had been a fellow-creature. I saw that it was excellent, and was very glad to know that it was so cheap. A scientific *explanation,* as it is called, would have been altogether out of place there. That is for pale daylight. Science with its retorts would have put me to sleep; it was

> the opportunity to be ignorant that I improved. It suggested to me that there was something to be seen if one had eyes. It made a believer of me more than before. I believed that the woods were not tenantless, but choke-full of honest spirits as good as myself any day, — not an empty chamber, in which chemistry was left to work alone, but an inhabited house, — and for a few moments I enjoyed fellowship with them. Your so-called wise man goes trying to persuade himself that there is no entity there but himself and his traps, but it is a great deal easier to believe the truth. . . .

Once again on a midwinter afternoon he walked to Fair Haven by the Musketaquid. As he started out, he felt the cutting edge of the wind, though the earth was quickened by the sun. In the furrows of the ploughed land lay freshly melted soil. Silvery down was perceptible on the catkins of the willow twigs rising out of the ice by the river, and both the greenbriar and the sassafras shoots were green. Along the way he saw several light ash-colored cocoons of the Promethea moth on a button-bush. They were quite remarkably disguised by withered and faded leaves wrapped around them. Penetrating their disguise, he glimpsed what seemed to him nature's prevision.

> Though the particular twigs on which you find some cocoons may never or very rarely retain any leaves, — the maple, for instance, — there are enough leaves left on other shrubs and trees to warrant their adopting this disguise. Yet it is startling to think that the inference has in this case been drawn by some mind that, as most other plants retain some leaves, the walker will suspect these also to. Each and all such disguises and other resources remind us that not some poor worm's instinct merely, as we call it, but the mind of the universe rather, which we share, has been intended upon each particular object. All the wit in the world was brought

> to bear on each case to secure its end. It was long ago, in a full senate of all intellects, determined how cocoons had best be suspended, – kindred mind with mine that admires and approves decided it so.

Three years later, on a January day, during one of his afternoon walks up the Assabet on the ice, he saw again the dirty-white cocoons concealed by the clusters of leaves on the alders, black willows, and white maples along the stream. Most of the cocoons were empty, as though a foe had attacked and devoured them. Their appearance set him wondering. "What kind of understanding," he inquired thoughtfully, "was there between the mind that determined that these leaves should hang on during the winter, and that of the worm that fastened a few of these leaves to its cocoon in order to disguise it?"

Quite as revelatory as his reflection upon the phenomenon of the Promethea cocoons was his penetrative insight into the phenomenon of the Norway cinquefoil. One late August day he found the alternate five leaves of the calyx of the Norway cinquefoil – now nearly out of blossom – closing over the seeds to protect them.

> This evidence of forethought, this simple *reflection* in a double sense of the term, in this flower, is affecting to me, as if it said to me: "Even I am doing my appointed work in this world faithfully. Not even do I, however obscurely I may grow among the other loftier and more famous plants, shirk my work, humble weed as I am. Not even when I have blossomed, and have lost my painted petals and am preparing to die down to my root, do I forget to fall with my arms around my babe, faithful to the last, that the infant may be found preserved in the arms of the frozen mother." . . . Nature ordered this bending back of the calyx leaves, and every year since this plant was created her order has

been faithfully obeyed, and this plant acts not an obscure, but essential, part in the revolution of the seasons. I am not ashamed to be contemporary with the Norway cinquefoil. May I perform my part as well! . . . The fall of each humblest flower marks the annual period of some phase of human life, experience. I can be said to note the flower's fall only when I see in it the symbol of my own change. When I experience this, then the flower appears to me.

4

When Robert Frost once remarked that "observation covers both sight and insight," he meant the invisible world is as real as the phenomenal world of earth, flower, bird, cloud, tree, or grass. Our observation covers both sight, by which we perceive objects in the visible natural universe, and insight, by which we detect a metaphysical fact beyond a material one. Is it not apparent that Thoreau exercised the faculty of insight when he apprehended a reality within the phenomenal world? If his nature mysticism signifies anything to us, it is that the visible world is but the threshold of an invisible one.

It is apparent from his insights into nature that he assumed a divine intelligence at work. His viewpoint is essentially teleological, and the quandary arises, whether he exhibits a valid insight or merely ingenuity in the reading of nature. Is what he sees part of the truth or is it *his* truth? Naturally, his sincerity is above challenge. The only question is whether the subjective and personal method can carry much authority when challenged by experimental science. Both methods — the poet's and the scientist's — may inevitably lead to an assurance in a divine plan or belief in some shrewd guiding force directing our destiny, but, to the scientist, the poet's insight may appear fanciful and frivolous, while to the poet the scientist's viewpoint may be narrow and non-human.

How did Thoreau reconcile the ubiquitous aspect of evil with his teleological belief? The fact is he believed the omnipresent force at the core of the universe was essentially beneficent, although at times its acts appeared ruthlessly savage. Less insistent than Melville on the violent elemental temper in nature, nevertheless he was cognizant of ruthless savagery and violence in nature on the animal and elemental levels. He saw a mother woodchuck push out her little ones to save herself, when her burrow was opened and dug out with the aid of a dog. He saw a painted tortoise with its head outstretched and its shell partially empty where some bird with a long, powerful bill had disemboweled it. He found a large closed box trap in which lay the remains of a rabbit which had been starved to death in its living tomb. Unlike Melville, who in *Mardi* concluded that "evil is the chronic malady of the universe," he did not consider the force at the core of nature as essentially malevolent. There was no subtle demonism in nature so far as he could perceive. In consequence his faith was strongly tenoned in purposive design, and when nature appeared so proliferant that myriads of tadpoles were gobbled up by herons, and when vultures grew strong feeding on carrion, he was assured only of "the strong appetite and inviolable health of Nature." The impression made on a wise man, he concluded – so at variance with Melville's impression of the "horrible vulturism of earth" – was one of nature's universal innocence. Certainly he recognized the dual impact of nature upon man: its life-sustaining force and equally its life-denying force represented by drought, storm, or scourging insect pest. He knew that nature was not bound to be kind to man, but he was far less insistent on nature's violence than on its beneficence. He did not, like Melville in *Moby Dick,* assume the insuperable force of the natural universe to be latently evil simply because there was a potential violence in nature. The skepticism in Melville's attitude toward nature finds no counterpart in Thoreau. Nor did he try to placate nature by primitive ritual. He was an intelligent, uncredulous man.

One has only to turn to Thoreau's contemporary Francis Parkman to find a realistic account of the effect upon man of the unloosed forces of nature. In *The Oregon Trail* (1849), Parkman shows us the pent-up fury of western thunderstorms, the horror of quicksand traps, the omnipresent fear of thirst and hunger, the terror from the wide-sweeping prairie fires, and the danger of blasting sun, barren desert terrene, venomous rattlesnakes, attacking buffaloes, and grizzly bears. To Parkman the wild and stern associations with primitive nature reduced society to its original elements; "for here," as he wrote of the Great Plains, "each man lives by the strength of his arm and the valor of his heart . . . the whole fabric of art and conventionality is struck rudely to pieces, and men find themselves suddenly brought back to the wants and resources of their original natures." The reckless independence, the haughty self-reliance, and the sense of irresponsible freedom which elsewhere he noted as engendered by the forest life made civilization seem flat and stale.

Thoreau undoubtedly measured his life by the discovery of the significance to himself of natural phenomena such as the strange, suggestive, white, slumbering light of the phosphorescent moosewood, or the disguised cocoons of the

Promethea moth, or the curled calyx leaves of the Norway cinquefoil; of so many discoveries were the seasons of the mind composed, and in the seasons of the mind we read the history of the nature mystic's inner life. Such phenomena provided symbols for his thought. Not only a poet analogist but a moralist as well, he sought the *ethical* significance of the object observed. Yet he was not didactic; he did not insist that we imitate the actions of the moths or the cinquefoil. He was personal without being doctrinaire. When, for example, in spring he sat on some distant hillside overlooking a meadow, he was struck by the vivid green tips of the sedge as they pushed up out of the brown and sere tussock. Here was the first phalanx of spring's forces. Here was the contrast of life with death. Here was the renewal of life. Now, there is, of course, an observation involved here, a poetic one, not a scientific one. No contribution is made to science by his observation. Yet the charm of the poetic is that it relates us directly with nature. Life is organic and natural, and as we are related to nature what goes on in it has a counterpart within ourselves. We, too, feel a vernal resurgence. Yet nowhere does Thoreau *insist* upon this inference; he simply suggests it.

We come closer to his essence when we consider him not as a master mind discerning an ulterior meaning in the universe unvouchsafed to others, and regard him, more simply, as a transcendental nature mystic aware of a spiritual reality, and a poetic naturalist in his correspondence with nature. By juxtaposing a dream of Emerson's with one of Thoreau's, the difference between two mystical attitudes becomes perceptible. Thoreau's aspirative tendency differs markedly from Emerson's serene assurance.

Once Emerson dreamed that as he floated at will in the great Ether, he saw the world floating near him shrunken in size to that of an apple. "Then," as he recalled, "an angel took it in his hand and brought it to me and said, 'This must thou eat.' And I ate the world." Indeed, his life and his work, which embodied the infinitude of the private man, are implicit in the dream. He wrote in "colossal cipher" and gossipped for his hour concerning the "eternal politics." The medium of an oracle, he spoke oracularly. In Emerson there was a serene benevolence which arose as from an ordained faith, for had he not eaten the world like an apple?

On the other hand, Thoreau, who read nature in the original, met life at all points *ex tempore* with a readiness the moment required, and stepped forward like one who had a destination in mind. To him both direction and intention were clear. He searched for Reality, and the touchstone by which he would know it was the spirit within. He countered the serene benevolence of Emerson by an austere independence. An aspiring seeker, he once dreamed he was ascending a mountain through a dark, unfrequented wood at its base, and passed rocky ridges, stunted trees, the haunts of wild beasts, until he crossed an imaginary line that separated the mountain from the upper air and clouds, and, at once, experienced "a superterranean grandeur and sublimity." There were two ways of access to the mountain – through the dark wood or through the sunny pasture. "Why is it," he queried, "that in the lives of men we hear more of the dark wood than of the sunny pasture?" Usually he ascended through the dark wood. When he had reached the dream-mountain's top, he was surprised to find how imminent to the top lay his native fields. At the top his thoughts became purified and sublimed. It was as though he had been translated. "And are there not such mountains, east or west, from which you may look down on Concord in your thought, and on all the world?" he inquired.

VIII

The Anatomy of Nature

It is imposible for the same person to see things from the poet's point of view and that of the man of science.

JOURNAL, February 18, 1852

THE VIEWPOINT of the Calvinistic Puritans, who considered natural science as irrelevant to their interests and problems, and nature as suggesting "the hidden mysterious operations of designing agents," contrasts sharply with Thoreau's view. Similarly the viewpoint of the eighteenth-century rationalists and deists who saw the natural universe as a world-machine, and the viewpoint of some contemporary thinkers who regard nature as mainly utilitarian – that is, good enough to raise wheat and corn and potatoes – also differ widely from Thoreau's viewpoint. Natural science was not irrelevant to him, and in this respect his viewpoint differed from the Puritan's attitude. Neither did he assume that "designing agents" manipulated nature at will; he was not superstitious. Nor did he believe that nature was in the least mechanical; it was, instead, sentient and organic. As for prevailing contemporary viewpoints, he would not have approved the crassly utilitarian, nor the frivolous "just-so-much-weather" aspect, nor relentless scientific materialism which sees nature only as an embodiment of inexorable law. He was too truly religious, and perhaps too wise, to justify all data merely by verification of the senses, when he realized "the things that are seen *are* temporal; but the things which are not seen *are* eternal." Was it simply impertinence or evidence of what Aunt Mary Moody Emerson referred to as "the fatal gift of penetration" that prompted him to inquire, "With all your science can you tell how it is, and whence it is, that light comes into the soul?" Frequently that light is difficult to verify by the senses. Certainly he would have distrusted Thomas Henry Huxley's statement, "that natural knowledge, seeking to satisfy natural wants, has found the ideas which can alone still spiritual cravings."

The point is, Thoreau's attitude toward nature is that of a poet and not that of a scientist. Doctor J. Arthur Thomson maintains that the scientist is "more concerned with knowing Nature than with enjoying her." "His main intention," Doctor Thomson continues, "is to describe the sequences in Nature in the simplest possible formulae, to make a working thought-model of the known world." Presumably the scientist coolly, dispassionately, and impersonally observes the forces of nature. As Madame Curie said to a journalist, "In science we must be interested in things and not in persons." The scientist is governed by the idea of explaining what he finds out about the sequences of nature through carefully planned investigations of natural phenomena. He collects and relates facts, and by the method of analysis and induction he seeks to apprehend general laws. Doctor Julian S. Huxley, in *Essays of a Biologist*, takes special pains to correct a general misapprehension of a law of nature. "A law of Nature," he says, "is not something revealed, not something absolute, not something imposed on phenomena from without or from above; it is no more and no less than a summing-up, in generalized form, of our own observations of phenomena; it is an epitome of fact, from which we can draw general conclusions." When the scientist's observations are accurate, his experimentation thorough, and his verification successful, he formulates the facts into an abstract statement. And, as a general law, the abstract statement forms a component part of the "working thought-model of the known world."

The object of the scientist is, then, to apprehend the laws of nature, find out how they work, and then apply them for man's advancement. His goal is the construction of a unified system which will represent in exact terms all the phenomena of nature. What the scientist builds empirically through observation and analysis is the structure of reality. It is apparent that he has not thrown much light on the substance of reality. His problem has been limited to how the forces of nature operate. As I. A. Richards points out in *Science and Poetry*: "For science, as our most elaborate way of *pointing* to things systematically, tells us and can tell us nothing about the nature of things in any *ultimate* sense. It can never answer any question of the form: *What* is so and so? it can only tell us *how* such and such behave." Benjamin Franklin thought it was sufficient to recognize the workings of natural laws. " 'Tis enough," said he, "if we know the laws themselves. 'Tis of real use to know that china left in the air unsupported will fall and break; but *how* it comes to fall, and *why* it breaks, are matters of speculation. 'Tis a pleasure indeed to know them, but we can preserve our china without it."

Poetry, on the other hand, as distinguished from science, is not an impersonal and objective description of the working of the forces of nature. It is a subjective interpretation of human experience. The poet is not always cool, dispassionate, and impersonal. On the contrary, since he is concerned with the relation of facts to the emotional nature, his emphasis is personal and impassioned, though not necessarily always subjective. It is the poet's special ability to communicate the quality of experience through metaphoric or connotative language. By whetting the sensibilities, by intensifying the feelings, by quickening the perception of beauty, and by arousing one to acts of moral good, the poet makes man more responsive to the emotional, intellectual, and ethical values implicit in experience. The attitude of the poet is, then, not antagonistic but complementary to the attitude of the scientist. The ultimate end of each may be the same; the approach and emphasis only differ.

By relating his observations directly to man, by humanizing knowledge, by emphasizing the subjective value of the facts of experience, the poetic naturalist is distinguished from the scientific naturalist. To the scientific naturalist who counts, analyzes, and measures every part of a flower, the poetic naturalist remonstrates: "But what is that to the purpose?" To the poetic naturalist the ultimate transcends the immediate means; analysis, measurement, and classification are subordinate; the chief aim is to determine the value and significance of the flower to man.

Because he was primarily concerned with the simple enjoyment of nature and with the relation of its phenomena to the moods and visions of his private imaginative experience, Thoreau is the poetic naturalist. He proposed as one of the salients of his life "to observe what transpires, not in the street, but in the mind and heart of me!" Aware that the relationship with natural phenomena should be humanized, he asserted: "A fact stated barely is dry. It must be the vehicle of some humanity in order to interest us. . . . A man has not seen a thing who has not felt it."

Thoreau went so far as to declare, "It is impossible for the same person to see things from the poet's point of view and that of the man of science." He assumed it was necessary to forget one's learning before one could begin really to know. An introduction by some learned man did not enable man to get closer to a natural object. In order to conceive of it with "a total apprehension," it was necessary to approach it as something "totally strange." Scientific terms and distinctions only prejudiced one's approach, and consequently he advised forgetting the botany book if one would make acquaintance with the ferns. It was easy to find out what was the position of the fruit-dots or the character of the indusium; such information was in the scientific books. But where would one turn in order to learn how to be affected by ferns? How was one to find in them "another sacred scripture and revelation" that redeemed one's life? The scientist only described natural phenomena whose reality Thoreau made us feel.

He thought science was interested chiefly in classification; it did little to clarify ultimate meaning. It could tell you what the various kinds of sentences were, but it could not illuminate the meaning of any. It knew how and where, but it could not answer why. When he told people that he had visited a mountain, their leading inquiry was whether or not he took a field-glass with him. But he did not go to the mountain-top to perceive particular objects more distinctly; he went in order that he might obtain an elevated position from which to see "the peculiar beauty and grandeur of the view." "It was not to see a few particular objects, as if they were near at hand, as I had been accustomed to see them, that I ascended the mountain, but to see an infinite variety far and near in their relation to each other, thus reduced to a single picture." Since only the higher view of things really counted, he refused to be confined to the horizontal field of sight. No matter how deeply absorbed he became in the examination of natural phenomena — of skunk cabbage or frog-spittle or water-beetles — he never forgot that each was not an end in itself, but only a part of the total phenomena of life — "a single picture."

When the secretary of the Association for the Advancement of Science at Washington wrote to Thoreau requesting information about the branch of science he was especially interested in, he felt some constraint in answering. If he truly reported his particular department of inquiry — his mystical, transcendental, natural philosophic interest — he felt the statement would make him the laughing-stock of the scientific community. Since there was no place for the poetic naturalist in the Association for the Advancement of Science, it indicated to him the limitation of science.

By temperament and inclination he was a poet rather than a scientist. His attitude was far more that of the Chaldean shepherd, who looked at the stars with wonder, than that of the learned astronomer, who, with his proofs and figures, charts and diagrams, added, divided, and measured the heavenly spheres. His skepticism was not prompted by any doubts of the empirical scientist's intellective capacity to submit the facts of life to an unflinching scrutiny. It was prompted by the inherent shortcomings of the scientist; the failure of the scientist to see the real significance of knowledge through its humanization. "It may happen," Thoreau conjectured, "that the stars are more significant and truly celestial to the teamster than to the astronomer," for the simple reason that the astronomer was more concerned with a few imposing statements respecting size and distance of stellar bodies than he was with man.

In failing to show the relationship of scientific discoveries to man, Thoreau thought that science stopped short of a real contribution. Apparently it did not occur to him that the scientist, philosopher, and poet were complementary, not antagonistic partners in the search for understanding and application of human knowledge. "The natural system may tell us the value of a plant in medicine or the arts or for food, but neither it nor the Linnaean, to any great extent, tells us its chief value and significance to man, which in any measure accounts for its beauty, its flower-like properties. . . ." The truest description of a flower consisted, did it not, in "the unmeasured and eloquent one which the sight of it inspires?" He considered the delight which observers drew from natural objects to be complete and final in itself. Not how did an object in nature appear to man, but how did it affect him; there was the leverage. So, as we note, the white water-lily was emblematic of purity to him and the purple poke of a successful life; the earth-song of the cricket set him moralizing, and the gospel of the wood thrush made a Sabbath out of a weekday. What was true of the flowers was also true of plants and of trees and of the grasses and of the creatures in the fields and in the woods and in the water and in the air. When the poetic faculty was fertile, the marriage of the soul with nature fertilized the intellect and invigorated the imagination.

What Thoreau sought in nature, then, was the personal affiliation — the highest quality of the animal, vegetable, or mineral inhering in its relation to man. All else was mechanical and non-human. As a poet it was his self-assumed task to wrest significance from natural phenomena by observing genuinely and accurately all natural objects as they lay in the range of his vision and by associating his observation with humanity. All nature composed the wide angle of his vision, but man was properly the focus.

In further clarification of Thoreau's attitude, let us juxtapose the viewpoints which I. A. Richards has referred to as "the Magical View" and the scientific. The magical view arose in primitive times in consequence of an increase in man's knowledge of and command over nature, and, in time, it was superseded by an extension of that knowledge of and command over nature. The change was effected by what Richards calls "the Neutralization of Nature," by which he means the transference from the magical view of the world, with its belief "in a world of Spirits and Powers which control events, and which can be evoked and, to some extent, controlled themselves by human practices," to the scientific view of the world which seeks by reason to understand and co-ordinate forces rampant in nature.

These two viewpoints are juxtaposed in Clarence King's book *Mountaineering in the Sierra Nevada.* Geologist King, a week after climbing Mount Whitney in the Inyo Range of the Sierra Nevada, lay on the desert sand at the foot of the range, and looked upward where the moving shadows of drifting clouds darkened Mount Whitney's sun-bright serenity. How would Thoreau have reacted had he lain on the desert sand and looked toward Mount Whitney? Would he not have listened tolerantly to an Indian, even as King did, who told him that the peak was an old man who watched the valley and cared for the Indians, shaking the country with earthquakes to punish the white man for injustice to his tribe? Would he with the disappearance of the Indian have felt the liberating power of modern culture that frees the white man from such self-made myths? Would Mount Whitney have embodied for him the magical view which feels inwardly "the greatness of a natural object, and forever after endows it with consciousness or power"? Or would he have seen, as the scientist sees, "a splendid mass of granite 14,887 feet high, ice-chiselled and storm-tinted"?

Thoreau was no obscurantist, yet he would have felt inwardly the greatness of the mountain without ascribing animistic power to it. He would not have seen it naïvely as valley-watcher and Indian-protector. He did not believe in spirits in the air. He was no primitivist who raised his voice either in placative or in supplicatory invocation before mysterious forces in a quasi-intelligible world. What he represents is that aspect of human nature which seeks emotional satisfaction concomitantly with the expansion of knowledge. He did not deny the verifiable truths of science nor did he try to correct science. He embodies, instead, the effort of the human spirit to make itself at home in our universe. It is as though Thoreau said: "Science can give us the facts and it can systematize its findings, but of what use are its laws even when applied if man has no capacity for enjoying what he has?" It is significant to know how the mountain is constructed. It is less significant to know that once upon a time man ascribed irrational powers to it. It is more important – much more, indeed, for the growth of the human spirit – to feel neighborly with the granitic mass of Mount Whitney, or with Chimborazo or Kilimanjaro or Popocatepetl or the Jungfrau. It is the poetic naturalist who warms with the human spirit what else might stand named and measured but unfelt.

2

Thoreau's indictment of science was a formidable though an astigmatic one. It was formidable because of his unwavering adherence to the position of the poetic naturalist. The first count in his arraignment of science was its failure to satisfy equally the demands of the imagination and the reason. He thought it impossible for the same person to see things from the poet's point of view and from that of the man of science. A botanist absorbed in the pursuit of grasses would not distinguish the grandest pasture oaks. Once from a perch on Fair Haven Cliff he saw a crimson cloud in the distant horizon. Now any scientist, he thought, would explain the crimson cloud simply as a mass of vapor which absorbed all other rays and reflected the red, and that would be the end of it. The scientific account certainly did not stir the blood, though it informed the understanding. Only the beauty of the red vision touching the imagination, and suggesting something unexplainable, excited a poet and made his thoughts flow. "What sort of science is that which enriches the understanding, but robs the imagination?" Thoreau inquired with some feeling. He did not forget to add, "Just as inadequate to a pure mechanic would be a poet's account of a steam-engine."

When the scientific naturalist saw the bream and considered it merely as another species of fish, Thoreau was aroused. What really interested mankind about the fish was hardly the co-operative effort of science, where one scientist counted the fin-rays, where another measured the intestines, and where a third daguerreotyped a scale, but rather the fact that in the fish man recognized "a living contemporary." When he saw the beauty of the little striped bream poised in Walden's glaucous waters, the place of the fish in a system – class, order, family, genus, species – was comparatively of little importance to Thoreau. "Its life no man can explain more than he can his own. I want you to perceive the mystery of the bream. I have a contemporary in Walden. It has fins where I have legs and arms. I have a friend among the fishes, at least a new acquaintance. Its character will interest me, I trust, not its clothes and anatomy. I do not want it to eat. Acquaintance with it is to make my life more rich and eventful."

Science also failed to explain adequately the relationship between moral and natural laws. How inadequate science was when one sought to explain the phenomena of nature! As a percipient sensibilitist he saw that any classification of natural phenomena which failed to indicate the ultimate moral relationship was of no great significance. He took the civilized viewpoint that a knowledge of the laws of nature did not suffice. Such knowledge certainly did not prevent man's acting perversely. Man might still use these laws for acts of cruelty, bloodshed, and stupidity, or for betrayal of and hatred toward his fellow-men. There must be a desire to act in harmony with these laws of nature. His problem as he saw it was complementary to the scientist's: the problem of interpretative evaluation and speculation as to the ultimate motivation of the forces of nature. What the substance of the great force at work in the universe is, who shall say? but our way of life depends upon our viewpoint toward it. During a walk to Lincoln, Thoreau saw a large white ash tree that had been riven by lightning. In the livid streak furrowing the tree, he observed the brute force of nature, and wondered if it were not possible to explain the lightning stroke on moral rather than natural grounds. "Is this of the character of a wild beast, or is it guided by intelligence and mercy? If we trust our natural impressions, it is a manifestation of brutish force or vengeance, more or less tempered with justice. Yet it is our own consciousness of sin, probably, which suggests the idea of vengeance, and to a righteous man it would be merely sublime without being awful. . . . Science affirms too much. Science assumes to show *why* the lightning strikes a tree, but it does not show us the moral *why* any better than our instincts did."

Science was deficient in another way. It failed when it became narrowly preoccupied with details. He observed that the man of science who did not seek for expression, but for a fact to be expressed merely, studied nature as a dead language. Evidence of the "cribb'd, cabin'd, and confined" viewpoint of science came directly from his own experience. It was the effect of an unrelaxed attention to nature upon his own part that forced the issue. He was disturbed by his preoccupation with such short commons and innutritious study as the inspection of the granules of lichens on the bark of trees. "Surely I might take wider views. The habit of looking at things microscopically, as the lichens on the trees and rocks, really prevents my seeing aught else in a walk. Would it not be noble to study the shield of the sun on the thallus of the sky, cerulean, which scatters its infinite sporules of light through the universe? To the lichenist is not the shield (or rather the apothecium) of a lichen disproportionately large compared with the universe? The minute apothecium of the pertusaria, which the wood-chopper never detected, occupies so large a space in my eye at present as to shut out a great part of the world." So he commented in March, 1852. A year later he was still troubled by the danger of shutting out a great part of the world. "Man cannot afford to be a naturalist, to look at Nature directly, but only with the side of his eye. He must look through and beyond her. . . . I feel that I am dissipated by so many observations. . . . I knock the back of my hand against a rock, and as I smooth back the skin, I find myself prepared to study lichens there. I look upon man but as a fungus. . . ." He knew inward experience did not so much depend upon the outward experience as the outward upon the inward, and since an obsession with the outward clouded the clarity of the inward, he cherished such inward experience as would make nature significant.

The fourth count in his indictment of science was its inhumanity. "The inhumanity of science concerns me," he said, "as when I am tempted to kill a rare snake that I may ascertain its species. I feel that this is not the means of acquiring true knowledge." Or, again: "I have just been through the process of killing the cistudo for the sake of science, but I cannot excuse myself for this murder, and see that such actions are inconsistent with the poetic perception, however they may serve science, and will affect the quality of my observations. I pray that I may walk more innocently and serenely through nature. No reasoning whatever reconciles me to this act. It affects my day injuriously. I have lost some self-respect. I have a murderer's experience in a degree."

3

No one who reads Thoreau can long remain unaware of the intense struggle that took place within him between the scientific impulse and the poetic. During most of his life he was a transcendental poet whose observation of nature was a matter of seeing and regarding nature as a symbol of the human mind. His *Journal* and published works are records of his search in nature for analogues which co-ordinate a natural fact with a mental association. In his *Journal* for 1862, Bronson Alcott recorded: "Like Homer, Hesiod, and the earliest poets, Thoreau saw and treated Nature as a symbolism of the mind, as a physiological theology. His mysticism is alike solid and organic, animal and ideal. He is the mythologist of these last days — reminds more of the ancients in his mode of seeing and saying than any recent naturalist and poet." Illustrations from Thoreau's works which confirm Alcott's observation occur many times at random and confirm the transcendental aspect of his relationship to nature. The transcendental belief held, as Emerson's little book *Nature* explains, that every part of nature is an emblem, symbol, or analogue of a spiritual or intellectual truth.

While this transcendental aspect of his relationship to nature is quite apparent, there is in his writings an equal and almost contrary tendency to see nature, not alone with his imagination as he preferred to see it, but also with his reason. He knew that by deducing only what the facts impelled him to deduce could he truthfully trace the operations of the forces of nature. The objective of the scientist is to find out what these natural forces are and how they work in order that he may discover at long last why they operate. The scientist may, of course, confirm with his reason what the poet with his imagination has already guessed, but at least the scientist will have the assurance of knowing by what method he learned how to observe and investigate. The scientist's respect for reason gripped Thoreau and confounded him when the transcendental imagination conflicted with it. Bronson Alcott remarked of Thoreau in his *Journal* in 1859: "He is less thinker than observer; a naturalist in tendency but of a mystic habit, and a genius for detecting the essence in the form and giving forth the soul of things seen. He knows more of Nature's secrets than any man I have known, and of Man as related to Nature." In the phrase "a naturalist in tendency but of a mystic habit" we most clearly apprehend the conflict between the empirical scientist and the imaginative poet in Thoreau.

Although he distinguished sharply between the poet's

and the scientist's viewpoint, Thoreau was preoccupied frequently with the scientist's method and viewpoint. When he was in uninterrupted relationship with nature, he found his intellectual life becoming more obedient to nature and less obedient to spirit. The memorable seasons in his inner life diminished. When, on one early April morning in 1852, he went to the Sudbury meadows, he started some woodcock in a wet place in Hi Wheeler's stubble-field, and he counted six spotted tortoises on the shore by the Hubbard Bridge causeway. But it was too late for the early morning inspiration. The bird-song was less joyous and earnest. In a way the advancing morning represented his own plight. The heaven of susceptibility that lay about him in his youth had disappeared, but, compensatorily, his powers of discrimination were stronger. "What," he wondered suggestively, "if there were united the susceptibility of youth with the discriminations of age?" Once he was part and parcel of nature, but now he was observant of her. He measured his descent by the fact that he grew less poetic and more scientific.

Perhaps the vigor of his opposition to the scientific viewpoint arose from a conscious knowledge that the method of the scientific naturalist gripped him too insidiously. A conflict within his temperament, a tendency toward cool, impersonal, scientific observation and examination sometimes clashed with ardent poetic humanism. It was necessary, therefore, occasionally to stop and ascertain the virtue of his methods as well as the purity of his motives. "I fear that the character of my knowledge is from year to year becoming more distinct and scientific; that, in exchange for views as wide as heaven's scope, I am being narrowed down to the field of the microscope. I see details, not wholes nor the shadow of the whole. I count some parts, and say, 'I know.'"

Frequently in the *Journal* we find notations far from poetic. The following entry could have been recorded only under the dry light of the scientist's lens, at such variance is it from the iridescent light of the poet's mind:

> A eupatorium from Hubbard's Bridge causeway answers to *E. purpureum,* except in these doubtful points, that the former has four leaves in a whorl, is unequally serrate, the stem is *nearly* filled with a thin pith, the corymb is not merely terminal, florets eight and nine. Differs from *verticillatum* in the stem being not solid, and I perceive no difference between calyx and corolla in color, if I know what the two are. It may be one of the intermediate varieties referred to.

Further evidences of the scientist's dry light in the *Journal* appears as he inventoried swamps, analyzed birds' nests, examined crow-droppings, or studied the flourishing growth and beauty of lichens, remarking how he could study a single piece of bark for hours. He measured the depth of snow; he took the temperature of Concord springs; he traced the physiography of Concord River; he counted the rings of tree-stumps; he compiled lists of plants. Apparently there was no end to his private quests into the manifold phases of nature. No professional naturalist ever applied himself to nature's varied phenomena any more assiduously than he did. An essential part of his equipment was a measuring tape or a footrule. One January afternoon when it showered, he went to Clintonia Swamp, and there, while he sat under his umbrella in the warm rain, he studied the genesis of birch fungus on a dead *Betula alba.* He was startled a little later when he found that he was studying fungi under the light of his lamp. He felt as if he were stooping too low and should next be found classifying carbuncles and ulcers.

> Why wilt thou examine every little fibre of my soul,
> Spreading them out before the sun like stalks of flax to dry?
> The infant joy is beautiful, but its anatomy
> Horrible, Ghast, and Deadly,

exclaimed Blake.

4

Thoreau thought he detected some sort of preparation and faint expectation preceding every discovery he made. Yet he knew that one might look too steadily actually to see. Since the woodchopper, who passed so much of his time in the woods, picked up unconsciously what the naturalist missed by trying to find it consciously, Thoreau advocated relaxed attention. Although in the discovery of new plants "a thrilled and expectant mood" was a chief factor, he learned to walk with relaxed senses and cultivated "a true sauntering of the eye" – that is, "seeing with the side of the eye."

While sauntering in the woods and fields he found that he never blundered into discoveries. For years he had searched vainly for Indian hemp. Then one day he read of it again, that its blossoms were very small, and this distinction continually recurring inclined him to regard closely the size of the flowers he saw, though he did not believe that the hemp could be found in Concord. In a day or two he saw it in three different places, each place having a different variety. Once again, when searching for a new plant, lo and behold, he found dyers'-green-weed. Having discovered the water-arum at the south end of Gowing's Swamp, he proceeded to find it in another locality. Upon returning from an up-country trip with his sight whetted by expectation, he detected two new plants, and he thought he had detected them first abroad because he had been looking for the strange. The existence of the remarkable Indian relics that he found in Concord soil were, as he noted, first divined; the discovery was planned. "Frequently I have told myself distinctly what it was to be before I found it." Apparently he possessed, within human limits, the uncanny knack of knowing where to find the objects of his expectation. He knew that the discoverer must take his discovery into his head first: "He must all but see it." Objects were not seen, he thought, even though they fell within one's visual ray, simply because they had not come within range of an intellectual ray. "So, in the largest sense, we find only the world we look for." He apprehended with the feelers of the imagination, but he also grasped by the forceps of the intellect.

In a passage in the *Journal* which clarifies his method, he declared:

> Objects are concealed from our view not so much because they are out of the course of our visual ray as because there is no intention of the mind and eye toward them. We do not realize how far and widely, or how near and narrowly, we are to look. The greater part of the phenomena of nature are for this reason concealed to us all our lives. . . . There is just as much beauty visible to us in the landscape as we are prepared to appreciate,—not a grain more . . . we can hardly see anything else. In my botanical rambles I find that first the idea, or image, of a plant occupies my thoughts, though it may at first seem very foreign to this locality, and for some weeks or months I go thinking of it and expecting it unconsciously, and at length I surely see it, and it is henceforth an actual neighbor of mine. This is the history of my finding a score or more of rare plants which I could name.

> . . . And so it is with him that shoots at beauty. Not till the sky falls will he catch larks, unless he is a trained sportsman. He will not bag any if he does not already know its seasons and haunts and the color of its wing, — if he has not dreamed of it, so that he can *anticipate* it; then, indeed, he flushes it at every step, shoots double and on the wing, with both barrels, even in corn-fields. . . .

In an effort to attain that correspondence with nature in which he was at home in her, he remarked how closely and how long a man must attend nature. He must know when and where and how to look for natural phenomena, for it was necessary to anticipate nature a little if one would make any discoveries. Expectation was important in the relationship of man to nature; it intensified his sensitive awareness.

A second factor in the technique by which he approached and studied the language of nature was curiosity. When, on a January day, near the town line, in Heywood's wood by the Pond, he found the lichens looking rather bright, he inquired, "When they are bright and expanded, is it not a sign of a thaw or of rain?" While searching about on the cliffs, he asked, "What is the little chickweed-like plant already springing up on the top of the Cliffs?" In fact, there was no end to his insatiable curiosity. "Are those large scarred roots at the bottom of the brooks now, three inches in diameter, the roots of the pickerel-weed?" "What kind of blackberry did I find in blossom in Hubbard's Swamp?" "To what sparrow belong the coffee-colored eggs in Hubbard's field by the brook?"

He fairly itched with inquiries: "What is that small insect with large, slender wings, which I see on the snow or fluttering in the air these days?" Walking along a path he saw some rank thimbleberry shoots covered with a hoary bloom and he remarked on the singularity of such a delicate outer coat. "What is this bloom," he inquired, "and what purpose does it serve? Is there anything analogous in animated nature?" And he thought, "It is the *coup de grâce*, the last touch and perfection of any work, a thin elysian veil cast over it, through which it may be viewed." He noticed, too, how timid birds were of man's presence, and he inquired: "What does this fact signify? Does it not signify that man, too, is a beast of prey to them? Is he, then, a true lord of creation, whose subjects are afraid of him, and with reason? They know very well that he is not humane, as he pretends to be."

Quite as important as curiosity in the technique by which he approached nature is patience. Patience was as important in the stalking of the fauna as expectation in the discovery of the new botanical plants. Emerson thought: "The charm which Henry uses for bird and frog and mink, is Patience. They will not come to him, or show him aught, until he becomes a log among the logs, sitting still for hours in the same place; then they come around him and to him, and show themselves at home." The naturalist accomplished much by patience. "He must take his position," he declared, "and then wait and watch. It is equally true of quadrupeds and reptiles. Sit still in the midst of their haunts." It was so he studied the reddish-brown, bushy-tailed, blunt-nosed mink that encountered him in its maraudings; and so he studied a single piece of bark—patiently—for hours. When he approached a spring and watched a frog hop in, he sat down to wait patiently for its reappearance. Fifteen minutes later the frog rose to the surface, eyeing its observer steadily. "At length he becomes as curious about you as you can be about him. He suddenly hops straight toward [you], pausing within a foot, and takes a near and leisurely view of you. Perchance you may now scratch its nose with your finger and examine it to your heart's content, for it is become as imperturbable as it was shy before. You conquer them by superior patience and immovableness; not by quickness, but by slowness; not by heat, but by coldness."

The capacity to see an animate object from the object's point of view without sacrificing one's identity is experiencing full and completely. When, for example, Thoreau saw a muskrat come out of a hole in the ice, he thought, "While I am looking at him, I am thinking what he is thinking of me." This quotation contains, I think, the key of his mastery of nature's fauna. Through patience and immobility he aroused the curiosity of the smaller creatures and lured them to him. He whetted the interest of a woodchuck or a fish in himself, the better to scrutinize it, the while he remained calmly observant, simulating inanimation. He did not adopt the attitude of the observed, who has aroused the curiosity of the object of his inquiry, and who observes at his leisure the creature that scrutinizes him so closely. This was his skill; the birds, animals, and fishes approached him in order to see what he was doing, and through arousing their interest he gleaned the information about them that he so much desired. It is worth while pointing out how his adroitness consisted in *looking from* the woodchuck's or the fish's or the bird's position as though at himself – reporting how *he* affected the woodchuck or bird or fish, not merely how the bird or woodchuck or fish affected him.

5

Thoreau's skill and capability as a naturalist cannot be ignored. Nor should we ever misrepresent the end for which he intensified his interest in nature: to realize a functional relationship with his natural environment. He had the naturalist's bent as well as the poet's temperament. But we should remember that there was nothing magical about his skill. As John Burroughs remarked, "Of course, Thoreau could do nothing with the wild creatures that you or I could not do under the same conditions." He knew where and when to look for things – whether birds' nests, snow fleas, painted tortoises, or insects. He knew where to find the marsh hawk's nest. He knew how to handle the creatures of nature; he plucked the young gray squirrels from their nest of twigs in the maple tree and they clung to his hands with their claws, their eyes as yet unopened. He shinnied up a middling-sized red oak that had a hole in one side, about fifteen feet from the ground, glimpsed a salmon-brown owl filling the interior of the hole, put in his hand and stroked it repeatedly until it reclined its head and closed its eyes.

Thoreau picked up snapping turtles from the wet mud. He thrust his arm down two-thirds its length into a hole at the bottom near the shore of Wyman's meadow, and plucked a pout by its head without resistance, from its firm-walled nest of weeds and fibrous mud, and then felt in the nest the flattish mass of dull-yellowish ova, the size of small buckshot, which he lifted out to examine at his leisure. He stroked familiarly the bream steadily poised over its nest hollowed in the sand by the river-bank, and raised it gently out of the water with his hand. He stroked away the constraint of a woodchuck, and once he picked up a partridge chick which squatted in his hand without winking. He raised large wood frogs from the sod and studied them at leisure while they squatted cold and moist in the middle of his palm, panting naturally.

He found the deer mouse snugly settled in a little nest of hypnum and dirty-white wool-like pappus of some plant, sixteen feet up an oak tree, in an owl's nest. He picked up a screech owl, which was sitting on the edge of a hollow hemlock stump, rolled it up in his handkerchief and carried it home. He buried small tortoise eggs on the fifteenth of June and dug them up on July tenth, and though the head was formless and the body was only a mass of yellow yolk, the eye was remarkably developed, and he noticed a very distinct pulsation where the heart should be. He found a fawn-colored flying squirrel in the bottom of a hemlock stump, rolled it up in his handkerchief, carried it home in his hand three miles in spite of its struggles, released it in his room and observed its movements, especially its inobvious "sails." The next day he carried the flying squirrel back to the woods, replaced it on the stump from which he had taken it, and watched it fly through the air. "It sprang off from the maple at the height of twenty-eight and a half feet, and struck the ground at the foot of a tree fifty and a half feet distant, measured horizontally . . . it skimmed much like a hawk," curving in its flight. He knew that Audubon and Bachman had seen the flying squirrel skim "about fifty yards."

When he was about twenty, he used Bigelow's *Plants of Boston and Vicinity* mainly for the popular names of the plants and for their localities. He learned the names of the plants, but he did not use any system. Nor did he pluck the flowers he found. When he was about thirty-five, he became more methodical, sought plants and brought them home to study. Yet he wondered if he should ever become familiar with the species of every twig and leaf in the swamps (where plants were so abundant). He learned most of the flowers and all but half a dozen shrubs, and then, one by one, he conquered the plants of his neighborhood. He persisted in the acquisition of botanical knowledge of his environment without any system. He only wanted to know his neighbors — to get a little nearer them.

> I soon found myself observing when plants first blossomed and leafed, and I followed it up early and late, far and near, several years in succession, running to different sides of the town and into the neighboring towns, often between twenty and thirty miles in a day. I often visited a particular plant four or five miles distant, half a dozen times within a fortnight, that I might know exactly when it opened, beside attending to a great many others in different directions and some of them equally distant, at the same time. At the same time I had an eye for birds and whatever else might offer.

He was interested in each contemporary plant in his neighborhood and attained a degree of acquaintance with it for the simple reason that it was a cohabitant of this planet.

While traversing Nut Meadow or Jimmy Miles's road, he saw the sulphur lichens on the rails brightening with the moisture and he felt like studying them as a relisher or tonic, "to make life go down and digest well, as we use pepper and vinegar and salads." Because the study of lichens whetted his relish for nature, he persisted in cultivating an intimacy with them. "A taste for this study is an evidence of titanic health, a sane earthiness. It makes not so much blood as soil of life. It fits a man to deal with the barrenest and rockiest experience. A little moisture, a fog, or rain, or melted snow makes his wilderness to blossom like the rose. . . ." He welcomed the lichen days. "The bank is tinged with a most delicate pink or bright flesh-color — where the *Baeomyces roseus* grows. It is lichen day. The ground is covered with cetrariae, etc., under the pines. How full of life and of eyes is the damp bark! It would not be worth the while to die and leave all this behind one." In the appearance of the lichens and mosses — the early and hardy cryptogamous vegetation — he *experienced* "a flowering of the crust of the earth." There were the Baeomyces — which he would name popularly "pink shot" or "eggs" — brightened by the rain, and the cladonias, and the red- and yellow-stemmed mosses, and the earthy lichens. The presence of these enabled him the better to sympathize with the earth. It indicated, not only how attractive the earth was, but also how full of life it was. The crust of the earth was actually "a very sensitive cuticle, teeming with life." As for the ferns, when he scented them, he felt like Antaeus touching the earth, and he bounded up with renewed strength "like a chamois, or mountain goat." There were also the buds and sprouts — "the impregnable, vivacious willow catkins, but half asleep under the armor of their black scales, sleeping along the twigs; the birch and oak sprouts, and the rank and lusty dogwood sprouts; the round red buds of the blueberries; the small pointed red buds, close to the twig, of the panicled andromeda; the large yellowish buds of the swamp-pink." "What," he exclaimed with the enthusiasm of a poetic naturalist, "what a rich book might be made about buds, including perhaps, sprouts!"

His natural discoveries were manifold. On a late March day, while walking along the edge of a meadow under Lupine Hill, he slumped through the sod into a muskrat's nest. He proceeded to lay it open with his hands, traced its galleries, and in the course of his examination made an interesting find — what he took to be beautiful frost crystals of rare form — like bodkins clustering around the fine white roots of the grass. A closer examination, during which he felt and tasted them, showed him that they were not frost, but "a clear, crystalline dew in almost invisible drops, concentrated from the dampness of the cavern, and perhaps melted frost still reserving by its fineness its original color, thus regularly arranged around the delicate white fibre; and, looking again, incredulous, I discerned extremely minute white threads or gossamer standing out on all sides from the main rootlet in this form and affording the core for these drops." He was greatly impressed with such a wonderful piece of chemistry: "that the very grass we trample on and esteem so cheap should be thus wonderfully nourished, that this spring greenness was not produced by coarse and cheap means, but in sod, out of sight, the most delicate and magical processes are going on.... The process that goes on in the sod and the dark, about the minute fibres of the grass, — the chemistry and the mechanics, — before a single green blade can appear above the withered herbage, if it could [be] adequately described, would supplant all other revelations. We are acquainted with but one side of the sod."

While surveying the windings of several brooks, he discovered that their meanders were not such regular serpentine curves as was commonly supposed. Their flow was as much in a zigzag as in a serpentine manner. "The eye is very much deceived when standing on the brink, and one who had only surveyed a brook so would be inclined to draw a succession of pretty regular serpentine curves. But, accurately plotted, the regularity disappears, and there are found to be many straight lines and sharp turns." Inspection of a little dried and bleached tortoise shell, an inch and three-quarters long, showed how much an architect might learn from a faithful study of it. "It is wonderful to see what a perfect piece of dovetailing his house is, the different plates of his shell fitting into each other by a thousand sharp teeth or serrations, and the scales always breaking joints over them so as to bind the whole firmly together, all parts of his abode variously interspliced and dovetailed." So nature made an arch. Even the appearance of some green galls on a goldenrod revealed how intimate the relationship between animal and vegetable life can be, since the little worms within the galls were completely changing the destiny of the plant. "The animal signifies its wishes by a touch, and the plant, instead of going on to blossom and bear its normal fruit, devotes itself to the service of the insect and becomes its cradle and food." It suggested to him that nature was a kind of gall, "that the Creator stung her and man is the grub she is destined to house and feed."

Thoreau's knowledge of nature was not merely speculative. When a fellow-townsman asked him to identify a spine and broken skull, he determined by its teeth that it was a muskrat. When he found some animal's cache in a perpendicular hole drilled for blasting in a sliver of rock, he determined that it was the hole of a deer mouse by examining closely with a microscope some scratches he found on chestnuts taken from the cache. "I now had no doubt that they were made by the incisors of a mouse, and, comparing them with the incisors of a deer mouse (*Mus Leucopus*) whose skull I have, I found that one or two of the marks were just the width of its two incisors combined (a twentieth of an inch), and the others, though finer, might have been made by them."

6

There were, however, limits to the accuracy of his scientific knowledge of natural phenomena. His observations were sometimes embarrassingly inaccurate. He attributed the white-throated sparrow, or Peabody-bird's, song to the myrtle warbler. When he heard the bittern, or stake-driver, make its curious sound, "like that made by a man pumping in a neighboring farmyard, watering his cattle, or like chopping wood before his door on a frosty morning," without observing it in the act of making its sound, he assumed that it sucked in and threw out water. "It is not easy," he said, "to understand how so small a creature can make so loud a sound by merely sucking in or throwing out water with pump-like lungs." Of course it was hard to understand if that was what the bittern did. It remained for an observer like William Brewster to describe for us the true story of the bittern's, or stake-driver's, pumping.

> At length [Brewster reported in *October Farm*] the head came slowly back. . . . Then the bill opened and shut five times in succession, with a spiteful snapping motion, the white throat dilating and flashing between each snap as if the bird were gulping in air, the usual *plumping* sound accompanying each gulp. The snaps became more and more rapid and emphatic until, immediately after the fifth and last, the bird pumped three times. With the first syllable (*pump*) the bill was opened wide and jerked downward a little below the horizontal; at the next syllable (*er*) it was tossed upward, apparently closed or nearly so; at the last syllable (*lump*) it was opened very wide and brought abruptly down to a little below the horizontal again. The bird did not lengthen his neck nor change his crouching attitude perceptibly while pumping. Indeed, the motions which accompanied the sound were much less energetic and pronounced than those which I have observed on former occasions. The position when at rest was nearly horizontal.

Thoreau's nature lapses were John Burroughs's despair. The latter was not disturbed about the former's ignorance of the fact that he had never seen phosphorescent wood until he went to the Maine Woods at forty, but he fairly snorted with amazement at Thoreau's failure to identify the little brown mate of the indigo bunting. (Thoreau called the black-throated blue warbler its mate.) Further, he failed to identify the mysterious "night warbler" as the oven-bird, or wood-accentor. Nor did he discriminate the song of the hermit thrush from that of the wood thrush. He never observed that the yellow-bellied woodpecker, not the downy woodpecker, was responsible for the rings of small holes in the bark of the apple tree, nor that the bird was feeding upon the milky cambium layer of the inner bark and not looking for grubs or insects, as he supposed. He thought, wrongly again, that it was more difficult to secure the swarm of the hive bee in seasons of much clover bloom than in seasons of scarcity. "Did he fancy that hunger would make the bees more docile and willing to be hived?" exclaimed the exasperated Burroughs. "Did he not know that, in a dearth of honey-producing flowers, as in times of great drought, the hive will not cast a swarm, and will kill the unhatched queens?" Soundly, too, Burroughs took exception to Thoreau's statement that once he stood in "the very abutment of a rainbow's arch." "How he could be aware that he was standing at the foot of one leg of the glowing arch is to me a mystery," asserted Burroughs; for, as the latter knew, the law of optics proved that one never saw a rainbow either to the right or to the left, but always facing the bow. Thus, "no two persons ever see exactly the same bow." It is impossible to flank it, let alone stand in its "very abutment."

7

In extenuation but not in apology for Thoreau's lapses, we must remember that his avidity for natural phenomena had as its ultimate objective, not a classifying of the natural phenomena, but a sympathetic relationship to it. His lapses hurt no one but himself. For better or worse, the poetic viewpoint always took precedence over the scientific viewpoint in his temperament. He used his senses imaginatively as a poet does; they were not always leashed to his intellect. He believed in the reality of the intuition, while the scientist believes in the reality of the concrete world of actuality.

An example of the use of imagination applied to scientific inquiry — a characteristic lacking in many scientists but not in the greatest — appeared in a *Journal* entry toward the end of his life. "The old naturalists were so sensitive and sympathetic to nature that they could be surprised by the ordinary events of life. It was an incessant miracle to them, and therefore gorgons and flying dragons were not incredible to them. The greatest and saddest defect is not credulity, but our habitual forgetfulness that our science is ignorance." In recognizing life as organic, dynamic, progressive, he saw that what we know is slight compared with what we do not know. The most refreshing and inspiring knowledge is, "in reference to important things, whose knowledge amounts to more than a consciousness of his ignorance?" The man who knew nothing about a subject and knew he knew nothing about it seemed to Thoreau to have a great advantage over the man who really knew something about it but thought that he knew all. "I do not know that knowledge amounts to anything more definite than a novel and grand surprise, or a sudden revelation of the insufficiency of all that we had called knowledge before; an indefinite sense of the grandeur and glory of the universe." Like Socrates, Thoreau cultivated his ignorance. He was an inquirer, a seeker who realized, as in the Tao philosophy, that life was a *way* to truth. Life was the *Tao* — the way to truth; truth was a state of mind and spirit – a state of expectation and receptive awareness and a realization of the immensity of life and of the untapped potentiality and resources latent in the commonplace phenomena of nature.

A confutation of Thoreau's way of life – the poetic way – will occur to the perverse critic who wishes to maintain a contrary assertion. He will concede that Thoreau in his relationship with nature attained a harmony with natural phenomena, not simply through the projection of sensibility upon insensate things, but through a close study and understanding of the actual ways of life. He will agree that Thoreau derived an aesthetic pleasure from his relationship with nature – shown so clearly and vigorously in his writings. He will affirm that Thoreau was intimately acquainted with nature in its modes of expression and various phases. He will accede that Thoreau did not avoid or ignore or omit the struggle for survival – the cunning stratagems of reptiles, plants, birds, and animals, to get their prey. He will admit that Thoreau observed widely, within the boundaries of his Concord environment, infrequently extended, and he will point out that, as in Noah's Ark, Thoreau included about two of everything in the copious tabulations of his *Journal*. "But" – and here the critic will raise his voice assertively – "but what right has Thoreau to assume that his philosophizings about nature are the truth, when, actually, he was essentially a poet rather than a scientist?" "Certainly," continues the trenchant critic, "Thoreau's descriptions and assertions are mainly subjective and romantic and as such are, strictly speaking, invalid as science. It is quite permissible for Walt Whitman to indulge in impressionistic reveries because he only wished to be regarded as a poet. As for Thoreau, did he assume, through mystical vision, that he transcended the world of actualities and discovered the ultimate values of life? If so, isn't his vision somewhat suspect? How is its validity to be tested when he accepted life on faith, and without testing his sense-data by empirical methods?" As a thoroughgoing romanticist did Thoreau make the error of romanticism? According to Doctor John Herman Randall, in *The Making of the Modern Mind,* the error "would consist in believing that these self-made worlds are factually true in a scientific sense"; while they are as interpretations of human experience in terms of its significance "true beyond question."

Our answer is brief enough: Thoreau did not aim at being a scientist. Nor did he expect to be evaluated scientifically. He aimed at being a human being who realized as completely as possible – and not wholly without the benefit of science, as his use of Asa Gray's *Manual* and Alphonse Wood's *Class-Book* and his perusal of Wilson and Nuttall indicate – the correspondence of nature and himself. If we can be convinced that he achieved such *rapport* with nature, this and this only is his private success. If his achievement appears positive to us, it suggests the degree to which we too might experience life if our sensibility were as intensely responsive. His success would then be important to us, not because he formed a self-created world out of nature, but because he achieved a perfect correspondence – a true vitalizing relationship with nature, going and coming "a part of herself," and because he left us an animated record interpreting the significance of his experience.

IX

The Sinews of Style

My work is writing, and I do not hesitate, though I know that no subject is too trivial for me, tried by ordinary standards. . . .

JOURNAL, October 18, 1856

EACH DAY Thoreau recorded in a journal the incidents and observations that impressed him on his walks. Without ennui, impatience, or dissatisfaction, he went into the field, wood, swamp, and pasture, or along the river highways, and returned at nightfall with abundantly detailed notes of what he had seen and thought. A careful observer, he perceived a life within nature peculiarly independent of ours. It is of this life within nature, the forces at work in the animal, vegetable, and mineral kingdoms – the little striped breams, cladonia lichens, wood thrushes, willow twigs, the color of shrub-oak leaves and the beauty of the freckled greenbriar leaves – that he gives us memorable glimpses. Though his life, seclusive, persistent, and independent, was important to him only as it related to man, either to mirror human actions or to replenish and reinvigorate the spirit, he revealed it with distinction: as simply, clearly, and precisely as he encountered it. He thought, in fact, that he resembled a clerk in the counting-room of the gods who at evening transferred his accounts from daybook to ledger.

The next day he reviewed what he had recorded the previous day, and saw that frequently he had omitted the most poetic part. As he pointed out, "It is not easy to write in a journal what interests us at any time, because to write it is not what interests us." Yet the ulterior motive in recording his experiences was the idea of publication. He worked up journal entries into lectures, and, in turn, polished and elaborated these lectures into essays. "And at last they stand," he said, "like the cubes of Pythagoras, firmly on either basis." In a way the *Journal* is his master work, for it is, as he maintained a journal should be, "a record of experiences and growth, not a preserve of things well done or said." As in the records of other journal-keepers like Amiel, Sénancour, Maurice de Guérin, Emerson, Alcott, and Hawthorne, it shows the tendency of the mind in mood, thought, and event.

According to Ellery Channing, Thoreau employed a method similar to Emerson's in journal-keeping. He read with pen in hand, jotting notes and citations in what he called his Factbooks. Later these quotations were included in the daybook journals which he kept regularly from year to year. Of all the journal-keepers he must be considered one of the most indefatigable in the history of American letters. His first diary — the Big Red Journal — contained 546 pages and extended from October 22, 1837, until June 11, 1840. He drew upon it for *The Service, Sir Walter Raleigh,* and for passages in *A Week* and *Walden.* Then he destroyed it and started another in which he recorded the intimacies of his private experience until his death in 1862.

After his death the manuscript journal, consisting of thirty-nine blank books of all shapes and sizes packed in a strong wooden box constructed by him, was given by his sister Sophia to Harrison G. O. Blake of Worcester, Massachusetts. Blake selected and published four volumes (1881–1892) of journal notes which related to the seasons. Later, the complete *Journal* was edited by Bradford Torrey and published in 1906 in fourteen volumes. The complete *Journal,* which represents an aggregate of about two million words, exemplifies, as one critic remarked, a typical example of Yankee devotion to duty. Its effect is the incremental one of mass.

Daily, Thoreau sauntered along old, meandering, uninhabited highways, like the Marlborough road, which led away from town. His spirits kindled as he turned from the beaten way and entered the open fields where the sky had a new appearance. Wherever he could breathe fresh air, whether beyond the piece of tillage, in the woodland stand, on some distant hillside pasture, or by a meadow brook, his mind opened like a wildflower. The impulse was an imperious one which sent him out-of-doors to get acquainted with the varied phases of nature. The aim was compelling which prompted him to try to communicate the essential quality of the acquaintanceship in his writings. Impulse and intention pulled conjunctively as the stern-and-bow paddles of a canoe.

Even as the whole physical being of a man responds in the act of walking, so the senses conspire with the intellect in thinking. Expression, like walking and thinking, to be vigorous must be the act of the whole man so "that our speech may be vascular." When Thoreau's legs began to move, his thoughts began to flow. He said: "Only while we are in action is the circulation perfect. The writing which consists with habitual sitting is mechanical, wooden, dull to read." He knew that what he wrote would have life in it only when he had life in him, and that the life would show only when natural sights and sounds stirred him responsively. So what he recorded in journal, essay, or book was the concrete embodiment of this acquaintanceship with nature as it touched the inward life of the spirit. He was one of the receivers in life who take into the mind what has been seen, felt, heard, and contemplated in the visible universe. From adventures with the homely, everyday phenomena which surrounded him he drew his themes. He wrote of autumnal tints, wild apples, the succession of forest trees, walking on a winter's day, a bean-field, the Concord River. "To improve from day to day just that soil and fertility which he has, to harvest that crop which his life yields, whatever it may be," he considered a great art in the writer.

Experience gathered from the earth and its ways settled in his stored memory until it was enkindled by the spark of creative imagination. Then it was communicated by the quickened mind in steady, supple expression. What had been observed was seen as clearly as his eye could see the object and recorded as directly as his intellect could express it. Although there is less emotion recollected in tranquillity in his writing than in many writers, it is still apparent that there was considerable interval between observation and expression. During this interval of reflection the thought was lengthened and its effect determined. It is for this reason that what he finally set down can be read many times over. Its pleasure is a multiple one of sound, sense, and suggestion.

In a letter which he wrote to his friend Harrison Blake, he suggested how a theme should be handled:

> Let me suggest a theme for you: to state to yourself precisely and completely what that walk over the mountains amounted to for you, — returning to this essay again and again, until you are satisfied that all that was important in your experience is in it. Give this good reason to yourself for having gone over the mountains, for mankind is ever going over a mountain. Don't suppose that you can tell it precisely the first dozen times you try, but at 'em again, especially when, after a sufficient pause, you suspect that you are touching the heart or summit of the matter, reiterate your blows there, and account for the mountain to yourself. Not that the story need be long, but it will take a long while to make it short. It did not take very long to get over the mountain, you thought; but have you got over it indeed? If you have been to the top of Mount Washington, let me ask, what did you find there? That is the way they prove witnesses, you know. Going up there and being blown on is nothing. We never do much climbing while we are there, but we eat our luncheon, etc., very much as at home. It is after we get home that we really go over the mountain, if ever. What did the mountain say? What did the mountain do?

So far as Thoreau's own compositions are concerned, is it not apparent that he really went over the mountain in *Walden* and *A Week* and *The Maine Woods* and *Excursions* and frequently in the *Journal*? It is more than apparent that he really went over the mountain only after he got home from the climb. Reflection is one of the chief qualities inherent in his books. He could sincerely say with Cardinal Newman, "Every thought I think is thought; and every word I write is writing." Much of contemporary writing is a matter of muscular impulse, literally first thoughts. Thoreau's writing is quintessential; it is an interwoven fabric of definitive thoughts. It is muscular and it is also cerebral. Reflection reinforces impulse. And further, it is in the ability to communicate without suspect device what it feels like to be alive and responsive that his power inheres. His writing stimulates us to take up a little life into our pores. The fact is, such a book as *Walden* is an act of life in two senses: in the actual experience and in the record. Together they constitute the deed.

One of the characteristic qualities of his skill as a writer consists in his knowledge of the earth and place of the natural fact in human experience. The way Paul Cézanne felt form in nature and projected his awareness in pictorial compositions – for example, in "L'Estaque" – was similarly felt and expressed by Thoreau. There is a sense of compositional effect, whether one reads the daily *Journal* entries or chapters in *Walden* or *A Week*. Reading Thoreau is like looking into the pocket of a vale where the fields are not seen separately as oblong or rectangular or polygonal patterns, where the watery patches are not isolated, or the trees as only particular oaks or beeches or maples. There is the sense, rather, of the field as it extends to the water and of the water as it is bordered by the trees, and of the vale in its compositional harmony. The suture of nature's seams is not an once apparent. We have at first a general impression in looking upon the natural scene, then we particularize and localize, and finally we re-establish the harmony of the separate objects in a total effect. The last is more than a sum of separate objects: it is a sense of the essential beauty of nature when realized as composition.

Thoreau started with the natural fact. It represented a point-of-reference definite and substantial, and when he soared into transcendental panegyric, it is still apparent that he started from the concrete. There is no ascent as by mythical ladders into heaven. His divinations are inductive – the ultimate significance is derived from close scrutiny of observable data. The habitual temper of his mind showed in what Matthew Arnold once called "the homely realism" of the German and Norse nature rather than in "the fairy-like loveliness" of the Celtic temperament. His intellect was nourished by direct association with the visible world – with huckleberries, rye-fields, thoroughwort, mizzling days, drumming partridges, orchises, snow crystals, owls and echoes; it was not animated with strange melancholy forms rising from the remote realm of a frenzied imagination as in the fantastic creations of some fellow-romanticist.

Yet he did not succumb to "the despotism of fact" for the simple reason that his devotion to sensuous beauty was imaginative. He was supremely the "poet-naturalist" with a sense of totality, that is, of the relationship of particular aspects to the living whole; of the Promethea moth to an Over-Mind kindred to his own; of the Norway cinquefoil to the great Fore-Thought; of the phosphorescent moose-wood to Reality; and of the signs in the snow to higher relationships, as in the following passage:

> The snow is the great betrayer. . . . Is there no trace of a nobler life than that of an otter or an escaped convict to be looked for in the snow? . . . Why do the vast snow plains give us pleasure, the twilight of the bent and half-buried woods? Is not all there consonant with virtue, justice, purity, courage, magnanimity? Are we not cheered by the sight? And does not all this amount to the track of a higher life than the otter's, a life which has not gone by and left a footprint merely, but is there with its beauty, its music, its perfume, its sweetness, to exhilarate and recreate us? Where

there is a perfect government of the world according to the highest laws, is there no trace of intelligence there, whether in the snow or the earth, or in ourselves? . . . The great game for mighty hunters as soon as the first snow falls is Purity, for, earlier than any rabbit or fox, it is abroad, and its trail may be detected by curs of lowest degree. Did this great snow come to reveal the track merely of some timorous hare, or of the Great Hare, whose track no hunter has seen? Is there no trace nor suggestion of Purity to be detected? If one could detect the meaning of the snow, would he not be on the trail of some higher life that has been abroad in the night? . . . A life which, pursued, does not earth itself, does not burrow downward but upward, which takes not to the trees but to the heavens as its home, which the hunter pursues with winged thoughts and aspirations, — these the dogs that tree it, — rallying his pack with the bugle notes of undying faith, and returns with some worthier trophy than a fox's tail, a life which we seek, not to destroy it, but to save our own. Is the great snow of use to the hunter only, and not to the saint, or him who is earnestly building up a life?

2

"How hard one must work in order to acquire his language, — words by which to express himself!" he commented. Basically words are of two sorts: exact and denotative on the one hand; suggestive and connotative on the other. The former are prosaic, explanatory, and rational in their effect; the latter are evocative and affective. The prosaic words are like blows; they have impact. The connotative words are poetic. They have a quality and tone which is resonant in combination as though a tuning-fork had been struck. Although he preferred poetic words like transport, rapture, ravishment, ecstasy, and flame ("What a good word is 'flame,' expressing the form and soul of fire, lambent with forked tongue!"), Thoreau thought the advantage in describing natural objects came from the use of words originally derived from nature. He, too, even as Emerson, would pierce the rotten diction, where all meanings were hazy and indefinite, and fasten words again to visible things. It was a poet who impressed the winds and streams into his service and who nailed words to their primitive senses.

It was the ability to fasten words to visible things in the talk of such countrymen as Rice and Minott that made their speech both piquant and poetic to Thoreau. "Very few men can speak of Nature with any truth," he said. George Minott could because he was an indigene whose speech savored of the natural sights and sounds of the broad earth and of his husbandry. When the ordinary man spoke of Walden Pond, Thoreau saw only "a shallow, dull-colored body of water without reflections or peculiar color," but when Minott spoke of it he saw "the green water and reflected hills at once, for he *has been* there." The expression of an indigene who spoke or wrote out of a full experience was quick with life. There was the rustle of the leaves from the wood through which he passed.

Thoreau attempted to nail words to their primitive senses. One way he had of re-allying words to their original meaning was by the inclusion of the Latin roots from which they flowered. Leaven, the soul of bread, was the *spiritus*. "The ear of wheat (in Latin *spica*, obsoletely *speca*, from *spe*, hope) should not be the only hope of the husbandman; its kernel or grain (*granum,* from *gerendo,* bearing) is not all that it bears." The hare was "lepus, levipes, light-foot, some think." "The value of these wild fruits is not in the mere possession or eating of them, but in the sight or enjoyment of them. The very derivation of the word 'fruit' would suggest this. It is from the Latin *fructus,* meaning that which is *used* or *enjoyed.*"

When literary language loses its tone and color from being used overlong in a particular way, the alert writer renews his expression by infusing it with the vigor of the popular speech. If he is a contemporary writer, like Sandburg or Frost or Mencken or Lardner, he might use such phrases as the following: "no depending on," "I don't get you," "put a crimp in," "where did he blow from?" etc. In Thoreau's own day there were proponents of American phraseology like Emerson, Davy Crockett, and Lincoln, and he also should be counted among those who stood for a living speech. He said characteristically enough: "It is too late to be studying Hebrew; it is more important to understand even the slang of today." By using the colloquial idiom he loosed the flex of the mother tongue. He called a load of wood a "jag." He referred to farms as "run out." It was the indigenous aspect of expression that interested him. He tethered his expression to the good earth. He had the writer's wisdom which is to use words that are part of one's actual experience. "Talk about learning our *letters* and being *literate!* Why, the roots of *letters* are *things.* Natural objects and phenomena are the original symbols or types which express our thoughts and feelings, and yet American scholars, having little or no root in the soil, commonly strive with all their might to confine themselves to the imported symbols alone. All the true growth and experience, the living speech, they would fain reject as 'Americanisms.' . . . When I really know that our river pursues a serpentine course to the Merrimack, shall I continue to describe it by referring to some other river no older than itself which is like it, and call it a *meander*? It is not more *meandering* than the *Meander* is *musketaquidding*." [1]

[1] That Thoreau favored the use of the American language, the following statement from *First and Last Journeys* (Bibliophile Society, Boston, vol. 1, p. 81) makes amply clear:

"We must look to the West for the growth of a new literature, manners, architecture, etc. Already there is more language there, which is the growth of the soil, than here; good Greekish words there are in abundance, — good because necessary and expressive; 'diggings,' for instance. If you analyze a Greek word you will not get anything simpler, truer, more poetical; and many others, also, which now look so ram-slang-like and colloquial when printed, another generation will cherish and affect as genuine American and standard."

The following reactions of Walt Whitman to a native idiom in *An American Primer* (*The Atlantic Monthly*, April, 1904) would have interested Thoreau greatly:

"The Americans are going to be the most fluent and melodious voiced people in the world — and the most perfect users of words. Words follow character, — nativity, independence, individuality."

"Mississippi! — the word winds with chutes — it rolls a stream three thousand miles long."

"I like limber, lasting fierce words."

"Do you suppose the liberties and the brawn of these States have to do only with delicate lady-words? with gloved gentleman words?"

"Monongahela: it rolls with venison richness upon the palate."

"Never will I allude to the English Language or tongue without exultation. This is the tongue that spurns laws, as the greatest tongue must. It is the most capacious vital tongue of all, — full of ease, definiteness, and power, — full of sustenance, — an enormous treasure

Thoreau chose carefully those words that added a general earthiness of tone and color to his writing. As the wind rose and the branches of the trees waved stiffly, he heard a *brattling* sound. When the wind blew strong and the atmosphere cleared brightly, it was a *washing* day, and the wind was a *washing* wind. Rain that fell thinly as a light mist was a *mizzling* rain, or *drisk.* September, the first month after the summer heat, a month of early frost, had a *burr* to it. Wild apples were *knurly*; cold days were *snapping* cold; the note of the toad was a *sprayey* one; the slate-colored snowbird had a *jingling* note; sparrows had *lisping* notes; the grasshopper's flight was a *crackling* one; and so on and on. Always the prose craftsman was finding the word that suited the particular matter about which he wrote. He listened to the gentle and uninterrupted *susurrus* of the wind. He admired Walden's *glaucous* water. He noted the woodchuck's *rufous* pelt. He *luted* his boat with grafting wax. When a coinage was needed he invented one. He referred to *realometers* by which he wished whimsically to measure realities. When the surface of Flint's Pond was yellow with the pollen of the white pines, he called it a *pollen-ometer.* Occasionally he used his Latin adroitly as when he described the hooting owl as "the very lingua vernacula" of Walden woods, or when he referred to himself hoeing his bean-field as "a very agricola laboriosus."

Old words made him prick up his ears. He liked such words as "kilter" that he found in Bradford's *History of the*

house or ranges of treasure houses, arsenals, granary, chock full of so many contributions from the north and from the south. . . ."

"Ten thousand native idiomatic words are growing, or are to-day already grown, out of which vast numbers could be used by American writers, with meaning and effect . . ."

Plymouth Plantation, or the origin of the word schooner, which he traced to the Indian schoon or scoot, meaning to rush, hence the schooner that schoons or rushes through the water. Yet he could not find the word in his dictionary. He was smitten with John Evelyn's expressive words and phrases in such discourses as the one on forest trees called *Silva,* especially the reference to oisers as fine for all wicker and twiggy works or the reference to the pines as "pearling out into gums" or to "a *sobbing* rain." He also liked what he called, in a hearty way, "lipped words," which, as he said, "like the lips of moose and browsing creatures, gather in the herbage and twigs with a certain greed." Words, for example, like tenacious, voracious, edacious, capacious, etc. He thought the termination *cious* added force to a word "like the lips of browsing creatures, which greedily collect what the jaw holds; as in the word 'tenacious' the first half represents the kind of jaw which holds, the last the lips which collect." He rejected words like tribal and ornamentation which dragged a tail around after them. Falsetto, still-born, wing-clipped, lame words were to be avoided. He contended that one reason why writers used torpid or wooden or lifeless words like humanitary, words which he said had a paralysis in their tails, was because the writer did not speak out of a full experience. There was no life in the writing because there had been an incomplete realization of life in the writer.

3

There is more to writing than vigor or clarity. There is beauty of phrasing, and his phrasing is often original and poetic. He said that his truest and most serene moments were too still for emotion; they had "woollen feet." The colors of the withered oak were "Quaker colors, sober ornaments." The constellation of the Lesser Bear represented "the everlasting geometry of the stars." He referred to the bluebird as "His Most Serene Birdship." He said, "The distant woods are but the tassels of my eye." His humorous reference to the bullfrog "with his sesquipedality of belly" is masterly.

One of the chief characteristics of his poetic energy is the way he illuminates actual phenomena by use of concrete images. These images are rarely fanciful or far-fetched. In the main they give the object a human appeal. Thus, a skunk "runs, even when undisturbed, with a singular teeter or undulation, like the walking of a Chinese lady." The common bladderwort was "like a sluttish woman with a gaudy yellow bonnet." The spathes of the skunk cabbage looked "like a monk in his crypt with powdered head."

One measure of a poet's skill is his ability to handle metaphor. Thoreau's similes are apt as the following group chosen from the *Journal* indicates. Ducks were like rolling-pins with wings. Lightning filled the damp air with light "like some vast glow-worm in the fields of ether opening its wings." The nuts were about as safe within the prickly bur of the chestnut until they matured "as a porcupine behind its spines." The leaves of the shrub oak hung on "like the perseverance of the saints." The huckleberry apple was as "a child with a great dropsical head, and prematurely bright." Maidenhair ferns were seen "unclenching their little red fists." Once he saw Wachusett like a right whale over the bow, "plowing the continent, with his flukes well down." He had a vicious look "as if he had a harpoon in him." When he found a bayonet rush piercing a lily pad, he was reminded "of the Saladin's cutting a silk handkerchief in the air with his cimetar." The red maple bore aloft "its scarlet standard for its regiment of green-clad foresters around." The lark flashed its white tail and showed its yellow breast "with its black crescent like an Indian locket." The first bluish haze was Nut Meadow's "blue feather." When the snow was falling he watched "the countless flakes, seen against the dark evergreens like a web that is woven in the air."

His auditive sense, especially as it reported the songs of the birds, was as responsive as his visual sense. He heard the note of the lark as it leaks up through the meadows, "as if its bill had been thawed by the warm sun." He heard the "seringo" sounding from the railroad "like the dropping of a file, or any bit of steel, on an anvil." He listened to the bluebirds, harbingers of serene and warm weather, whose "little azure rills of melody trickling here and there from out the air," were thawing the torpid mass of winter. The redwing rang his bobylee "as if he tossed up a fourpence and it rattled on some counter in the air as it went up." The brilliant jay's steel-cold scream sounded to him "as if it blowed [sic] on the edge of an October leaf," while the wood thrush discharged its song "like a bolas, or a piece of jingling steel."

4

Thoreau thought the fruit the writer bore was sentences — statements of opinions — and when these were truly expressive, they possessed the sum of the qualities one found in effective writing. They suggested more than they said; they had atmosphere. They did not merely report old impressions but new ones. They were durable "as a Roman aqueduct." They were seminal; they contained "the seed of other sentences." They had in them the germs of original virtues, fresh beginnings, new horizons. They were like roots with strength for centuries of growing in their fibres. The greatest of all sentences were the serene ones; such, for example, as one found in the Sacred Books of the East, for these sentences were conceived when the mind was in repose. Sentences which were durable, suggestive, seminal, concentrated, and, as Thoreau said, like so many resiliences from the spring floor of one's life, originated in the life of the writer. They were the product of mental energy and a galvanic temperament.

He was essentially an aphorist whose unit of writing was the epigrammatic sentence. A maker of arrowheadiferous sentences, he drove them home with resolution from the set bow of a determined mind. Their tone is the resonant bow-twangish one of an indigene who hit his target by intention not by chance. Certainly the idiomatic language by which feelings and thoughts are expressed is one of the earmarks of an original talent. Another is force and vigor, the source of which is the living spirit – the anima – of the writer.

Some of the sentences ring out like military commands on the parade ground, or like challenges along a picket line. "Read your fate, see what is before you, and walk on into futurity." Some, like rallying cries, commit us to decisive acts. "You must live in the present, launch yourself on every wave, find your eternity in each moment." Some are tart and crusty, plain and crisp. "Let every man mind his own business, and endeavor to be what he was made." "Nothing can shock a brave man but dullness." Some are pungently dry of wit. "Some circumstantial evidence is very strong, as when you find a trout in the milk." Some are psychologically discerning. "Who are the estranged? Two friends explaining." "The worst kind of *chigo,* or tick, to get under your skin is yourself in an irritable mood." "Wherever a man feels fear, there is an avenger." Some are highly personal declarations surcharged with personality. "I make my own time, I make my own terms. I cannot see how God or Nature can ever get the start of me." "I love a broad margin to my life." Some are cryptic. "My thought is a part of the meaning of the world, and hence I use a part of the world as a symbol to express my thought." "He that is not behind his time is swift."

Some are serene and oracular, like scriptural sayings, and quicken the spirit. They have vigor and purity and intensity that is auroral, as though the early morning light was reflected in them. "Our truest life is when we are in dreams awake." "Day would not dawn if it were not for the inward morning." "Only that day dawns to which we are awake." Some are poetic. "When man is asleep and day fairly forgotten, then is the beauty of moonlight seen over lonely pastures where cattle are silently feeding." "*There* are the stars, and they who can read them." Some are peculiarly and compactly phrased. "That kind of life which sleeping we dream that we live awake, in our walks by night we waking live; while our daily life appears as a dream." Some are allusive. "I see the northern lights over my shoulder, to remind me of the Esquimaux, and that they are still my contemporaries on this globe." Most of his sentences are direct, incisive, spiny, and sanguine, the product of sturdy, keen, affirmative intellection. "For an impenetrable shield, stand inside yourself." "It is life near the bone where it is sweetest." "We do not live by justice, but by grace." "I was not born to be forced. I will breathe after my own fashion." "The law will never make men free; it is men who have got to make the law free." There is nothing smug, docile, or sluggish about these sentences. Thoreau never drawled or whimpered in his writing. He was surely a maker of stirring sentences which command with the authority of conviction. The sentences have no currish bark. They do not snap at one's heels. Neither do they pule or whine. They are sure, sound, and firmly written as though truly he drew his furrow deep and straight to the end.

5

In the pattern of his writing, word and phrase fuse in the sentence, and the sentences unite to form an integral part of the paragraph. His substantial sentences fit together snugly like kernels on a cob of corn. He selected and arranged his material carefully. First he discovered as soon as possible what the best passages were, and then he eliminated the inessential until the best passages were given prominence. These were arranged so that the more mature sentences reflected life and color on the less successful ones. In the general pattern of his writing, naturalness, simplicity, and directness were the qualities he aimed for and attained in his style of expression. He wanted his writing to be as natural "as the voice of a brute or an interjection." No "mealy-mouthed enthusiasm" would do. Much to be preferred was the surliness with which the wood-chopper spoke of the wood he cut and trimmed and stacked. Naturalness was a prime quality and so too was simplicity. He deplored the fact that life was not simply expressed, that it was too often a long-winded speech into which life was occasionally injected. What was naturally and simply expressed should also be directly expressed. He wanted to feel in writing that what the writer had to say dropped as directly as a stone to the ground, and he advised against polishing the stone or giving it a peculiar turn in its descent. "Your polished stuff turns out not to be meteoric, but of this earth."

Consider the natural tone, the simplicity of expression, and the directness of progression in the following passage on the weather-wise wood frog. He had a feeling for the rhythm in the phrase, his inner ear was generally true; it caught and held the tune.

> Now, when the leaves get to be dry and rustle under your feet, dried by the March winds, the peculiar dry note, *wurrk wurrk wur-r-r-k wurk* of the wood frog is heard faintly by ears on the alert, borne up from some unseen pool in a woodland hollow which is open to the influences of the sun. It is a singular sound for awakening Nature to make, associated with the first warmer days, when you sit in some sheltered place in the woods amid the dried leaves. How moderate on her first awakening, how little demonstrative! You may sit half an hour before you will hear another. You doubt if the season will be long enough for such Oriental and luxurious slowness. But they get on, nevertheless, and by tomorrow, or in a day or two, they croak louder and more frequently. Can you ever be sure that you have heard the very first wood frog in the township croak? Ah! how weather-wise must he be! There is no guessing at the weather with him. He makes the weather in his degree; he encourages it to be mild. The weather, what is it but the temperament

> of the earth? and he is wholly of the earth, sensitive as its skin in which he lives and of which he is a part. His life relaxes with the thawing ground. He pitches and tunes his voice to chord with the rustling leaves which the March wind has dried. Long before the frost is quite out, he feels the influence of the spring rains and the warmer days. His is the very voice of the weather. He rises and falls like quicksilver in the thermometer. You do not perceive the spring so surely in the actions of men, their lives are so artificial. They may make more fire or less in their parlors, and their feelings accordingly are not good thermometers. The frog far away in the wood, that burns no coal nor wood, perceives more surely the general and universal changes.

The advantage of the poetic description over the scientific one consists in the zest and vivid imagery in the poet's lively description of natural phenomena, "as if he saw it for the first time, the novelty consisting not in the strangeness of the object, but in the new and clearer perception of it." The poet succeeds in giving us "the unmeasured and eloquent" description which the sight of the object inspired. What Thoreau saw was an animated object; what he heard was a different music; what he felt was the vibration in his own heart. When he praised Gerard, the herbalist, it was not only because he had heard of, seen, and raised plants, but because he had applied all his senses to the natural object he described. Gerard had also felt, smelled, and tasted the plant. He had not confined himself to systems and arrangements. It was as necessary to release the life — that is to say, the anima, or vital spirit — of the animal one described as it was to release one's own vitality in writing. "You must tell what it is to man," Thoreau counselled the writer. "A history of animated nature must itself be animated." But to make it animated, there must be vigor and what Lowell called "blood-warmth" in the words.

Thoreau's writing has atmosphere, rhythmic tension, and flexibility. His atmosphere varies with the subject-matter. Objects described in the daytime had the light of day in them. Nocturnal walks were to be described in sentences that were peculiarly dusky. The tempo depends upon mood and manner, whether eloquent, exclamatory, vascular, whether plain, terse, and direct. There is a supple flex in his most characteristic writing; a natural grace and vigor of mind and spirit. It has an easy gait and a natural emphasis "like a man's tread." It saunters along with an Indian's quiet tread, covering ground, making distance. In his own idiom, the following characteristic passage from *Walden* is composed of sentences which were written "while grass grew and water ran." The sentences spring "like the sward in its native pasture." The tint and fragrance and sap of natural things is in them:

> After a still winter night I awoke with the impression that some question had been put to me, which I had been endeavoring in vain to answer in my sleep, as what — how — when — where? But there was dawning Nature, in whom all creatures live, looking in at my broad windows with serene and satisfied face, and no question on *her* lips. I awoke to an answered question, to Nature and daylight. The snow lying deep on the earth dotted with young pines, and the very slope of the hill on which my house is placed, seemed to say, "Forward!" Nature puts no question and answers none which we mortals ask. She has long ago taken her resolution. . . .
>
> Then to my morning work. First I take an axe and pail and go in search of water, if that be not a dream. After a cold and snowy night it needed a divining-rod to find it.

> Every winter the liquid and trembling surface of the pond, which was so sensitive to every breath, and reflected every light and shadow, becomes solid to the depth of a foot or a foot and a half, so that it will support the heaviest teams, and perchance the snow covers it to an equal depth, and it is not to be distinguished from any level field. Like the marmots in the surrounding hills, it closes its eyelids and becomes dormant for three months or more. Standing on the snow-covered plain, as if in a pasture amid the hills, I cut my way first through a foot of snow, and then a foot of ice, and open a window under my feet, where, kneeling to drink, I look down into the quiet parlor of the fishes, pervaded by a softened light as through a window of ground glass, with its bright sanded floor the same as in summer; there a perennial waveless serenity reigns as in the amber twilight sky, corresponding to the cool and even temperament of the inhabitants. Heaven is under our feet as well as over our heads.

There is also a range to his writing as well as an inherent rhythm and a personal accent. It ranges from the lyrical and aspirative to impassioned incisiveness; from mystical transcendentalism to whimsical humor; from description and narration to dramatic action; from poetically evocative writing to cool, meditative monologues. Because he knew how to use the tool of common speech, he could make language curl in barbed backlash or pelt with stinging gibe and rejoinder. He is really good when you can hear him talking to you, or feel the intensity of his reaction to something. Then he is not trying to polish what he has to say; he is not even trying to wipe the film off the lens so that you can see more clearly; he is simply putting it down in hot haste with the impulse flaming. *A Plea for Captain John Brown* is audible. In *Walden* he ranged from the buoyant exclamation on Baker Farm to the cryptic declaration that "Time is but the stream I go a-fishing in." Bristly, he arraigned "that devilish Iron Horse." With a sense of drama he extirpated the weeds in the bean-field. Feelingly he described the hare: "One evening one sat by my door two paces from me, at first trembling with fear, yet unwilling to move; a poor wee thing, lean and bony, with ragged ears and sharp nose, scant tail and slender paws." He etched sharply the picture of the night fisherman "communicating by a long flaxen line with mysterious nocturnal fishes which had their dwelling forty feet below."

6

Every writer worth his salt has more than one resource: he is not alone sympathetic or imaginative or sensitive or enthusiastic or curious or humorous. When he can combine several of these resources, his writing intensifies in color and interest. Thoreau's sensitivity and enthusiasm, his imagination and curiosity are implicit in his writings; and so, too, is a sense of humor. Constance Rourke characterizes Thoreau's humor as, "Wry humor in slow prose arrangements; he kept the habitual composure." His humor was also characteristically dry as well as wry. When he asked one of his Indian guides in the Maine Woods, Tahmunt Swasen, how the name Quebec was derived, the Indian said, "Well, when the English ships came up the river, they could not go any farther, it was so narrow there; they must go back, – go-back, – that's Que-bec." Then Thoreau commented dryly, "I mention this to show the value of his authority in the other cases." On another occasion, he remarked how it was not the howling wilderness which did the howling, but, as he said, "It is the imagination of the traveller that does the howling." When on the trip up the Merrimack he noticed a barren place formed by the river-bank, someone told him that it had been caused by the sheep, who, worried by the fleas, pawed the ground, broke the sod, and so started the sand blowing over forty or fifty acres of land. "The fleas bit the sheep, and the sheep bit the ground, and the sore had spread to this extent. It is astonishing what a great sore a little scratch breedeth."

Whimsicality is as characteristic of his humor as dryness of wit. Once he coveted the Hollowell Farm, snugly retired two miles southeast of Concord, half a mile from the nearest neighbor, separated from the highway by a broad field, and bounded by the river. There it stood, the ruin of house and barn, securely concealed behind a dense grove of maples — a farm with hollow and lichen-covered apple trees gnawed by rabbits, with stone croppings in the fields, and birches seeding in the pastures.

> The nearest that I came to actual possession was when I bought the Hollowell place, and had begun to sort my seeds, and collected materials with which to make a wheelbarrow to carry it on or off with; but before the owner gave me a deed of it, his wife — every man has such a wife — changed her mind and wishes to keep it, and he offered me ten dollars to release him. Now, to speak the truth, I had but ten cents in the world, and it surpassed my arithmetic to tell, if I was that man who had ten cents, or who had a farm, or ten dollars, or all together. However, I let him keep the ten dollars and the farm too, for I had carried it far enough; or rather, to be generous, I sold him the farm for just what I gave for it, and, as he was not a rich man, made him a present of ten dollars, and still had my ten cents, and seeds,

and materials for a wheelbarrow left. I found thus that I had been a rich man without any damage to my poverty.

His humor also had an edge to it. He could be ironical or satirical as the circumstance demanded. He characterized the modern Christian as "a man who had consented to say all the prayers in their liturgy, provided you would let him go straight to bed and sleep quietly afterward. All his prayers begin with 'Now I lay me down to sleep.'" Satirically, he wrote about reformers in *Walden.* "If anything ail a man, so that he does not perform his functions, if he have a pain in his bowels even, – for that is the seat of sympathy, – he forthwith sets about reforming – the world. Being a microcosm himself, he discovers – and it is a true discovery, and he is the man to make it – that the world has been eating green apples. . . ." One of his weaknesses was the making of puns. Probably the prize one concerned an Irish gardener familiarly called Hugh. "The Ethiopian cannot change his skin nor the leopard his spots, nor indeed Hugh – his Hugh," punned Thoreau, whose power of resistance at least for once was rather below normal.

7

Conscious of a literary excellence to be striven for in prose writing, he criticized Ellery Channing's "sublimo-slipshod style." He suggested that a wayward poet ought to write Latin (he practised what he preached) in order to discipline his style. On occasion he lapsed into the sublimo-slipshod: "My dear, my dewy sister, let thy rain descend on me. I not only love thee, but I love the best of thee; that is to love thee rarely. I do not love thee every day. Commonly I love those who are less than thou. . . ." However, through revision and an insistence upon self-discipline he purged much dross from his writings.

When he corrected his manuscripts, he found the good along with the bad, and after "having purified the main body and thus created a distinct standard for comparison," he once more considered the rejected sentences and detected those which he thought deserved to be readmitted. He trusted his finer instincts. Details not questioned at first, when sent off to the publishers or printer, obtruded themselves on his attention with force. When the manuscript returned, he revised once more. When he stood a little distance from his composition, he could criticize it best. He found that the distraction of surveying enabled him to take new points of view toward his writings. He said, "A day or two surveying is equal to a journey." He served his thoughts as he did tumblers; he rapped them to see if they would ring. And he found that often what he told another was worth telling himself, that is to say, it was worth including in his *Journal.* This was a further value of companionship. The main thing was to save the life – his life – or private experience. The talent as such could go, but not the private experience.

His most glaring faults he faced with considerable sense of self-criticism. The tendency to moralize he discovered to be a defect in his work and he deprecated its presence. "What offends me most in my compositions is the moral element in them. The repentant say never a brave word," he commented. He compiled a list of faults, doubtless to make himself so conscious of these faults that he might avoid them.

My faults are: –

Paradoxes, – saying just the opposite, – a style which may be imitated.

Ingenious.

Playing with words, — getting the laugh, — not always simple, strong and broad.

Using current phrases and maxims, when I should speak for myself.

Not always earnest.

"In short," "in fact," "alas!" etc.

Want of conciseness.

Many examples might be found to prove that he was correct on every count in his self-arraignment, but the clearness, force, and beauty of his average writing is sound evidence that he was a sturdy prose craftsman.

8

The kind of work Thoreau wanted to do — "A book of the seasons, each page of which should be written in its own season and out-of-doors, or in its own locality wherever it may be" — he achieved in the *Journal,* and more, he succeeded in giving us the natural history of a whole township. After conquering the wilderness of Concord, he extended his horizon to include the wilderness reaches of the Maine woods and the seaward reach of Cape Cod. His general theme was the outdoors, and his writing amplified his subject-matter, for in the essay he discovered a form through which to communicate natural beauty latent in such commonplaces of life as a wayside ditch or a fallow field. His selection of themes was constitutional. Outdoors meant health and well-being to him; indoors meant sluggishness and sickness. He contended that a great part of our trouble was attributable to our indoor way of living. He thought he might undertake a crusade against houses, and in a way his books represent just such a crusade. In his writings he tried for what he called a hypaethral character, "to use," as he explained, "an epithet applied to those Egyptian temples which are open to the heavens above, under the *ether*." He didn't want his books to smell of the study or library, but rather of the fields and woods. He wanted them to be unroofed – hypaethral. Considerably more hypaethral than *A Week* are *Walden* and the *Journal*. They are resinous and earthy enough, and almost entirely unroofed. Surely they are as permeated with the outdoors as a sugar maple with streaming sap in March.

Reading Thoreau's writings inspires a reserved but sterling admiration that advances steadily a degree at a time. They draw us quietly but insistently outdoors, into the fields and wood paths, along the country brooks, toward upland vistas. There is a tang to the writing like that of wild apples in late autumn – the tang of the natural life in the open air. The fruit of his mind – those hardy, well-ripened thoughts – were seasoned in the wind and frost and rain and sunshine, until they absorbed the qualities of their natural environment. In the field and woods they are spirited and racy; indoors they might be found harsh and crabbed to the delicate, house-bred palate. They represent his essential qualities – tanginess and tartness.

In the history of letters his contribution consists in the fact that he gave the relationship of man to nature, already firmly embodied in literature, clearer definition and a fresher and more vigorous expression. As a prose craftsman he possessed the ability to communicate with poetic imagination his sensitive response to nature's essential beauty, disclosing to us the seclusive life of the creatures of nature, like the old pout and her fry, or like the nascent life forming in a clutch of turtle eggs, or like the bream which when raised from its nest keeps up a sculling motion, "for unlike ours, the element in which they live is a stream which must be constantly resisted." His prose is, in effect, the product of a vigorous if somewhat perversely independent thinker, who seasoned his individualistic thought in contemplation, who unsheathed his emotions reservedly, and who loosed his conviction with defiance. One criterion by which one judges good prose writing is whether or not, when simply and clearly recorded, it takes hold by its own energy. By such a token Thoreau's writing excels. It represents muscularity of thought and a constitutional earthiness. The energy of the earth is in all that he had to say.

He was essentially a poetic proseman, if we accept his definition of poetry as "a true account of the actual," for whom living was the reception and communication of thoughts. This he says was his salient: to communicate those parts of his life which he would gladly live again. No wonder his writings are tonic and enheartening to the crippled or wounded spirit and invigorating to those who stand in need of inspiration. The natural vigor which emanates from his writings is as refreshing "as if a green bough were laid across the page." His record imparts courage and well-being.

He thought there was no more Herculean task than to think a thought about this life and then get it expressed. This was what he lived for, why he walked and talked and used his hands in manual labor, why he disciplined his senses, and why he practised with such patience and determination the arduous craft of writing. His writing does represent the fusion of an independent way of seeing life with an idiomatic way of expressing himself. His skill is shown in the degree to which he successfully mastered thought and feeling so that he neither blurred the clarity of the one nor diminished the intensity of the other through facile and inexact use of words. It is apparent also that he avoided overintensification of the personal pressure in expression which results only in mannered writing. Because the substance of his thought is rooted in a way of life with which he was intimately familiar, the reader is constantly reassured by "the warrant of life and experience" in what he reads.

His books, like his sentences, were the result of a long probation. It took seven years for the experience at Walden Pond and ten years for the voyage on the Concord and Merrimack Rivers to settle. Both *Walden* and *A Week* represent the crystallization of multiple experience, but *Walden* represents greater concentration of energy; each chapter is compounded experience. Its effect is linear; the effect of *A Week* is less so because it is less selective and orderly. The former has the Indian feel of nature; the latter is filled with unfolding vistas as of a boatman on a winding stream. There is a deliberate tread in the prose rhythm of each book, a pinch of the east wind in the expression, and a telling restraint.

It is in what his writings show of man's relationship to the New World environment that the significance of the experience chiefly inheres. The land is our heritage, and the basic desire of the American has been to realize in relationship to it a greater freedom for the human spirit. It is precisely because Thoreau's writings show under what conditions and on what terms the human spirit can most completely fulfil itself in the new world that he is one of our most influential writers. In the detailed record of a passionate attachment to his environment Thoreau shows us what it means to be naturalized in the New World. Nothing native was alien to him. Through a sensitive and imaginative sympathy he assimilated and he contained the naturistic tradition. He succeeded also in renewing it through the male energy of his prose.

Walden, more organic in structure and more compelling in its thought than *A Week,* is well established as the most indigenous nature classic in American literature. It is one of America's indispensable books. Its auroral atmosphere – "Rise free from care before the dawn, and seek adventures" – is like a morning song. Its content is affirmative, tangy, and surcharged. Its essence consists partly in the superb articulation of Thoreau's correspondence with nature, partly in the vindication of solitude and contemplation, partly in the exaltation of individualism, but mainly its essence consists in the galvanizing challenge of Thoreau's personal "awakeness" to those who have not yet learned how to emancipate their lives from material possessions. A challenge to conventional existence, *Walden* reflects its author's brag – a brag, by the way, for humanity and not alone for himself. "If I seem to boast more than is becoming," he said, "my excuse is that I brag for humanity rather than for myself; and my shortcomings and inconsistencies do not affect the truth of my statement."

9

His passion for nature was very strong, as vigorous certainly as Whitman's passion for democracy, and as intense as Poe's passion for supernal beauty, but because his imagination was practical it restrained the powerful emotional surge to earth-ways. In Emerson's *Journals,* Thoreau is quoted as saying, "I wish so to live as to derive my satisfactions and inspirations from the commonest events, so that what my senses hourly perceive, my daily walk, the conversation of my neighbors, may inspire me, and I may dream of no heaven but that which lies about me." His interest in the concrete was only the focus of his experience. What did he see? What vision of reality had he? He made no notable discovery, like blind Huber's, that some species of ants practise slavery. Nor did he, like Swammerdam, fix the identity of the Queen Bee. He devised no scheme similar to Linnaeus' classification of plants in the *Systema Naturae*, (which, in spite of obvious limitations, was at least a scientific handle), nor did he originate a way of systematizing nature as Lamarck did by differentiating between the animals that were vertebrate and those that were invertebrate. Nor did he compose detailed studies such as Fabre painstakingly produced in his *Souvenirs entomologiques*. Thoreau did none of these things, yet his accomplishment and contribution to literature and philosophy, if not to science, was equally significant. In attaining a correspondence between natural phenomena and his inner moods, he released the possibility of inward growth, not alone for himself, but for all men, and a continual renewal of the intellectuality of civilization through a harmony of the human spirit with untamed nature. Civilized men he thought should never alienate themselves from nature, the original source of their physical, moral, and intellectual health. One of the main Thoreauvian emphases is the realization of joy and power originating in the organic functional relationship of a man with his natural environment.

To realize the wisdom of the natural ways, Thoreau did not reject the arts, techniques, and contributions of civilization. He did not advocate a return to the primitive way of life. Such an attitude he would have considered as irrational and obscurantist. He did not, like D. H. Lawrence, renounce the domination of the intellect and concomitantly proclaim the doctrine of the free, uninhabited action of the primal, intuitive forces in our blood-stream. He would have given an emphatic negative to the inquiry in *Women in Love*: "Isn't the mind . . . our death? Doesn't it destroy all our spontaneity, all our instincts? Are not the young people growing up to-day, really dead before they have a chance to live?" He did not believe in the surrender of the conscious will to primitive impulse. He did not believe that intellect negated spontaneity of natural response. What he did believe was that there were plenty of champions of the civilized life. He wished only "to speak a word for Nature, for absolute freedom and wildness, as contrasted with a freedom and culture merely civil." This is his statement. It is direct and clear enough. It does not exclude or reject civilization; it speaks only for the other side.

Thoreau's writings celebrate neither the primitive nor the sophisticated, but the simple life. To the sociologist they are an interesting reflection of the mutually harmonious relationship of the organism and its environment. In order to share what Thoreau experienced, one must be able to imagine what he lived, because his writings are the condensation of his mental and physical experience. Among those writings which originate in the experience of the American people and which reflect the acclimatizing of the American in his environment, Thoreau's are foremost. Our country will be completely the homeland of the American people when each region is as cherishable and rewarding spiritually as Concord was for Thoreau. For generations European stock transported to the New World had taken possession of America, but it is not until Thoreau speaks out that one has the sense of an American's passionate attachment to his region. He represents a stake-in-nature. There is a natural authority in what he says by right of being on the ground. He had lived here long enough for his foundations to settle; they rested on the security of the American earth.

What Henry Thoreau assures the enlightened citizen of the western world is the certainty that nature quickens and renews the human spirit through sympathetic relationship. By discovering and recording his association with the chief phases of nature in the progression of its seasonal cycles, he indicated a way for Americans to become naturalized in the American environment. His acquaintance with New England drift boulders, cattle fairs, meeting-houses, thin sandy soil, scrub oak, sweet fern, lilacs, swamp pinks, northeasters, huckleberries, hermit thrushes, bobolinks, rather than with skylarks and fieldfares, redstarts and meadow pipits, downs and coombes, heather and furze, billberries and haws of Old England, make his contribution as redolent of the New World as buckeyes are indigenous to Ohio or burr oaks to Illinois or redwoods to California. Though Concord only happened to be his meeting-place with nature, nevertheless he readily identified himself with it and sprang up like a natural shoot in its generous soil. It was his victory to be naturalized without succumbing to domestication. In a sense he was committed, yet free. He was committed to the regional spirit of place, but he was elemental like the prevailing wind. He was, in the true sense of the word, an elemental saunterer in Concord, and the world of nature was resonant in his ears, sensitive to his touch, graphic to his eye, pungent to his nostrils, savory on his tongue. "Of thee, O earth, are my bone and sinew made. . . . Here have I my habitat. I am of thee."

THE END

KEY

Unless otherwise indicated the references cited are to be found in the following writings of Thoreau and Emerson.

TW Henry David Thoreau, *Writings* (Boston: Houghton Mifflin; 1906), edited by Bradford Torrey.

TJ Henry David Thoreau, *Journal* (Boston: Houghton Mifflin; 1906).

EJ *Journals of Ralph Waldo Emerson*, edited by Edward Waldo Emerson and Waldo Emerson Forbes (Boston: Houghton Mifflin; 1909-1914).

Numerals at the left refer to pages in this book. The words of each reference indicate the beginning and end of the passage in the text to which it is related, except for occasional other references which are described in detail.

I *The Saunterer*

1	"I . . . live."	TJ VIII, 204.
	"A . . . are."	Ibid., VI, 275.
2	"Olympus . . . everywhere."	TW II, 94.
3	"with . . . warrior."	Ibid., I, 10.
	"like . . . scattered."	TJ XIII, 116.
	"where . . . anything."	TW I, 374.
4	"near . . . leaves."	TJ V, 310.
	"The . . . latitude."	TW IV, 349.
	"sawyer-like strain."	TJ II, 9.
	"far off . . . picture."	Ibid., II, 423.
5	"with . . . nest."	EJ IX, 45.
6	"along . . . sides."	TJ XII, 26.
7	"the . . . experience."	TW X, 210.
	"which . . . seasons."	Ibid., II, 20.
	"for . . . open."	TJ XIII, 111.
8	"a . . . skies."	Ibid., II, 436.
	"a . . . Holy-Lander."	TW V, 205.
	"For . . . Infidels."	Ibid., V, 206.
	"fleets . . . boughs."	Ibid., II, 223.
	"where . . . Valhalla."	Ibid., II, 223.
	"round . . . gods."	Ibid., II, 223.
8, 9	"like . . . imps."	Ibid., II, 223.
9	"These . . . pines."	Ibid., II, 224.
	"in . . . adventure."	Ibid., V, 207.
	"I . . . Europe."	Ibid., V, 218.
	"retracing . . . free."	Ibid., V, 218.
9, 10	"as . . . adventure."	Ibid., V, 218.
10	"From . . . kind."	Ibid., V, 224.
	"to . . . manners."	TJ VIII, 221.
10, 11	"a . . . nature."	Ibid., I, 209.

11	"primeval . . . Nature."	TW III, 77.
	"the . . . man."	Ibid., III, 78.
	"Talk . . . we?"	Ibid., III, 79.
	"The . . . animals."	TJ VIII, 220.
	"impervious . . . quaking."	TW V, 226–27.
12	"It . . . it!"	TJ IX, 41.
	"vast . . . Nature."	TW V, 237.
	"A . . . lichen."	TJ II, 97.
13	"It . . . peat."	Ibid., III, 353.
	"To . . . tree."	Ibid., IV, 118.
14	"a . . . ruminating."	Ibid., I, 132.
	"Take . . . weary."	Ibid., IX, 198.
	"When . . . estate."	Ibid., III, 444.
15	"to . . . territory."	Ibid., III, 367.
	"evidences . . . divines."	Ibid., X, 212.
	"What . . . is."	Thoreau, "The Moon" (Boston: Houghton Mifflin; 1927) p. 10.
	"for . . . day."	Ibid., p. 54.
15, 16	"I . . . day."	Ibid., pp. 12, 13.
16, 17	"Let . . . life."	E. Harlow Russell, "A Bit of Unpublished Correspondence Between Henry D. Thoreau and Isaac Hecker" (Worcester, Massachusetts, 1902).

II *Nature's Eye-Witnesses*

18	"How . . . poetry!"	TJ X, 69.
26	"I . . . appreciation."	Ibid., XI, 277.
34	"to . . . panther."	TW III, 242.

III *Nature and Natural Men*

52	"I . . . even."	TJ IX, 151.
	"Nature . . . well-head."	Ibid., II, 170.
	"But . . . world."	Ibid., XII, 443.
53	"It . . . objects."	Ibid., XII, 447.
	"Nature . . . significant."	Ibid., IV, 163.
	"It . . . other."	Ibid., III, 400.
54	"I . . . her."	Ibid., IV, 445.
	"absolute . . . things."	Ibid., IX, 362.
	"to . . . again."	Ibid., IX, 362.
	"Most . . . things."	TW IV, 469.
54, 55	"I . . . wayside."	TJ III, 382.
55	"holy . . . heroic."	Ibid., II, 384.
	"simple . . . natural."	Ibid., I, 471.
56	"He . . . contemplating."	Ibid., IX, 46.
	"I . . . shore."	Ibid., IX, 47.

56, 57	"They . . . afternoons."	Ibid., XII, 333.
57	"unless . . . abound."	Ibid., IX, 200.
58	"Why . . . trust."	Ibid., III, 115.
58, 59	"These . . . connections."	Ibid., III, 115.
59	"It . . . office."	Ibid., IX, 209-10.
	"as . . . water."	Ibid., IX, 210.
60	"a . . . pasture."	Ibid., I, 254.
	"flux . . . streams."	Ibid., I, 149–50.
	"that . . . unconscious."	TW II, 85.
	"like . . . duckling."	Ibid., II, 169.
61	"whose . . . it."	Ibid., II, 169.
	"like . . . shop-window."	TJ XII, 31.
	"out . . . hand."	Ibid., XII, 31.
62	"puffballs . . . ashes."	Ibid., VI, 200.
	"very . . . particular."	Ibid., VIII, 246.
	"when . . . it."	Ibid., XIV, 104.
	"But . . . soft."	Ibid., V, 506.
63	"So . . . fibre."	Ibid., V, 10.
	"I . . . live."	Ibid., II, 207.
64	"Undoubtedly . . . level."	Ibid., II, 192.
	"I . . . myself."	Ibid., VIII, 19.
65	"Some . . . World-ridden."	Ibid., IX, 362.
	"only . . . together."	Ibid., I, 213.
	"Why! . . . content."	Ibid., IX, 206–07.
65, 66	"Perhaps . . . money-getting."	Ibid., XI, 196.
	"literally . . . up."	Ibid., XII, 342.
67	"I . . . moose."	Ibid., I, 143.
68	"Heaven . . . avoid."	Ibid., XI, 127.
	"in . . . green."	Ibid., X, 50, 51.
	"We . . . us."	Ibid., XII, 170.
69	"He . . . bidding."	Ibid., XIV, 130–31.
	"overseers . . . husbandmen."	Ibid., XIV, 131.
	"for . . . sum."	Ibid., XIV, 306.
70	"of . . . Lady's-Finger."	Ibid., IX, 384.
71	"There . . . succession."	Ibid., X, 173–74.
72	"dusky . . . smoke."	Ibid., III, 49.
73	"As . . . continually."	Ibid., XI, 424–25.
	"awkward . . . loose-hung."	Ibid., IX, 148.
	"as . . . hillside."	Ibid., IX, 148.
	"He . . . war."	Ibid., IX, 148.
	"No . . . behind."	TW II, 235.
74	"like . . . nut."	TJ X, 110.
	"like . . . around."	TW III, 34.
	"petticoat government."	Ibid., IV, 81.
	"A . . . find."	Ibid., II, 160.
75	"he . . . other."	Ibid., II, 165.
	"suggested . . . muddy."	Ibid., II, 166.
	"the . . . satisfaction."	TJ III, 41.
76	"half-stocked."	Ibid., XI, 108.

	"belcher-squelcher."	Ibid., III, 69.
76, 77	"As . . . suppose."	Ibid., XI, 109.
77	"and . . . Middlesex."	Ibid., IV, 194.
	"He . . . life."	Ibid., IV, 194.
	"like . . . happiness."	Ibid., III, 485.
	"human . . . Hosmer."	Ibid., VIII, 245.
78	"You . . . them."	Ibid., VIII, 26.
	"To . . . it."	Ibid., VIII, 26, 27.
	"would . . . savages."	Ibid., VIII, 46.
	"who . . . day."	Ibid., III, 244.
	"now . . . nature."	Ibid., III, 244.
79	"the . . . us."	Ibid., II, 492.
	"little . . . life."	Ibid., II, 492.

IV *An Indian Memory*

80	"For . . . own."	*The First and Last Journeys of Thoreau,* ed. F. B. Sanborn (Boston: 1945) I, 36.
81	"the . . . men."	TJ XII, 92.
	"fossil thoughts."	Ibid., XII, 91.
81, 82	"I . . . transmuted."	Ibid., XII, 91.
82, 83	"great . . . rabbits."	TW III, 122.
83	"peculiar . . . ground."	Ibid., III, 124.
	"No . . . once."	Ibid., III, 125.
	"Altogether . . . years."	Ibid., III, 150.
	"as . . . did."	Ibid., III, 151.
84	"We . . . had."	TJ IX, 486.
	"vague . . . responsibility."	TW III, 180.
85	"Indians . . . ado."	Ibid., III, 300.
	"somewhat . . . thunder-spout."	Ibid., III, 300.
	"he . . . moment."	Ibid., III, 205.
86	"It . . . himself."	Ibid., III, 320.
	"a . . . lips."	Ibid., III, 228.
	"I . . . me."	Ibid., III, 228.
86, 87	"free . . . Nature."	TJ I, 253.
87	"We . . . Indian."	TW I, 55.
	"bow-arrow tang."	Ibid., III, 187.
88, 89	"How . . . is."	TJ X, 294–95.
89	"It . . . extermination."	Ibid., V, 526.
90	"Foresake . . . country."	Ibid., I, 444.
	"A . . . husbandmen."	Ibid., I, 445.
	"the . . . gets."	Ibid., I, 446.
	"The . . . dance."	Ibid., I, 446.
91	"a . . . Nature."	TW I, 55.
	"We . . . distance."	Ibid., I, 55.

V *The Machine Age and Man*

99	"Let . . . machine."	TW IV, 368.
	"a . . . wealth."	Ibid., VI, 9.
100	"to . . . lives."	Ibid., VI, 9.
	"to . . . pay."	Ibid., IV, 280.
	"It . . . little."	Ibid., IV, 280.
	"for . . . ends."	Ibid., IV, 286.
101	"O . . . offered."	Ibid., IV, 291.
	"by . . . crank."	Ibid., IV, 295.
	"We . . . Industry."	Ibid., IV, 297.
102	"Three . . . centuries."	Ibid., IV, 298.
	"Nothing . . . enterprise."	Ibid., IV, 299.
	"Faith . . . reform."	Ibid., IV, 300.
	"one . . . men."	Ibid., IV, 301.
	"slow . . . world."	Ibid., IV, 301.
103	"Undoubtedly . . . alone."	Ibid., IV, 302.
103–04	"Love . . . yet."	Ibid., IV, 304.
104	"improved . . . end?"	Ibid., II, 58.
105	"the . . . labor."	Ibid., IV, 457.
106	"Do . . . it."	Ibid., IV, 459.
107	"I . . . life."	Ibid., II, 100–01.
108	"quiet desperation."	Ibid., II, 8.
	"It . . . affairs."	Ibid., IV, 373.
109	"I . . . it."	Ibid., I, 310.
	"to . . . universe."	TJ III, 133.
	"to . . . fact."	Ibid., III, 208.
	"a . . . things."	Ibid., IX, 362.
	"elevated . . . views."	Ibid., XI, 277.
	"as . . . fingers."	TW II, 65.
	"a . . . one."	Ibid., II, 62.
110	"voluntary poverty."	Ibid., II, 16.
	"By . . . organized . . ."	TJ IX, 246.
	"The . . . still."	TW II, 40.
110-11	"To . . . those . . ."	Ibid., VI, 259.
112	"had . . . one."	Ibid., II, 355.
	"new . . . laws."	Ibid., II, 346.
	"with . . . beings."	Ibid., II, 356.
114	"the . . . sensitive."	Ibid., II, 242.
	"home–cosmography."	Ibid., II, 353.
	"In . . . do."	Ibid., II, 78.
	"One . . . instead."	Ibid., II, 78.
115	"as . . . centre."	Ibid., II, 12.
116	"There . . . pathetic."	Ibid., I, 55.
117	"They . . . is."	TJ XI, 227–28.
118	"We . . . myself."	TW II, 51.
120	"Let . . . friction."	Ibid., IV, 281.

VI *Nature Mysticism*

122	"The . . . them."	TW I, 408.
122–23	"I . . . frog."	EJ IX, 153.
123	"Nature . . . lived."	TJ V, 323.
124	"some . . . him."	Ibid., IX, 209.
	"Live . . . health."	Ibid., V, 394–95.
125	"I . . . herself."	TW II, 143.
	"At . . . tree."	TJ X, 305.
	"I . . . it."	TW II, 149.
125–26	"The . . . things."	Ibid., II, 109.
126	"though . . . iteration."	TJ V, 478.
	"let . . . it."	Ibid., III, 157.
127	"You . . . leaf."	TW II, 338.
	"This . . . vineyards."	Ibid., V, 340.
127–28	"For . . . weather."	Ibid., I, 309–10.
128	"The . . . man."	TJ I, 265.
129	"stark . . . thoughts."	Ibid., III, 122.
	"Come . . . gone."	Ibid., IX, 363.
	"The . . . eternally."	Ibid., IX, 363.
	"I . . . nature."	Ibid., III, 368.
131	"It . . . me."	Ibid., X, 164–65.
	"I . . . sky."	TW VI, 36.
132	"the . . . winter."	TJ VIII, 42.
132–33	"What . . . snow!"	Ibid., VIII, 42.
133	"to . . . significance."	Ibid., VIII, 44.
	"My . . . feel."	TW VI, 108.
140	"Nearest . . . are."	Ibid., II, 148.
141	"In . . . shrine."	Ibid., I, 65.
	". . . Now . . . God . . ."	TJ II, 392.
	"God–propped."	Ibid., I, 296.
141–42	"to . . . nature."	Ibid., II, 472.
142	"the . . . God."	Ibid., I, 302.
	"I . . . with."	TW I, 182.
143	"I . . . witness."	TJ IX, 364.

VII *Correspondence with Nature*

144	"The . . . her!"	TJ X, 127.
	"The . . . being."	Ibid., III, 185.
	"Our . . . body."	Ibid., I, 147.
145	"Perhaps . . . senses."	*First and Last Journeys of Thoreau* I, 61.
	"One . . . invitation."	TJ IV, 433.
146	"rank . . . life."	TW II, 232.
	"The . . . us."	Ibid., II, 243.
147	"I . . . that."	TJ VIII, 242.
	"My . . . battery."	Ibid., VIII, 44.

	"The . . . soundness."	Ibid., I, 27.
148	"brazen . . . jay."	Ibid., I, 70.
	"a . . . makes."	Ibid., VI, 52.
	"the . . . nature."	TW V, 114.
	"I . . . music."	*The Moon,* p. 31.
	"the . . . been."	TJ II, 12.
	"patiently . . . eyes."	Ibid., II, 72.
148–49	"How . . . fury."	Ibid., III, 11.
149	"There . . . is!"	Ibid., II, 330.
149–50	"I . . . worn."	TW II, 188.
150	"to . . . sometime."	TJ IV, 403.
151	"soft . . . custard."	Ibid., II, 127.
	"Let . . . hang."	Ibid., II, 127.
	"a . . . trustworthy."	Ibid., IV, 40.
	"Yet . . . sweeter."	Ibid., IV, 59.
152	"It . . . sweet."	Ibid., V, 165.
	"I . . . plant."	Ibid., VII, 361.
153	"There . . . smell."	Ibid., IV, 27.
	"As . . . it."	Ibid., XII, 353.
	"Today . . . earth."	Ibid., V, 27.
154	"Yet . . . village."	Ibid., VIII, 158.
	"though . . . it."	Ibid., XII, 444.
	"The . . . shadow."	Ibid., XI, 99.
	"What . . . varnished?"	Ibid., III, 56.
155	"What . . . plant . . ."	Ibid., II, 490.
	"as . . . tints."	Ibid., XII, 41.
	"ceaselessly . . . off . . ."	TW II, 208.
	"a . . . dot."	TJ VI, 60.
156	"the . . . senses."	Ibid., V, 17.
	"His . . . body."	Ibid., V, 17.
157	"surrounded . . . leisure."	Ibid., I, 356.
	"You . . . mind."	Ibid., X, 188.
	"June . . . time?"	Ibid., IX, 32, 33.
157–58	"Catch . . . you."	Ibid., III, 182.
158	"Whole . . . fortune."	TW I, 314.
	"a . . . sea."	TJ I, 54.
	"rapt . . . revery."	TW II, 123.
	"like . . . night."	Ibid., II, 124.
159	"I . . . highway."	TJ I, 477.
	"If . . . myth."	Ibid., V, 135.
161	"a . . . nature."	TJ IX, 407.
	"the . . . partridge."	Ibid., V, 144.
	"the . . . music."	Ibid., V, 292.
	"perfect . . . tire."	Ibid., VIII, 87.
	"with . . . air."	TW II, 349.
162	"Only . . . expressed."	TJ II, 291.
	"a . . . life."	E. H. Russell: "A Bit of Unpublished Correspondence."

163	"No . . . come."	TJ I, 352.
	"It . . . light . . ."	Ibid., VI, 194.
	"to . . . plain."	Ibid., I, 92.
	"as . . . ear."	Ibid., VI, 265.
163–64	"to . . . last."	Ibid., VII, 56.
164	"The . . . see."	Ibid., II, 373.
	"I . . . being."	Ibid., VI, 206.
	"an . . . fish."	Ibid., III, 437–38.
165–66	"It . . . truth."	TW III, 198–201 (incl.)
166–67	"Though . . . so."	TJ VI, 131–32.
167	"What . . . it?"	Ibid., IX, 221.
167–68	"This . . . me."	Ibid., II, 430–31.
169	"the . . . Nature."	TW II, 350.
172	"Then . . . world."	EJ V, 485.
	"a . . . sublimity."	TJ X, 142–43.

VIII *The Anatomy of Nature*

173	"It . . . science."	TJ III, 311.
174	"the . . . penetration."	EJ IX, 201.
	"with . . . soul?"	TJ II, 307.
176	"to . . . me."	Ibid., II, 469.
	"A . . . it."	Ibid., XIII, 160.
177	"It . . . science."	Ibid., III, 311.
	"a total apprehension."	Ibid., XII, 372.
	"the . . . view."	Ibid., IV, 392.
	"It . . . picture."	Ibid., IV, 392.
178	"a single picture."	Ibid., IV, 392.
	"It . . . astronomer."	Ibid., IV, 470.
179	"The . . . properties."	Ibid., III, 252–53.
	"the . . . inspires."	Ibid., XIV, 117.
182	"What . . . imagination?"	Ibid., III, 156.
	"Just . . . steam–engine."	Ibid., III, 156.
	"a . . . contemporary."	Ibid., XI, 360.
182–83	"Its . . . eventful."	Ibid., XI, 359.
183	"Is . . . did."	Ibid., IV, 165–67.
184	"Surely . . . world."	Ibid., III, 336–37.
	"Man . . . fungus . . ."	Ibid., V, 45.
185	"The . . . knowledge."	Ibid., VI, 311.
	"I . . . degree."	Ibid., II, 452.
187	"What . . . age."	Ibid., III, 378.
	"I . . . know."	Ibid., II, 406.
188	"A . . . to."	Ibid., II, 389.
189	"a . . . mood."	Ibid., IX, 54.
	"a . . . eye."	Ibid., IV, 351.
	"seeing . . . eye."	Ibid., IV, 351.
190	"Frequently . . . it."	Ibid., XIV, 60.
	"He . . . it."	Ibid., XIV, 267.
	"So . . . for."	Ibid., IX, 466.

190–191	"Objects . . . corn–fields."	Ibid., XI, 285–86.
191	"When . . . rain."	Ibid., III, 234.
	"What . . . Cliffs?"	Ibid., III, 345.
	"Are . . . pickerel-weed?"	Ibid., III, 349.
	"What . . . Swamp?"	Ibid., IV, 76.
	"To . . . brook?"	Ibid., IV, 76.
	"What . . . days?"	Ibid., VII, 103.
192	"What . . . nature."	Ibid., X, 161.
	"It . . . viewed."	Ibid., X, 161.
	"What . . . be."	Ibid., VII, 510.
	"The . . . home."	EJ IX, 153–54.
	"He . . . haunts."	TJ X, 369.
192–93	"At . . . coldness."	Ibid., X, 375.
193	"While . . . me."	Ibid., II, 111.
195	"It . . . hawk."	Ibid., VII, 266.
196	"I . . . offer."	Ibid., IX, 158.
	"to . . . salads."	Ibid., XI, 439.
	"A . . . rose . . ."	Ibid., XI, 440.
196–97	"The . . . one."	Ibid., VII, 105.
197	"a . . . crust."	Ibid., XII, 110.
	"a . . . life."	Ibid., XII, 353.
	"like . . . goat."	Ibid., XII, 353.
	"the . . . swamp–pink."	Ibid., X, 258.
	"What . . . sprouts!"	Ibid., X, 258.
197–98	"a . . . drops."	Ibid., V, 68.
198	"that . . . sod."	Ibid., V, 68, 69.
	"The . . . turns."	Ibid., V, 401.
198–99	"It . . . dovetailed."	Ibid., V, 41.
199	"The . . . food."	Ibid., V, 349.
	"that . . . feed."	Ibid., V, 349.
	"I . . . them."	Ibid., X, 180.
200	"like . . . morning."	Ibid., II, 255.
	"It . . . lungs."	Ibid., II, 255.
202	"The . . . ignorance."	Ibid., XIII, 180.
	"in . . . ignorance."	Ibid., II, 150.
	"I . . . universe."	Ibid., II, 168.
204	"a part of herself."	TW II, 143.

IX *The Sinews of Style*

205	"My . . . standards . . ."	TJ IX, 121.
206	"It . . . us."	TW I, 354.
	"And . . . basis."	TJ I, 413.
	"a . . . said."	Ibid., VIII, 134.
207	"that . . . vascular."	Ibid., II, 441.
207–08	"Only . . . read."	Ibid., II, 405.
208	"To . . . be."	Ibid., XI, 304.
209	"Let . . . do?"	TW VI, 320.

211–12	"The . . . life?"	TJ VI, 43–45.
212	"How . . . himself!"	Ibid., XI, 137.
213	"What . . . tongue!"	Ibid., IV, 443.
	"very . . . truth."	Ibid., I, 237.
	"a . . . there."	Ibid., X, 168.
213–14	"The . . . bears."	TW II, 184.
214	"lepus . . . think."	Ibid., II, 310.
	"the . . . *enjoyed.*"	TJ XIV, 273.
	"It . . . today."	TW V, 223.
214–15	"Talk . . . *musketaquidding.*"	TJ XII, 389–90.
216	"the . . . vernacula."	TW II, 300.
	"a . . . laboriosus."	Ibid., II, 173.
	"kilter."	TJ., IX, 177.
217	"like . . . greed."	Ibid., II, 443.
218	"woolen feet."	Ibid., I, 174.
	"Quaker . . . ornaments."	Ibid., XI, 337.
	"the . . . stars."	Ibid., IV, 402.
	"His . . . Birdship."	Ibid., XII, 5.
	"with . . . belly."	Ibid., IV, 125.
	"runs . . . lady."	Ibid., VI, 161.
	"like . . . bonnet."	Ibid., IV, 91.
	"like . . . head."	Ibid., VIII, 249.
	"like . . . wings."	Ibid., II, 321.
	"as . . . spines."	Ibid., IX, 120.
	"like . . . saints."	Ibid., IX, 185.
	"a . . . bright."	Ibid., V, 269.
	"unclenching . . . fists."	Ibid., VI, 270.
	"plowing . . . down."	Ibid., VI, 30.
218–19	"as . . . him."	Ibid., VI, 30.
219	"of . . . cimetar."	Ibid., VI, 399.
	"its . . . around."	Ibid., X, 43.
	"with . . . locket."	Ibid., VI, 336.
	"blue feather."	Ibid., VIII, 253.
	"the . . . air."	Ibid., VIII, 45.
	"as . . . sun."	Ibid., I, 330.
	"like . . . anvil."	Ibid., IV, 18.
	"little . . . air."	Ibid., V, 23.
	"as . . . up."	Ibid., VI, 202.
	"as . . . leaf."	Ibid., XI, 279.
	"like . . . steel."	Ibid., II, 280.
220	"as . . . aqueduct."	Ibid., II, 418–19.
	"the . . . sentences."	Ibid., II, 419.
	"Read . . . futurity."	TW II, 123.
	"You . . . moment."	TJ XII, 159.
	"let . . . made."	TW II, 358.
220–21	"Nothing . . . dullness."	Ibid., I, 304.
221	"Some . . . milk."	TJ II, 94.
	"Who . . . explaining."	Ibid., II, 146.
	"The . . . mood."	Ibid., III, 173.
	"Wherever . . . avenger."	Ibid., IV, 157.

	"I . . . me."	Ibid., I, 294.
	"I . . . life."	TW II, 123.
	"My . . . thought."	TJ IV, 410.
	"He . . . swift."	Ibid., IV, 350.
	"Our . . . awake."	TW I, 316.
	"Day . . . morning."	Ibid., I, 313.
	"Only . . . awake."	Ibid., II, 367.
	"Where . . . feeding."	TJ II, 260.
	"*There* . . . them."	TW II, 113.
	"That . . . dream."	*The Moon*, p. 60.
	"I . . . globe."	Ibid., p. 40.
221–22	"For . . . yourself."	TJ I, 106.
222	"It . . . sweetest."	TW II, 362.
	"We . . . grace."	TJ I, 412.
	"I . . . fashion."	TW IV, 376.
	"The . . . free."	Ibid., IV, 396.
	"as . . . interjection."	TJ XI, 386.
	"mealy-mouthed enthusiasm."	TW I, 111.
223	"Your . . . earth."	Ibid., VI, 312.
223–24	"Now . . . changes."	TJ XII, 79.
224	"as . . . it."	Ibid., XIV, 120.
	"the . . . eloquent."	Ibid., XIV, 117.
	"You . . . man."	Ibid., XIII, 154.
224–25	"A . . . animated."	Ibid., XIII, 154.
225	"like . . . tread."	TW I, 106.
	"while . . . ran."	Ibid., I, 106.
	"like . . . pasture."	Ibid., I, 106.
225–26	"After . . . heads."	Ibid., II, 312.
227	"Time . . . in."	Ibid., II, 109.
	"that . . . Horse."	Ibid., II, 213.
	"One . . . paws."	Ibid., II, 310.
	"communicating . . . below."	Ibid., II, 194.
	"Well . . . Que–bec."	Ibid., III, 158.
	"I . . . cases."	Ibid., III, 158.
228	"It . . . howling."	Ibid., III, 242.
	"The . . . breedeth."	Ibid., I, 209.
228–29	"The . . . poverty."	Ibid., II, 91.
229	"a . . . sleep."	TJ XII, 419.
	"If . . . apples . . ."	TW II, 85.
	"The . . . Hugh."	Ibid., VI, 140.
	"sublimo–slipshod style."	TJ III, 118.
	"My . . . thou . . ."	Ibid., II, 78.
230	"having . . . comparison."	Ibid., VI, 146.
	"A . . . journey."	Ibid., VI, 190.
	"What . . . word."	Ibid., I, 316.
230–31	"My . . . conciseness."	Ibid., VII, 7, 8.
231	"A . . . be."	Ibid., II, 239.
232	"to . . . *ether*."	Ibid., II, 274.
233	"for . . . resisted."	TW I, 25.
	"a . . . actual."	Ibid., I, 347.

	"as . . . page."	Ibid., I, 107.
234	"the . . . experience."	Ibid., I, 107.
235	"Rise . . . adventures."	Ibid., II, 230.
	"If . . . statement."	Ibid., II, 55.
235–36	"I . . . me."	EJ IX, 440.
237	"to . . . civil."	TW V, 205.
238	"Of . . . thee."	TJ III, 95.

INDEX